Tchaikovsky's Last Days

TCHAIKOVSKY'S LAST DAYS

A Documentary Study

———

ALEXANDER POZNANSKY

CLARENDON PRESS · OXFORD

1996

Oxford University Press, Walton Street, Oxford OX2 6DP

Oxford New York
Athens Auckland Bangkok Bogota Bombay
Buenos Aires Calcutta Cape Town Dar es Salaam
Delhi Florence Hong Kong Istanbul Karachi
Kuala Lumpur Madras Madrid Melbourne
Mexico City Nairobi Paris Singapore
Taipei Tokyo Toronto
and associated companies in
Berlin Ibadan

Oxford is a trade mark of Oxford University Press

Published in the United States
by Oxford University Press Inc., New York

British Library Cataloguing in Publication Data
Data available

Library of Congress Cataloging in Publication Data
Poznansky, Alexander.
Tchaikovsky's last days : a documentary study / Alexander Poznansky.
p. cm.
Includes bibliographical references (p.   ) and index.
1. Tchaikovsky, Peter Ilich, 1840–1893—Death and burial.
2. Composers—Russia—Biography. I. Title.
ML410.C4P856 1996 780'.92—dc20 [B] 96–13332
ISBN 0–19–816596–X

1 3 5 7 9 10 8 6 4 2

Typeset by Graphicraft Typesetters Ltd, Hong Kong

Printed in Great Britain
on acid-free paper by
Biddles Ltd
Guildford & Kings Lynn

Preface

Nearly as much as his music, Tchaikovsky's very personality persists in haunting our contemporary imagination. It is now widely recognized that the popularity of Tchaikovsky's music is comparable only to that of Mozart. Although his reputation within professional circles in the West has until recently tended to vacillate, a series of in-depth studies has resulted in the growing consensus that he belongs among the foremost composers in European history. His life seems amply documented, including several volumes of letters, diaries, a host of memoirs, not to mention the monumental biography by his brother Modest. Nevertheless, as in the case of Mozart, not only Tchaikovsky's life but also his death from cholera has, despite the considerable publicity given to it at the time, become clouded in myth.

Tchaikovsky's 'private life was always surrounded by kind of haze and mysterious mist', as one contemporary suggested.[1] Such a perception is understandable. Tchaikovsky's homosexuality and the secrecy it entailed necessarily created about him an aura of something unexpressible yet meaningful, giving rise to all manner of rumour and gossip.

This does not mean, however, that such rumours and gossip, or the legends and myths they have engendered, should be taken as historical truth. Material of this nature, which is much like folklore, must be subjected to rigorous scrutiny before any responsible judgement can be made.

There was nothing secret about Tchaikovsky's actual death: he was being treated by four physicians and was surrounded by a crowd of relatives and friends. The progress of his illness was reported in daily bulletins as well as in the newspapers. Indeed, his may well be one of the most

---

[1] *VC* (1980), 345.

thoroughly recorded deaths of prominent cultural figures in modern times. All this, however, was not enough to prevent the spread soon after his death of rumours of suicide, which has only intensified over the decades.

First there was the claim derived mostly from Tchaikovsky's music, that the composer was tormented by his sexual preferences and that this torment was responsible for his tragic end. Later someone reported that the composer was poisoned on direct orders from Alexander III; another held that he took his life, of his own volition, from fear of an imminent homosexual scandal, which would have exposed his involvement with, according to one version, a young member of his own family or, according to another, the Imperial family, or according to a third version, the son of a street-sweeper (indeed, quite a social sweep!); while yet another tale contends that he was forced to commit suicide by none other than his own brothers Modest and Anatoly, to save the honour of the family.

The most recent version to acquire notoriety in the West brought into circulation new elements to the story of poison and murder. Shortly before his death, we are told, Tchaikovsky entered into an affair with a young nobleman and was threatened with exposure. To avoid an impending scandal that might have affected the prestige of the School of Jurisprudence, from which he had graduated more than thirty years earlier, he was subjected to a self-appointed 'court of honour' composed of a group of his former classmates and forced to take his own life by poison, death from cholera being a fabrication of his brother Modest and the doctors, who resorted to this conspiracy in order to save the reputation of the Tchaikovsky family.[2]

Surprisingly, this complex legend, despite its sheer implausibility—or perhaps because of it—has cast a spell, which has allowed it to find its way into even the most respectable of scholarly publications.[3]

An uncritical acceptance of the so-called new 'findings', based only on rumour and third-hand information and never on hard evidence, coupled with ignorance about Tchaikovsky's private life and the social and cultural context of the times, led some recent biographers to give this version of the suicide 'theory' undeserved credit.[4]

Richard Taruskin correctly observed that 'the persistence of these

---

[2] Alexandra Orlova, 'Tchaikovsky: The Last Chapter', *Music & Letters*, 62 (1981), 125–45; Alexandra Orlova, *Tchaikovsky: A Self-Portrait* (Oxford, 1990), 406–14.

[3] Cf. e.g. *The New Grove Dictionary of Music and Musicians* (20 vols.; London, 1980), xviii. 626; David Brown, 'Tchaikovsky', in *The New Grove: Russian Masters 1* (London, 1986), 143–250.

[4] Alan Kendall, *Tchaikovsky* (London, 1988), 241–4; David Brown, *Tchaikovsky: A Biographical and Critical Study*, iv: *The Final Years (1885–1893)* (London, 1991), 478–88; André Lischke, *Piotr Ilyitch Tchaikovski* (Paris, 1993), 309–35; David Brown, *Tchaikovsky Remembered* (London, 1993), 206–26; Anthony Holden, *Tchaikovsky* (London, 1995), 352–400.

preposterous unsubstantiated stories of pederastic affairs, threatened
exposure and suicide at the behest of an honor court is symptomatic of
the unfortunate climate surrounding Tchaikovsky criticism to this day,
in which the art is to a sometimes childish extent read as clandestine auto-
biographical effusion, and the composer's artistic success . . . measured in
terms of primitive emotional identification'.[5]

A few years ago I published an article based on extensive historical and
biographical research, where I demonstrated that the entire theory of
conspiracy and suicide is not in any way compatible with Tchaikovsky's
character, his environment, Russian social customs, the circumstances of
his death, the medical records, or, last but certainly not least, common
sense.[6] Since that time, I have discovered in the Russian archives many
more documents related to Tchaikovsky's last days.[7] It was then that
I conceived the idea of conducting a sort of formal inquest, that is, of
collecting all the available information on the composer's death in one
volume, on a larger scale than was suitable for the purpose of the Tchaikovsky biography, so that readers might judge for themselves whether the
evidence leaves any room for undocumented speculation.

Consequently, the present book invites those interested to undertake a
new and free investigation. Every effort has been made to provide full
coverage of the composer's activities and whereabouts, beginning on the
eve of his arrival in St Petersburg in October 1893, where he was to conduct the première of his Sixth Symphony just a few days before the onset
of his fatal illness.

The material offered here is arranged chronologically and consists of
eyewitness accounts, newspaper reports, memoirs, documents, and medical records, much of it hitherto unavailable in English, and some of it
unearthed from the Tchaikovsky archives during my recent visits to Klin
in Russia and therefore altogether unknown. My intention has been to
allow many voices to speak even at the cost of occasional repetition. To
proceed otherwise risked the loss of a nuance or a detail where often it is
precisely such a nuance or detail that matters most. At the same time, it
is important to realize that in terms of factual accuracy many of these
texts must be treated with some caution. Most of the memoirs were written long after the events they describe, and not only reflect the personal

---

[5] *The New Grove Dictionary of Opera* (4 vols.; London, 1993), iv. 664.
[6] Alexander Poznansky, 'Tchaikovsky's Suicide: Myth and Reality', *19th Century Music*, 11
(1988), 199–220; also Alexander Poznansky, *Samoubiistvo Chaikovskogo: mif i realnost'* (Moscow,
1993); Alexander Poznansky, 'Tchaikovsky as Communist Ikon', *For SK: In Celebration of the
Life and Career of Simon Karlinsky* (Berkeley, 1994), 233–46.
[7] Alexander Poznansky, 'Tchaikovsky: The Man behind the Myth', *Musical Times*, 4 (1995),
175–82.

bias of their authors but may also contain erroneous statements, particularly with regard to dates, places, and the names of participants. Each such case will be checked against the other evidence and commented on in the remarks at the end of each chapter.

One would expect the account of Tchaikovsky's last days written by his brother Modest to play an important role in our investigation, and so it does, but only to a degree. A close reading reveals Modest's narrative to be in several respects self-serving, since he wished to present his own behaviour in the best possible light. At the same time, we possess a number of other eyewitness testimonies which appeared before Modest's version was published. Some of these served as the basis for the anonymous newspaper reports which, as is often the case in journalism, were not entirely devoid of conflated and confusing information. Still, these eyewitness accounts by physicians, relatives, and friends who were present at the bedside of the dying man produce a coherent picture of what happened. A certain degree of apparent contradiction is only natural, as legal investigation often show us, for a witness will tend to emphasize only those aspects of an event which particularly caught his or her attention and disregard those that did not. Thus, even if at first glance two or more eyewitness accounts may appear to conflict with one another in some detail or other, in the final analysis they prove to be complementary rather than contradictory.

In treating Tchaikovsky's death, since the official cholera version is now questioned and nefarious intentions from various quarters are now implied, a combination of approaches, the historical and the detective, is needed. This latter presupposes the consideration of both external, or circumstantial, evidence and inner motivation as a prerequisite for solving criminal cases. In the event that all external and circumstantial evidence against a suspect is successfully refuted, he must then be acquitted, whatever motives he may have had for committing the alleged crime. *Mutatis mutandis*, the same principle has to be followed in the case of suspected suicide: if the actual evidence for suicide is disproved, the existence of a motive becomes irrelevant. The weight of refutation should therefore be placed on demolishing the presumed evidence of a conspiratorial plot and the subsequent suicide by poison put forward by the supporters of the suicide theory. In the end, one must bear in mind the old criminological maxim that if a single fact cannot be encompassed by a theory, that theory has then to be unequivocally rejected.

Since two aspects of Tchaikovskian rumour—homosexuality and suicide—are linked from earliest documentation it is important first of all to clarify the status of homosexuals in nineteenth-century Russia, to examine Tchaikovsky's psychosexuality, and to summarize the events in the

composer's life in 1893 up to October. This will be done in the Introduction. These three elements provide the key to a proper understanding of
the vicissitudes of the composer's private and inner life, including his
attitude towards suicide. The assumption of his perennial homosexual
torment is somewhat superficial: he was far too complex a personality to
be reduced to such a stereotype. Here for the first time will be quoted in
full Tchaikovsky's revelatory letters to his brothers Modest and Anatoly,
which were published only in part in all previous studies of the composer;
excerpts from Modest's own autobiography, long suppressed in Tchaikovsky's archives; and some as yet unknown documents and memoirs of his
contemporaries.

The last chapter will deal with the oral material—rumour, gossip, hearsay—which cannot be precisely dated and which serves, in fact, as the
sole source for the promoters of the suicide theory. The chapter will enquire into the nature of that phenomenon, summarize the implausibilities
of the oral tradition, and discuss, in terms of probability, when, why, and
through whom this oral tradition originated and spread and thus allow the
reader the ultimate choice of accepting or rejecting the conclusion there
reached.

During my recent visits to the Tchaikovsky archives in Klin I was
pleased to discover that a thorough research on Tchaikovsky's last illness, supported by documentation, had been undertaken by the late
Russian microbiologist Nikolay Blinov and that, independent of my own
endeavours, the conclusions Blinov has reached are identical to mine.[8] In
the present book I have followed the practice of referring to those documents which I found and examined *de visu* before I had an opportunity
to acquaint myself with Nikolay Blinov's materials, as well as to those
that he does not mention, by their archival number. In cases where I first
learned of them from his publication, I refer also to that.

Dates in the book are Old Style, which is twelve days behind the
Western calendar in the nineteenth century. Transliteration of Russian
sources, quoted in the abbreviations, the footnotes, at the end of the
documents, and in the Select Bibliography are given according to the
Library of Congress system. Russian names in the main body of the text
are spelled so that the sound of the Russian variant is preserved without
an eccentric appearance: Alexander instead of Aleksandr, Yury instead
of Iurii, or Meshchersky instead of Meshcherskii. The Russian patronimics
in most cases are dropped, with the noticeable exception of Russian royalty and Pyotr Ilyich Tchaikovsky.

---

[8] Nikolay Blinov's partially finished work was published in 1994 as *Posledniaia bolezn' i smert'
P. I. Chaikovskogo* [*PBC*].

In the course of preparing this study I have been assisted by many individuals and the staff of many institutions.

I owe a debt to Ralph C. Burr, Jr., for his major contribution in translating large documentary portions of the text; to Leonard Forman for keeping me up to date with every development in the realm of Tchaikovskiana; to Vasily A. Rudich, who never failed to provide help and advice in a moment of need; to Mary Weigand who carefully read and edited the entire manuscript and offered numerous suggestions for improvement; to the late Lowry Nelson, whose insights, criticisms, and patient encouragement have proved again of immeasurable value.

I feel particularly grateful to Joanna and Daniel Rose for their generous material and moral support.

For unfailing help and interest in my work I am further indebted to the following:

In Russia: Galina Belonovich, Polina Vaidman, Lyudmila Shapovalova, Sergey Ganus, and the friendly staff of the Tchaikovsky Archive and House Museum at Klin; Irina Medvedeva and Nataliya Tartakovskaya of the Glinka State Central Museum of Musical Culture, Ludmila Korabelnikova of the Institute of Art Sciences, Anatoly Altshuller and Galina Kopytova of the Russian Institute of the History of Arts in St Petersburg, the directors and staff of the State Archive of the Russian Federation, the manuscript and newspaper departments of the Russian National Library and the Russian State Library, the State Central Archive of Literature and Art, the State Historical Archive of St Petersburg, the St Petersburg Theatre Museum; Irina Barsova of the Moscow Conservatoire, Valery Smirnov of the St Petersburg Conservatoire, Valery Sokolov, Boris Nikitin, Igor Kon, Larisa Sergeyeva, Ivan Darenkov, Kirill Balabaev, Lev Kuliavin, Alexander Laskin, Anatoly Matlashenko, and, especially, to the late Xeniya Davydova, Tchaikovsky's great-niece.

Special thanks are due to present residents of Tchaikovsky's last apartment in St Petersburg on Malaya Morskaya Street: Yuliya and Yakov Mezeyas, Vladimir and Nataliya Kliushkin, and Elena Kolvarsky, who kindly allowed me to spend a few hours there.

In Finland: to the staff of the University of Helsinki Slavic Library. In Germany: Thomas Kohlhase and the Tchaikovsky Society (Tübingen). In the Netherlands: Elisabeth Riethof-van Heulen.

In the United Kingdom: Helen Foster, Janet Moth, Bruce Phillips, John Warrack, Mary Worthington, and Henry Zajaczkowski.

In the United States and Canada: the late Nina Berberova, Malcolm H. Brown, Simon Karlinsky, Joseph Kerman, Stephen Oyler, Richard Taruskin, Mary Woodside, the International Research and Exchange

Board, the New York Foundation for the Arts, and Yale University Sterling Memorial Library staff.

I owe my wife Elena and son Philip paramount gratitude for their patience, affection, and encouragement throughout the time when this book was being written.

ALEXANDER POZNANSKY

Hamden, Connecticut
July 1995

Acknowledgements

I am grateful for permission to quote from the following copyright material (detailed source references are given at the end of each extract): Richard Buckle, *Diaghilev* (Weidenfeld & Nicolson, London, 1979); Alexandra Orlova, *Tchaikovsky: A Self-Portrait* (Oxford University Press, Oxford, 1990); Galina von Meck, *Pyotr Ilyich Tchaikovsky: Letters to his Family: an Autobiography* (Dennis Dobson, London, 1981); Igor Stravinsky and Robert Craft, *Expositions and Developments* (Faber & Faber, London, 1962).

Every effort has been made to contact the copyright holders of material reproduced in this book, but in some cases without success. The publishers will be pleased to hear from anyone I have not acknowledged above.

Contents

Illustrations

Picture credits: The Tchaikovsky State Archive and House Museum (Klin): 3, 4, 8; The Russian Institute of the History of the Arts (St Petersburg): 1, 6, 7, 10, 16; The Glinka State Museum of Musical Culture (Moscow): 2, 5, 12, 14; Alexander Poznansky's collection: 9, 13, 15, 20; The Hulton-Deutsch collection (London): 11; The State Central Archive for Cinematographic, Photographic and Phonographic Documents (St Petersburg): 17, 18, 19.

Abbreviations

BV	*Birzhevye viedomosti* [*Stock Exchange Register*]
d.	*delo* (file)
ed. kh.	edenitsa khranenniia (storage unit)
f.	*fond* (collection)
GARF	Gosudarstvennyi arkhiv Rossiiskoi Federatsii [The State Archive of the Russian Federation], Moscow
GDMC	Gosudarstvenyi arkhiv doma-muzeia P. I. Chaikovskogo [The Tchaikovsky State Archive and House Museum], Klin
GGTMMK	Gosudarstvennyi tsentral'nyi muzei muzykal'noi kul'tury imeni M. I. Glinki [M. I. Glinka State Central Museum of Musical Culture], Moscow
GR	*Grazhdanin* [*Citizen*]
IRLI	Institut russkoi literatury, Otdel rukopisei [Institute of Russian Literature, manuscripts department], St Petersburg
IV	*Istoricheskii viestnik* [*History Herald*]
l., ll.	*list, listy* (folio, folios)
LU	*Luch* [*Ray*]
MV	*Moskovskie viedomosti* [*Moscow Register*]
MZ	*Muzyka i zhizn'* [*Music and Life*]
NBG	*Novosti i birzhevaia gazeta* [*News and Stock Exchange Gazette*]
ND	*Novosti dnia* [*News of the Day*]
NV	*Novoe vremia* [*New Times*]
NZ	*Novyi zhurnal* [*New Review*]
OL	*Odesskii listok* [*Odessa Leaflet*]
op.	*opis'* (inventory)
PBC	N. O. Blinov, *Posledniaia bolezn' i smert' Chaikovskogo* [*Tchaikovsky's Last Illness and Death*] (Moscow, 1994)
PG	*Peterburgskaia gazeta* [*Petersburg Gazette*]
PL	*Peterburgskii listok* [*Petersburg Leaflet*]

PR	P. I. Tchaikovsky, *Pis'ma k rodnym* [*Letters to relatives*] (2 vols.; Moscow, 1940), i
PZ	*St Petersburger Zeitung* [*Petersburg Gazette*]
PSS	P. I. Tchaikovsky, *Polnoe sobranie sochinenii: Literaturnye proizvedeniia i pis'ma* [*Complete Collected Works: Literary Works and Correspondence*] (17 vols.; Moscow, 1953–81)
RGALI	Rossiiskii gosudarstvennyi arkhiv literatury i iskusstva [The Russian State Archive of Literature and the Arts], Moscow
RGB	Rossiiskaia gosudarstvennaia biblioteka, Otdel rukopisei [The Russian State Library, Manuscripts Department], Moscow
RGIA	Rossiiskii gosudarstvennyi istoricheskii arkhiv [The State Russian Historical Archive], St Petersburg
RIII	Rossiiskii institut istorii iskusstv [The Russian Institut of the History of Arts], St Petersburg
RMG	*Russkaia muzykal'naia gazeta* [*Russian Musical Gazette*]
RMS	Imperial Russian Musical Society
RNB	Rossiiskaia natsional'naia biblioteka, Otdel rukopisei [The Russian National Library, Manuscripts Department], St Petersburg
RO	*Rossiia* [*Russia*]
RU	*Rannee utro* [*Early Morning*]
RZ	*Russkaia zhizn'* [*Russian Life*]
SO	*Syn otechestva* [*Son of Fatherland*]
SPV	*Sankt-Peterburgskie viedomosti* [*St Petersburg Register*]
SR	*Solntse Rossii* [*Russian Sun*]
SV	*Sviet* [*The World*]
TG	*Teatral'naia gazeta* [*Theatrical Gazette*]
TZ	*Teatr i zhizn'* [*Theatre and Life*]
VC	V. V. Protopopov (ed.), *Vospominaniia o P. I. Chaikovskom* [*Recollections of Tchaikovsky*], 1st edn. (Moscow, 1962); 4th edn., (Leningrad, 1980)
ZC	M. I. Chaikovskii, *Zhizn' P. I. Chaikovskogo* [*The Life of P. I. Chaikovskii*], (3 vols.; Moscow, 1900–2), iii

1. Tchaikovsky in Odessa, 20 January 1893

Introduction

The little that at first sight seems plausible about the suicide theory derives from two premises, which need to be examined and refuted: first, that late nineteenth-century Russia was a sexually repressive society in which sexual conduct that did not conform to the established standards was sternly penalized; and second, that Tchaikovsky all his life, and more than anything else, feared the exposure of what he allegedly saw as his abnormal, as well as immoral, inclinations. As a result, it is argued, under the threat of punishment and disgrace, the highly neurotic composer would have been compelled to take his life.

One must turn, however, to a study of Russia's social history in order to determine the interplay of the apparent and the real regarding sexuality and sexual mores in the period of Tchaikovsky's lifetime.

Nineteenth-century Russia happened to have been a society considerably more permissive than, say, Victorian England. Russia did not have a ban on homosexuality until Peter the Great, that is, in the early eighteenth century. Even then homosexual activity was banned solely in the army. It was only in 1832, under Nicholas I, that Russian criminal legislation, as in all other European countries not affected by the Napoleonic Code, declared homosexuality, along with other 'sexual' or 'carnal' offences, to be a criminally punishable act. The relevant article of the Penal Code in effect in the early 1890s stated that 'a man convicted of the unnatural vice of *muzhelozhstvo* [buggery] shall for this be subject to deprivation of all rights of status and exile to Siberia. Furthermore, if a Christian, he shall submit to Church penance at the direction of his spiritual adviser.'[1] It would seem that the matter is clear. In reality, however, things were by no means so simple.

Complications began with the very determination of *corpus delicti*. This was emphasized by the well-known liberal jurist Vladimir Nabokov (father of the famous writer) in his article of 1902 on carnal offences in the new draft of the Criminal Code then in preparation.[2] The sometimes insurmountable legal complexities in establishing the fact, substance, and scope of the offence are for Nabokov one of the essential arguments in favour of the abolition of anti-homosexual legislation in general: 'What a vast and abundant field for blackmail and unpunished extortion, if we remember that legal evidence in this area, by its very essence, can very rarely possess the character of incontestable fact! What a temptation for enemies, who might easily ruin an opponent with malicious gossip!'[3]

However, a major argument for the repeal of anti-homosexual legislation in the Russia of that period was, as Nabokov saw it, 'one of the grossest evils of all: the virtual non-application of the law, the random and uneven nature of repression, which pounces on some, but spares others who are strong in their position, influence or connections. To point to all this is to speak of something long since known to all observers of our public life.'[4]

There can be no doubt whatsoever that in Russia, as throughout Europe at that time (and actually at all other times), there existed with regard to homosexuality a significant (and ever-increasing) gap between theory and practice, between the situation *de jure* and *de facto*. Similarly, in the Russia of those years repression had a 'random and uneven' character, or in other words, was extremely selective. The same passage quoted above provides a key to understanding the principle of this selectiveness: persons who were 'strong in their position, influence or connections' would not be prosecuted. Indeed this state of affairs was characteristic in Russia throughout the nineteenth century: those with power who had homosexual inclinations could with good reason feel quite secure, despite any rumours which might be circulating concerning them. A minimum of discretion was in these cases sufficient to avert even social scandal. In the very rarest instances, when such scandals did break out because of some indiscretion or misadventure, the authorities would make every effort to suppress them and to prevent any serious complication.

---

[1] *Svod zakonov Rossiiskoi imperii* [*The Code of Laws of the Russian Empire*] (St Petersburg, 1857), vol. xv, pt. 1, ch. 4. On homosexuality as a juridical subject in medieval Russian law see Eva Levin, *Sex and Society in the World of the Orthodox Slavs, 900–1700* (Ithaca, NY, 1989), 199–204; on 19th-c. Russian law: Laura Engelstein, *The Keys to Happiness: Sex and the Search for Modernity in fin-de-siècle Russia* (Ithaca, NY, 1992), 57–71.

[2] V. D. Nabokov, 'Plotskie prestupleniia po proektu ugolovnogo ulozheniia', *Sbornik statei po ugolovnomu pravu* (St Petersburg, 1904), 102–25.

[3] Ibid. 123.

[4] Ibid. 124.

There is not a single known prosecution for homosexuality during the entire century, in which the culprit was a more or less prominent individual—someone belonging to the higher official ranks or the cultural élite, or generally well established in fashionable society, not to mention of course anyone close to the throne. Within the framework of the present study, however, one need not illustrate this point in more detail.

In extreme cases, when or if an outside factor, such as a particular antipathy on the part of the authorities, a provocative life-style, or a major scandal, came into play, anyone of importance accused of such a crime was subject to so-called *administrative measures* (for example, confinement to one's estate, to a mental asylum, or to a monastery, exile from the capital to the provinces, banishment abroad). These measures, however, were by no means the result of legal proceedings and should be distinguished from criminal prosecution, being merely arbitrary acts carried out by the Imperial bureaucracy, to avoid the publicity inevitably resulting from legal action.

When one delves into the memoirs and diaries of the period, it becomes obvious that it was quite possible to do without judicial decisions or legal evidence in ascertaining unorthodox sexual tastes of this or that well-known person. Within the narrow circle of fashionable society these things were a matter of common knowledge: stories about them were spread (in most cases, quite good-natured), epigrams composed, and gossip spawned. The objects of this gossip were by no means subjected to ostracism or exclusion from the salons; on the contrary, they often acquired additional lustre because of them. Many homosexuals were so powerful that anyone wishing to hurt them might well have had to pay for it.

Given the close social relations which prevailed in fashionable society, little was needed in order to ascertain someone's sexual preferences: historically the life of the aristocracy, be it in London, Paris, or St Petersburg, was always out in the open for all to see. A pattern of behaviour, a primarily male circle, a predilection for the society of young men, an absence of amorous liaisons with women—for the truly intelligent and observant contemporary, this was sufficient to penetrate the intimate life of a fellow aristocrat. In essence, only this and nothing more was known to the fashionable circle as regards Tchaikovsky.

In Russian history of the nineteenth century, individuals unanimously declared by contemporaries to have been homosexuals held numerous responsible government positions, playing an important role in the political and cultural life of the country. One may quote the opinion of a contemporary on the reign of Alexander III, that is, the period in which Tchaikovsky lived:

The shameful vice was indulged by many well-known people in Petersburg: actors, writers, musicians, grand dukes. Their names were on everyone's lips, many would flaunt their way of life. Countless scandals were raised by the public disclosure of such adventures, but the filthy affairs usually did not go to trial. In this regard Alexander III lacked in resoluteness and tolerated within his own family members just as depraved, limiting himself to occasional dismissals of individual officers, whose deeds had already received widespread publicity.[5]

The glaring example was Prince Vladimir Meshchersky, publisher of the right-wing government-sponsored newspaper *Grazhdanin* (the *Citizen*), perhaps the most execrated public figure of the entire second half of the century. Meshchersky was, on the one hand, a schoolmate of Tchaikovsky from the School of Jurisprudence and once a close friend of the composer and of his brother Modest, and on the other hand, an agent of both Alexander III and Nicholas II, exerting a formidable influence upon the workings of the government.

'Prince of Sodom and citizen of Gomorrah' is what Meshchersky was dubbed by the poet and philosopher Vladimir Solovyev. The statesman Count Sergey Witte complained in his memoirs:

All his life Meshchersky has only concerned himself with his favourites. He makes of politics a trade in which he deals in the most unscrupulous manner to his own benefit and that of his favourites. Thus I can only say of Meshchersky that he is a most dreadful man. This is known by nearly all who have had dealings with him.[6]

In 1887 a vociferous scandal broke out around Meshchersky, who had been showing excessive attention to a trumpet-boy of the Guard's infantry battalion. This affair had significant consequences: the Prince's relatives publicly disavowed him. The Head Procurator of the Holy Synod (the highest religious authority), Konstantin Pobedonostsev, turning resolutely against him, spared no effort to have him disgraced. Yet Meshchersky proceeded to defend himself, and Alexander III took his side. Not only was the scandal suppressed with no repercussions for the culprit, but, what is more, 'at the height of his scandals Meshchersky . . . also reached the height of his power, for at this very moment he became a trusted counselor to the Tsar'.[7]

In 1889 the notorious Prince was again in homosexual trouble, finding himself implicated in an affair involving some two hundred other persons, members of the Guards and actors from the Alexandrinsky Theatre. The rumour was that he might be ordered to leave St Petersburg for a

---

[5] [V. P. Obninskii], *Poslednii samoderzhets* [Berlin, 1912], 34.

[6] S. I. Witte, *Vospominaniia* (3 vols.; Berlin, 1922), ii. 526.

[7] Igor Vinogradoff, 'Some Russian Imperial Letters to Prince V. P. Meshchersky (1839–1914)', *Oxford Slavonic Papers*, 10 (1962), 122.

time. In the end, however, nothing of the sort occurred, and this storm was safely weathered. As for yet another attempt on the part of Meshchersky's enemies to destroy him by turning over to the next sovereign, Nicholas II, the Prince's correspondence with his lover Burdukov, Alexey Suvorin, the influential publisher and editor-in-chief of the conservative paper *New Times* comments: 'The Tsar read the correspondence. He regards this "association" with indifference.'[8]

Such a situation is not surprising when one learns that at the top of the 'homosexual pyramid' in Tchaikovsky's time stood the Grand Duke Sergey Aleksandrovich, son of Alexander II and brother of the reigning Emperor. The Grand Duke's penchants were widely known. They were openly discussed in the salons of the capital and were the subject of various jokes. Mrs Alexandra Bogdanovich, wife of the general, in whose salon was heard all the latest news and gossip, recorded in her diary: 'Sergey Aleksandrovich is living with his adjutant Martynov, and has suggested to his wife more than once that she choose a "husband" from among her entourage. . . . One foreign newspaper has even written that *le Grand Duke Serge avec sa maitresse M-r un tel* has arrived in Paris.'[9]

Another source of information on similar mores within the court aristocrats is the diary of a distinguished court official, Count Vladimir Lamsdorf. Having first served as senior adviser to the foreign minister, Lamsdorf went on to hold the office of Minister himself from 1900 until his death. 'The Tsar calls Lamsdorf "madame" and promotes his lover Savitsky within the ranks of the count,' muses Alexey Suvorin privately: 'Lamsdorf boasts that he spent thirty years in the corridors of the Foreign Ministry. As he is a homosexual and all men are for him sluts, he thus spent thirty years in . . . [a bordello].'[10]

Tchaikovsky was a friend of Meshchersky and personally acquainted with the Grand Duke. His friend and classmate, the famed poet Alexey Apukhtin, led an openly homosexual life-style, embarrassed by nothing, fearful of nothing, and making this life-style the butt of his own jokes. If such people as Meshchersky, whom everyone hated, could not be harmed by their enemies, then certainly there was nothing for such a renowned and personally charming cultural figure as Apukhtin to fear, to say nothing of everybody's favourite, Tchaikovsky, who was relatively discreet.

Two circumstances relevant both to Tchaikovsky and Apukhtin made their position unassailable: first, they belonged to the privileged class and

[8] A. S. Suvorin, *Dnevnik* (Moscow/Petrograd, 1923), 316. For more on Meshchersky see W. E. Mosse, 'Imperial Favorite: V. P. Meshchersky and the *Grazhdanin*', *Slavonic and East European Review*, 59 (1981), 529–47.

[9] A. V. Bogdanovich, *Tri poslednikh samoderzhtsa* (Moscow/Leningrad, 1924), 68.

[10] Suvorin, *Dnevnik*, 316.

so shared with it the proper standards of political outlook (both were conservative and supported the official line), and second, they were judicious in their behaviour, avoiding excess and using the right measure of discretion, tact, and taste. Given these circumstances, fame, connections, and influential patronage were guarantees which would avert any sort of scandal in the unlikely event that such a threat were to present itself as the result of an isolated unfortunate incident.

The tradition of serfdom, even after it was abolished in 1861, continued to dominate the social behaviour of both upper and lower classes. According to the established patterns of conduct, the socially inferior were expected to submit to the wishes of the socially superior in every respect, including the gratification of sexual desire. Russian peasants were traditionally tolerant of all the varieties of sexual preferences shown by their masters and were often prepared to satisfy them on demand. This naturally resulted in boundless sexual exploitation, which at the same time elucidates sexual affairs with servants and other lower-class persons so characteristic of Tchaikovsky and his milieu—a sort of hierarchical sex. As one of Tchaikovsky's contemporaries put it, Russia was for him 'some Polynesian island' and it would not be an exaggeration to say that the deterrents and limitations which influenced sexual mores were less noticeable in nineteenth-century Russia than in England, France, or Germany.

If one reviews Tchaikovsky's outward situation towards the autumn of 1893, one must admit that it appeared in all respects splendid. By this time, after a triumphal tour in America and an honorary degree received at Cambridge University, he was a world celebrity. Within Russia his music was adored by all levels of the population, from the court to the common people. In our view, this status alone would already have ensured his safety—especially in Russia, where washing one's dirty linen in public was highly frowned upon. Let us not forget that all this took place before 1895, when the trial of Oscar Wilde shook the foundations of Victorian morality, and sparked off similar scandals elsewhere in Europe (with Friedrich Krupp and Philip zu Eulenberg in Germany, and Jacques d'Adelsvard-Fersen in France). Until that time—and this is essential to bear in mind—homosexual legislation had never been applied with respect to cultural figures of national, not to mention international, renown (thus, Paul Verlaine was tried not for homosexuality, but for attempting to shoot Arthur Rimbaud). It is impossible to assume that Russia would have been the first to break this unwritten rule, sacrificing with this not only her 'national treasure', but cultural prestige as well. Let us note that in contrast to Wilde, who consciously elected to *épater les bourgeois* and by this alone made countless enemies, Tchaikovsky's behaviour was invariably discreet, with strict observance of social conventions. So if the authorities had, in some hypothetical fit of madness, dared to subject the composer to criminal prosecution, they could not have counted even on that portion of support from Philistine-minded circles, which their British colleagues secured for themselves in Wilde's case. On the contrary, the slightest move against Tchaikovsky would have unleashed an outburst of public indignation. The measure of his extraordinary popularity was demonstrated by the people's reaction to his death. Finally, as everyone knows, Wilde actually brought catastrophe upon himself when he sued the father of his lover Alfred Lord Douglas for slander.

To all this one might answer that for the Russian government, as indicated above, it was not necessary to bring a court action against Tchaikovsky. To avoid a scandal, he could be punished administratively, banished to some estate for a period of time.

However, even administrative punishment could hardly have touched the composer. He had strong and powerful connections at court, where many were extremely well disposed towards him, starting with the Emperor, Alexander III. Even if one assumes (for which there are absolutely no grounds) that during the following five years relations between Tsar and composer did worsen, the act of granting a life pension (of 3,000 silver roubles) in 1888 is definitely significant. Despite the very different circumstances, this act bound the Emperor to Tchaikovsky in the same way as the Emperor's subsidy of the newspaper *Grazhdanin* forever cemented his relations with Meshchersky. In both cases this official financing set the Emperor's personal stamp of monarchical favour upon the recipients, making it quite difficult to disavow those so favoured under any circumstances whatsoever: any excess connected with them, if not hushed up, would cast a shadow on the Tsar. This state of affairs, as we know, played a saving role in the fate of Prince Meshchersky.

Cordial and even creative relations had existed also between Tchaikovsky and Grand Duke Konstantin Konstantinovich. The Grand Duke, using the pen name K.R. (Konstantin Romanov), was a fairly popular poet, pianist, and also a dilettante composer. Tchaikovsky composed six romances, Op. 63 (1887), and the chorus 'Blazhen kto ulybaetsia' [Blessed is he who smiles] (1887) on verses by K.R. In a letter to Nadezhda von Meck of 10 November 1886, where he describes his relations with the court, Tchaikovsky discloses: 'In the higher circles, besides the Emperor and Empress, who treat me with favour, I have a particular, special patron, namely the Grand Duke Konstantin Konstantinovich.'[11]

The Grand Duke described in his diary his first meeting in 1880 with the 40-year-old composer:

[11] *PSS* xiii. 493.

Pyotr Ilyich Tchaikovsky appears about 35 years old of age, even though his face and greying hair make him look older. He was educated at the School of Jurisprudence, he was very unhappy in his family life, and now he is preoccupied exclusively with music. Tchaikovsky was asked to play something from his work-in-progress, *Joan of Arc*; he sat at the piano and played the chorus of prayers. We were all intoxicated by this wonderful music.[12]

The last letters Tchaikovsky wrote to the Grand Duke are dated 21 and 26 September 1893—respectively, thirty-six and twenty-nine days before his death. They testify to the same high degree of favour which the Grand Duke Konstantin showed the composer and to the latter's charming manner of reciprocity.

In late February 1881, during his stay in Rome, Tchaikovsky was introduced to the Grand Dukes Sergey Aleksandrovich and his brother Pavel, a meeting about which the composer wrote most enthusiastically to his benefactress Mrs von Meck and to his brothers. The Grand Dukes were likewise charmed by their new acquaintance and even invited him to travel in their company, which invitation was gratefully accepted. Just at this time, however, there came the tragic news of the assassination of their father, Alexander II, and of course all such pleasurable plans were cast aside. Let us remember that in the early 1890s the Grand Duke Sergey Aleksandrovich stood particularly close to the throne and would not have hesitated to step forward, if need be, in defence of his good acquaintance and fellow homosexual. Not without reason did the wife of General Bogdanovich observe indignantly with regard to a homosexual scandal in 1889: 'It is said that the Grand Dukes will rush to suppress this story: many of them belong to this circle.'[13]

All this means that even if one assumes that Tchaikovsky indeed became involved in a relationship threatened with exposure—although no material evidence exists—the subsequent scenario had to have been far different from blackmail followed by suicide. Any provocation concerning the composer's sexual tendencies would seriously affect the prestige and interests of a whole string of powerful people right to the very summit of governmental hierarchy.

The Imperial court, where the composer had so many protectors, would have resorted, should the need have arisen, to any expedient measures to suppress an impending scandal—without even taking administrative action. It would have sufficed, for instance, to suggest to Tchaikovsky that he should go abroad for a while, which he would willingly have done, especially as he had by the same manœuvre avoided unpleasant disclosures

---

[12] GARF, f. 660, op. 1, d. 40.
[13] Bogdanovich, *Tri poslednikh samoderzhtsa*, 91.

at the time of his catastrophic marriage. And as for his possible accusers, irrespective of their social status, it was in their interest to hush everything up as quickly and quietly as possible.

Considering the external circumstances alone, a suicide theory cannot hold up under any serious examination. Even supposing the situation to have been such (and this remains to be proved) to have compelled Tchaikovsky to commit suicide, that would have been a last resort, when there was no other way out of a dead end. In the case of Tchaikovsky, however, even if you take the supposition of an impending homosexual scandal to be accurate, there were for him many possible ways out—from travel abroad to an appeal for help to his numerous (and among them most august) protectors.

II

The suicide theory might make some sense only in one case: if it were proved that the oppressive external circumstances which have been postulated for Tchaikovsky coincided with no less oppressive inner circumstances, that is to say, with a painful personal crisis, and that this combination prompted him to take his own life. We shall now turn to an examination of the composer's 'inner circumstances' towards the autumn of 1893. The thesis that throughout his life Tchaikovsky was 'cruelly tormented' by his homosexuality is central to the promoters of the suicide theory.

Every single one of the composer's letters which they cite to substantiate their point of view belongs, however, to the period 1876–7. During these years the composer did indeed experience a crisis intimately connected with the problem of homosexuality. In fact, this was a culmination of what had started in the early 1860s, when Tchaikovsky had just begun his music studies in the St Petersburg Conservatoire, and was a result of events about which we have learned only recently from documents in the Klin archives.

In his unpublished autobiography, which strikes one as remarkably candid, Modest Tchaikovsky first tells of the positive and poignant experience his brother underwent during his adolescence through the 'special friendship' with his schoolmate Sergey Kireyev, which I discussed in my biography of Tchaikovsky.[14] Modest writes:

That was the strongest, most durable, and purest amorous infatuation of Tchaikovsky's life. It possessed all the charms, all the sufferings, all the depth and force

---

[14] Alexander Poznansky, *Tchaikovsky: The Quest for the Inner Man* (London, 1993), 47–9.

of love, most luminous and sublime. . . . Anyone who doubts the beauty and high poetry of this 'cult' should be pointed to the best pages of Tchaikovsky's musical *œuvre* . . . which cannot be 'invented' without being experienced, and he never experienced later in life such powerful, lasting, and painful emotion. . . . They shared their feelings for a period of ten years.[15]

The significance of the Kireyev episode for the future composer cannot be underrated: it endowed him with a taste for living and a faith in the power of love which he never gave up, and also with an inner strength that stayed with him despite all later perturbations. As often happens, this early intense affair created in Tchaikovsky a pattern that resurfaced later in his brief relationship with Eduard Sack and, towards the end of his life, in his deep attachment to his nephew Bob Davydov.

While insisting on the romantic aspect of Tchaikovsky's relationship with Kireyev, Modest nevertheless admits that

Side by side with this adoration of Sergey Kireyev, Pyotr experienced many involvements of a different character, yielding to them unrestrainedly, and with the full fervour of his passionate and sensuous nature. Women were never the object of these infatuations; physically they evoked in him only detestation. . . . [On one occasion dinner guests at St Petersburg's restaurant Chautemps] were defamed throughout the whole city as buggers. Among them were Pyotr and Apukhtin, and they acquired forever the reputation of buggers. . . . The Chautemps affair had a significant effect on Pyotr. It was the first time that he had faced cruel injustice on the part of people who despised and were indignant about a situation that might have caused, if the matter had been clearly under-stood, at worst regret with regard to an irreversible natural defect. It goes with-out saying that the Chautemps scandal did not change Pyotr's inclinations—nor could anything else in the world—but he became more cautious in his amorous adventures and, hiding his offence, he began to avoid society where his reputa-tion could hurt his self-esteem, and at the same time to seek interests outside the *beau monde*. I also believe that while he recognized the injustice in society's con-demnation of what is beyond human powers to rectify, at the same time society's cruel attitude to pederasty affected to some extent Pyotr's fastidious attitude to himself. Despite the inner protest he could not help submitting to the influence of the general detestation of this very defect and, having looked at himself through the eyes of those unjust and merciless judges, he felt equally merciless in regard to his own infatuations so that he arrived at that point of despair, at that dis-pleasure with himself which worked the transformation of a young rake and so-cialite into a tender son and brother, of a bad public officer into a good musician.[16]

---

[15] GDMC, B², no. 21, 29–30.
[16] GDMC, B², nos. 21, 32. A thorough search, which I conducted in the Russian Archives on the 'Chautemps affair', regrettably did not yield any additional information. The police files for this period were actually destroyed during the turmoil accompanying the Revolution of 1917.

There is little doubt that this very experience prompted Tchaikovsky to reconsider his disorderly way of life as a 'young man about town' and led to his important decision to embark upon a career in music by enrolling in the newly founded St Petersburg Conservatoire. At the same time, both the threat of danger and the escape from it must have affected his manner of conduct in the years to come, by teaching him, on the one hand, the need to exercise caution, and, on the other, the need to survive, if similar occurrences were to befall him in the future.

A close study of the extant documentation leads inevitably to the conclusion that Tchaikovsky's attitude to his own homosexuality had undergone a significant—and even dramatic—change, in which the crisis of 1877–8, that is to say the collapse of his marriage to Antonina Milyukova proved a turning-point. The evidence makes it clear that during the years which preceded his attempt at matrimony, the composer experienced a growth of anxiety in regard to his sexual tastes, and, as Modest suggested, this was probably at least partly caused by the after-effects of the Chautemps scandal. This undoubtedly contributed to his fits of hypochondria as manifested, for instance, in his letter to his brother Anatoly of 9 January 1875:

I am very, very lonely here, and were it not for continual work, I should simply abandon myself to melancholy. But then it is true that my damned pederasty does form an unbridgeable abyss between me and most people. It imparts to my character an aloofness, a fear of people, an excessive shyness, in short, a thousand qualities which make me grow more and more unsociable. Imagine, I often dwell for hours now on the thought of a monastery or the like.[17]

This sense of dissatisfaction with his life-style, however, may actually have been the least prominent among the motives which compelled him to embark upon the matrimonial experiment. Although on several occasions Tchaikovsky bravely claimed that he did not care about public opinion, for the most part this was an exercise in self-persuasion. Apparently, he was sensitive to the possibility of his reputation being tainted, and even more to the harm this could have inflicted on the members of his family. Of the latter, his aged father seems to have been entirely unaware of his favourite son's inclinations and cherished a passionate desire to see him finally married. In the letter to Mrs von Meck of 3 July

---

[17] GDMC, A³, no. 1088; the phrase 'my damned pederasty' [*moia prokliataia bugromaniia*] is blotted out by someone in the original letter but reconstructable and omitted in *PR* 213–14; *PSS* v. 389–90 (partial). The word 'bugromaniia' is derived from two words: 'bugger' and 'mania'. My deepest gratitude goes to Valery Sokolov, who reconstructed all blotted lines in Tchaikovsky's letters and generously shared with me all his findings.

1877 Tchaikovsky admitted: 'My decision was supported by the fact that
my eighty-two-year-old father and all my relatives have set their hearts
on my marrying.'[18] The crucial letter to Modest of 28 September 1876
makes this mixture of feelings manifest:

You say that one should spit on *qu'en dira-t-on* [i.e. public opinion—A.P.] This is
true only to a certain degree. There are people who cannot despise me for my
vices only because they came to love me when they did not suspect that I am in
essence a man with a lost reputation. Sasha [Tchaikovsky's sister Alexandra—
A. P.], for instance, is one of these! I know that she guesses *everything* and *forgives*
everything. Thus am I treated by very many people whom I love or respect. Do
you really think that I am not oppressed by this awareness *that they pity and
forgive me*, when in fact I am guilty of nothing! And is it really not dreadful to
think that people who love me can ever *be ashamed* of me! But, you see, this has
happened a hundred times before and will happen a hundred times again. In a
word, I should like by my marriage or, in general, an open affair with a woman
to shut the mouths of various contemptible creatures whose opinion I do not
value in the least but who can cause pain to people close to me.[19]

The confession of 'vice' on the one hand, and claim of innocence on the
other reveal the extent of mental confusion and even anguish that he
must have temporarily experienced: he was 'innocent' since it was not his
fault that he had been born a homosexual, which none the less constituted a 'vice' in the eyes of those who held him dear. At the same time
there is every reason to believe that, up to a point, Tchaikovsky thought
his peculiarity to be something that he could potentially overcome if required to do so. Just such an attitude is evident in his letter to Modest of
10 September 1876: 'As for me, I shall do my utmost to get married this
very year, but if I've not the courage to do so, I am in any case abandon-
ing my habits forever and shall endeavour no longer to be numbered
among the company of Gruzinsky and Co. . . . I think solely of eradicat-
ing pernicious passions from myself.'[20]

Resolution, however, would at times fail, and a week later he again
wrote to Modest, far more judiciously: 'In this matter I do not intend to
be hasty, and you may be sure that if I do in fact bind myself to a woman,

---

[18] P. I. Tchaikovsky, *'To my best friend': Correspondence between Tchaikovsky and Nadezhda
von Meck, 1876–1878*, trans. Galina von Meck, ed. Edward Garden and Nigel Gotteri (Oxford,
1993), 24.

[19] GDMC, A³, no. 1467; *PR* 259–60; *PSS* vi. 76 (omitted). Cf. Modest's letter of 23 Sept. 1877:
'You will not be able to change the opinion about you on the part of those who know you well.
I do not mean the scum for whose sake you have married and who would hate you anyway since
you are better than they and they would look for pieces of mud to throw on you.' GDMC, A⁴,
no. 5097.

[20] GDMC, A³, no. 1465; *PR* 254; *PSS* vi. 69 (omitted). Pavel Gruzinsky was a fellow homosexual in Moscow.

I shall do it with the greatest circumspection.'[21] And, in more detail, to Anatoly: 'I felt I lied when I told you that I'd firmly decided on this abrupt revolution in my way of life. As a matter of fact, I have not yet decided on this at all. I am merely thinking seriously about it and am waiting for something to force me to act. . . . I repeat that I seriously intend to make a new man of myself, but I wish simply to prepare myself for this gradually.'[22]

Yet, the preparation proceeded sluggishly. In the same important letter to Modest from 28 September, following an argument to the effect that marriage is a necessity, we read:

In any event, do not be frightened for me, dear Modest. The realization of my plans is not nearly so close as you think. I am so set in my habits and tastes that it is not possible to cast them aside all at once like an old glove. And besides, I am far from possessing a will of iron, and since my last letters to you I have already surrendered some three times to the force of my natural tendencies. Would you imagine! One of these days I even went to *Bulatov*'s country estate, and his house is nothing but a pederastic bordello. As if it were not enough that I had been there, I *fell in love* as a cat with his coachman!!! So you are perfectly right when you say in your letter that it is not possible to restrain oneself, despite all vows, from one's weaknesses.[23]

Thus, in the course of less than a month and in spite of all his resolve and rhetoric, Tchaikovsky, as he confessed to his brother, had three homosexual contacts. Furthermore, the expression 'natural tendencies' (the very words Tchaikovsky consistently used in his letters to designate his sexual tastes) indicates that, all discomfort and anxieties notwithstanding, he did not regard them as an anomalous—in all his known writings there is nothing to suggest that he considered himself a sexually pathological individual. Further on in the same letter one reads:

And all the same I stand by my intentions and I assure you that somehow or other I shall carry them out. But I shall do this neither suddenly nor rashly. In any event, I do not intend to put on a yoke. I shall not enter any lawful or illicit union with a woman without having fully ensured my own peace and my own freedom.

Clearly freedom has already come to mean here also the freedom to indulge in those 'weaknesses', from which 'it is not possible to refrain, despite all vows'.

In his aspiration to reconcile this 'freedom' with the condition of

---

[21] *PR* 256; *PSS* vi. 71.

[22] *PR* 257; *PSS* vi. 72–3 (partially).

[23] GDMC, A³, no. 1467; *PR* 259–60; *PSS* vi. 76 (omitted). Mikhail Bek-Bulatov was Tchaikovsky's schoolmate in the School of Jurisprudence and also a fellow homosexual in Moscow.

matrimony, Tchaikovsky may well have been encouraged by the example of his married homosexual friends, such as Nikolay Kondratyev and Vladimir and Konstantin Shilovsky whose wives apparently tolerated the infatuations of their husbands. Combined, all these considerations prompted the composer to announce resolutely, in a letter to Modest of 19 August 1876: 'I have made up my mind to marry. It is unavoidable. I must do this, and not only for myself, but also for you, and for Anatoly, and for Sasha, and for everyone I love. For you in particular!'[24] The last phrase relates to yet another added factor of the whole affair, that is, to an association which had developed between Modest and his deaf-mute pupil Nikolay Konradi, and the trip abroad all three had taken together in the summer of that same year. It appears that Tchaikovsky was extremely uneasy about what was going on. In view of Modest's own homosexuality, the prospect of mutual relations between two of them entailed consequences that were unpredictable. This concern permeated a passage in another letter to Modest of 10 September 1876:

I have done a great deal of thinking during this time about myself and about you and about our future. The result of this deliberation is that starting today I shall seriously prepare to enter into lawful matrimony with whomever. I find that our *inclinations* are for both of us the greatest and most insurmountable obstacle to happiness, and we must fight our nature with all our strength. I love you very much, I love *Nikolay* very much, and for the good of you both I dearly hope that you never part, but a condition *sine qua non* of the durability of your relations is that you no longer be *that* which you have been until now. This is necessary not for the sake of *qu'en dira-t-on*, but for you yourself, for your own peace of mind. A man who, after parting with, as one might say, *his own* (he can be called your own) child [i.e. Nikolay Konradi] falls into the embraces of any passing trash can not be a real educator that you want and ought to become. At any rate, now I cannot imagine you without horror in Aleksandrovsky Garden walking with Okoneshnikov on your arm. You will say that at your age it is difficult to conquer passions; to this I shall answer that at your age it is easier to turn your tastes in a different direction. Here your religiousness should, I think, be a firm support to you.[25]

Obviously Tchaikovsky's intent was, once married, to become a model for his younger brother and thereby prevent a disaster in Modest's relations with his pupil. As he wrote earlier to the former on 19 August 1876: 'Pederasty and pedagogy cannot live in harmony with one another.'[26]

---

[24] GDMC, A³, no. 1464; *PR* 253; *PSS* vi. 66 (omitted).

[25] GDMC, A³, no. 1465; *PR* 254; *PSS* vi. 69 (omitted). Pyotr Okoneshnikov was Tchaikovsky's brother's society friend and fellow homosexual.

[26] GDMC, A³, no. 1464; *PR* 253; *PSS* vi. 66 (omitted). In the letter's original 'pederasty' is 'bugromanstvo'; this word was later blotted out by someone.

Ironically, by the end of the same year 1876, when Tchaikovsky had just completed *Francesca da Rimini*, the composer fell deeply in love with one of his own students at the Conservatoire, Iosif Kotek, of which affair he wrote most emphatically to Modest on 19 January 1877:

I am *in love* as I have not been for so long. . . . I have known him already for six years. I always liked him and a couple of times came close to falling in love with him. Those were rehearsals of my love. Now I have made a leap and have surrendered to it most irrevocably. When for hours I hold his hand and with anguish fight a temptation to fall at his feet . . . passion storms me with an unimaginable force, my voice trembles like that of a youth, and I speak some kind of nonsense.[27]

If on 4 May Tchaikovsky wrote with full detachment to his brother Anatoly on the subject of the 'candidate for marriage', former Conservatoire student Antonina Milyukova, whom he had known since 1872, the letter to his brother Modest of the same day described his relationship with Kotek in excited tones: 'My love for you know whom sparks with new and unprecedented strength! The reason for it is my jealousy. . . . I was not able to conceal my grief. I spent several terrible nights. . . . Later I got accustomed to this horrible situation, but my love burned even stronger than ever before. I see him every day, and he has never been so affectionate with me as now.'[28]

The wishful thinking regarding his capability of conducting a heterosexual way of life led Tchaikovsky to the impulsive project of marrying Antonina, which proved a major disaster. Here are quoted for the first time the most revealing letters of the composer to his brothers describing his first experiences as a newly-wed husband. It is known that Tchaikovsky went to St Petersburg immediately after the wedding on 6 July 1877. Full of hope, he wrote to Modest on 8 July:

We spent yesterday rather pleasantly; we had a carriage ride, also visited a place of entertainment on Krestovsky island, and the night passed very quietly. Defloration did not happen, however, and perhaps will not happen for quite a while. But I asserted myself in a such a manner that there is no need to worry. My wife has one huge merit: she blindly obeys me in everything, she is very neat, she is pleased with everything, and desires nothing but to feel happy for providing me with support and consolation. I cannot say yet that I love her, but I already feel that I will love her after we get accustomed to each other.[29]

Next day, 9 July, writing to his other brother, Anatoly, Tchaikovsky confessed:

[27] GDMC, A³, no. 1470; *PSS* vi. 110 (omitted).
[28] GDMC, A³, no. 1471; *PSS* vi. 130 (omitted).
[29] GDMC, A³, no. 1476; *PR* 288 (partially); *PSS* vi. 153 (omitted).

This night the first attack took place. The attack proved weak; it is true, it met no resistance, but in itself it was very weak. However, this first step accomplished a lot. It brought me closer to my wife, since I resorted to various manipulations which established intimacy between us. Today I feel in her regard incomparably freer.[30]

But Tchaikovsky's next letter, of 11 July to Anatoly, already betrays the signs of discouragement and confusion:

I am indeed living through hard moments in my life, but I feel that I will gradually get accustomed to the new situation. It would be utterly false and unbearable if I were to have deceived my wife, but I did warn her that she may count only on my brotherly love. The attack was not resumed. After the first attempt, my wife has became totally repugnant to me in the physical sense. I am sure that sometime later the attacks will resume and prove more successful, but now any attempts would be useless.[31]

It was shortly afterwards that Tchaikovsky, despite his desire to regard the situation optimistically, must have realized that their union would not work owing to psychological incompatibilities as well as irreconcilable differences of sexual orientation.

The peak of desperation was revealed in the next letter to his brother Anatoly, written on 13 July:

Yesterday was perhaps the most difficult day of all since 6 July. In the morning it seemed to me that my life was broken and I fell into a fit of despair. . . . Beginning today the terrible crisis has passed. I am recovering. But the crisis was *terrible, terrible, terrible*; were it not for my love for you and my other dear ones, which supported me in the midst of *unbearable mental torments*, it might have ended badly, i.e. with illness or madness.[32]

A couple of weeks later, after their return to Moscow from the capital, Tchaikovsky left his wife behind and rushed to recuperate at his sister's estate Kamenka in the Ukraine. Furthermore, it was there, in Kamenka, that Tchaikovsky eventually experienced, in his own words, 'the fullness of happiness'.[33] Again, he fell in love, this time, with Kamenka's man-servant Evstafy, which he bluntly admitted in a letter to Modest of 9 September 1877:

As regards my source of delight, about whom I cannot even think without being sexually aroused and whose *boots I would feel happy to clean all my life long*, whose chamber pots I would take out and I am generally ready to lower myself anyhow, provided that I could kiss, even *if only rarely his hands and feet*.[34]

[30] GDMC, A³, no. 1111; *PR* 289 (omitted); *PSS* vi. 154 (omitted).
[31] GDMC, A³, no. 1112; *PR* 290 (partially).
[32] *PSS* vi. 155.
[33] GDMC, A³, no. 1115; *PR* 296; *PSS* vi. 177.
[34] GDMC, A³, no. 1477; *PR* 294 (omitted); *PSS* vi. 173 (omitted).

This letter amply testifies to the fact that only a few weeks after his wedding Tchaikovsky felt no intention of seriously becoming strictly heterosexual, as some biographers want us to believe. It was then that he understood the impossibility of continuing to live with Antonina and started to count the days when he would be able return to his previous life.[35]

It is evident that on the eve of his wedding and in the course of his abortive marriage, the composer suffered considerable emotional turmoil, in varying degrees caused by the factors related to his sexual preferences. As is well known, his state of matrimony did not last and ended with his flight abroad under the pretext of a nervous breakdown. One observes, however, that Tchaikovsky himself never blamed his homosexuality for what happened, but rather his misguided urge to change himself, as he formulated it in a letter of 13 February 1878 to his brother Anatoly, and in which the composer arrived at an important conclusion: 'Only now, especially after the story of my marriage, have I finally begun to understand that there is nothing more fruitless than not wanting to be that which I am by nature.'[36]

This very recognition stayed with him for the rest of his life and helped him eventually to become reconciled with himself.

Thanks to the efforts of his family and friends no particular scandal resulted from the collapse of Tchaikovsky's marriage. That Antonina was well aware of the sexual basis of her husband's aversion to her is clear from passing remarks in Tchaikovsky's letter to Modest on 26 October from Clarens. Although an opportunity for blackmail thus presented itself to her (or at least this is what Tchaikovsky believed for quite a while) it never materialized, and he learned to laugh at his fears.

By this time Tchaikovsky could not help realizing that his sexual orientation became, if not exactly public property, at least common knowledge to a wider circle of people. There is evidence that it was by no means a secret to his friend and protector Nikolay Rubinstein and his publisher Pyotr Jurgenson. And Tchaikovsky was of course right in the assumption that his sister Alexandra had her own suspicions. This becomes clear from her letter to Modest dated 1 October 1877, immediately after Tchaikovsky's matrimonial fiasco:

Now I will tell you briefly what I think of Pyotr: his behaviour towards Antonina is very, very bad. He is not a young man any more and he must have understood that he does not possess the slightest capacity to become even a bearable husband. To take a woman, to attempt to make her a screen against one's own

---

[35] For further details on Tchaikovsky's abortive marriage and its aftermath, see V. Sokolov, *Antonina Chaikovskaia: Istoriia zabytoi zhizni* (Moscow, 1994).

[36] *PR* 374; *PSS* vii. 115 (partially).

debauchery and then to transfer to her that very hatred that should be directed at one's own behaviour is unworthy of so highly cultivated a man. I am almost convinced that his wife's personal characteristics play no role in his hatred of her—he would start to hate any woman who entered into an intimate relation-ship with him.[37]

Following Tchaikovsky's impetuous departure abroad in connection with the matrimonial catastrophe, Modest wrote to him that 'all Petersburg' was talking about it, which must have necessarily indulged speculations about his sexual tastes. Furthermore, Tchaikovsky even had to endure a public blow, when an article in the newspaper *New Times* of 26 August 1878 attacked the morals in the Conservatoire, alleging that its professors conducted love affairs with female students, as well as 'amours of a dif-ferent kind'. Even though the allusion to amours of different kind was made without naming any names, Tchaikovsky took it very personally. In a letter to Modest, written three days later he wrote:

The hint is clear. So, that which I fear more than anything else in the world, that sword of Damocles in the shape of newspaper insinuation, has again struck me in the neck. Even if the insinuation doesn't touch me personally this time, so much the worse. My pederastic reputation falls upon the entire Conservatoire, and this makes me feel even more ashamed and wretched. I endured this unanticipated passage heroically and philosophically . . . but inside I was sick at heart . . . *Après tout*, it's all for the best, and at the present moment I have already quite set my mind at rest so far as any newspapers are concerned. . . . At bottom it is all one, when there are people whom you love.[38]

Despite all the odds and considerable anguish, the composer in this period succeeded—and this was testimony to the ultimate strength of his character—to endure an accumulated tension arising from his sexual in-terests, which threatened him with the public scandal that he feared most. One must be reminded, furthermore, that at this period he was still a modest professor at the Conservatoire, struggling for recognition, so that any public unpleasantness could adversely affect his career. In 1893, on the other hand, there stands before us a world celebrity, a 'national treas-ure', protected by the favour of the Tsar and the Grand Dukes, with fame and productivity swiftly ascending. There can be no doubt that given these circumstances popular indignation in the event of a scandal would have fallen not on him, but on his persecutors.

The crisis of 1877–8 poignantly demonstrated to the composer the need for self-adjustment, both psychological and social, a predicament common to his numerous upper- and middle-class fellow homosexuals in Russia and Europe. The majority of them managed to discover some kind of

[37] GDMC, B[10], no. 1408.
[38] *PR* 442–3; *PSS* vii. 380–1. (omitted) In the original letter the phrase 'my pederastic repu-tation' ['moia bugrskaia reputatsiia'] was blotted out.

niche that allowed them to function and to indulge in their sexual activities with little risk of incurring harassment by society. Tchaikovsky also gradually succeeded in adjusting his inner circumstances to the societal conditions of his time without experiencing any serious psychological damage. As Malcolm H. Brown has correctly pointed out, 'Tchaikovsky made a highly adaptive, even successful adjustment to his psychological condition. An "extreme case" [as he is occasionally presented] would have ended in a mental institution, not in the halls of Cambridge University to receive a Doctor of Music degree, *honoris causa*.'[39] Moreover, contrary to popular opinion, there seem to have existed in the late nineteenth century several quiet patterns of accommodation for persons with outlawed erotic tastes who were not eager to display them openly. Such a view is argued by the social historian Peter Gay with respect to Victorian sensibilities: 'After all, behind the sheltering façade of discretion many nineteenth-century male and female homosexuals defining their own forbidden ways of loving, enjoyed a privileged space of impunity for their unorthodox amorous arrangement.'[40]

Tchaikovsky's eventual solution became, while often entertaining passionate and even sublime feelings for young males among his social peers, including his pupils, to gratify his physical needs by means of anonymous encounters with members of the lower classes.

An example is found in a letter to Modest of 16 September 1878, which describes a 'rendezvous' with 'one very nice youth of peasant origin serving as a butler', that was arranged by Tchaikovsky's old friend and full-time pimp, Nikolay Bochechkarov. The composer writes that in anticipation of this meeting 'his heart felt a sweet anguish' since at that point he was 'fully disposed to fall in love with someone'. And he continues: 'We arrive at the boulevard, get acquainted, and I immediately fell in love as Tatyana with Onegin. His face and his body—*un rêve* [like a dream], are the fulfilment of a sweet fantasy. After a walk and utterly infatuated, I invite him and Bochechkarov to a pub. We take a private room.'[41]

Henry Zajaczkowski pointed out that 'if the composer's response to possible sexual objects was whether to use and discard them or to idolize them, it shows that he was unable to form an integrated, secure relationship with another man'.[42] This may have constituted a source of frustration which must, however, have been considerably mitigated by Tchaikovsky's long-standing relationship with his manservant Alexey Sofronov, whose

---

[39] Malcolm H. Brown, 'Tchaikovsky: The Early Years, 1840–1874 by David Brown', *Journal of the American Musicological Society*, 33 (1980), 405.

[40] Peter Gay, *The Bourgeois Experience: Victoria to Freud*, ii: The Tender Passion (Oxford, 1986), 205.

[41] GDMC, A³, no. 1509; *PSS* vii. 401 (omitted).

[42] Henry Zajaczkowski, 'Tchaikovsky: The Quest for the Inner Man by Alexander Poznansky', *Musical Times*, 11 (1992), 574.

status changed over the years from one of bedmate to that of valued friend who eventually married with Tchaikovsky's blessing, but stayed in his household till the very end.

For the period subsequent to his failed marriage, there is no documentary material that could justify Tchaikovsky's portrayal (still recurrent in popular literature) as a lifelong sexual martyr. He certainly suffered periods of depression, as all of us do occasionally, even on sexual grounds, be it unrequited love or a sense of separateness and alienation, but the earlier and specifically 'homosexual anxiety' ceased to be a dominant feature of his inner life.[43]

In Tchaikovsky's entire post-marital correspondence, which is voluminous and almost not censored, there are found only very few passages manifesting a nostalgia for love of a woman, and in each case it is caused by his observation of, and immediate reaction to, prospective spouses or the newly wed. Thus, in a letter to Modest of 17 October 1881 the composer describes the arrival of their niece's fiancé:

How much in love he is! Just as I used to be. He devours her with his eyes, is angry and anguished as soon as she leaves him for a moment. Yet it's obvious that this is not merely infatuation, but genuine normal love. Modest, what poor fellows we are, you and I—why, we shall live out our whole lives without experiencing for a single second the full happiness of love.[44]

Another relevant passage comes in a letter to Anatoly of 8 February 1882, on the occasion of the latter's impending marriage: 'There is a certain kind of need for affection and caring, which only a woman can satisfy. I am seized sometimes by a mad desire to be caressed by a woman's hand. Sometimes I see kindly looking ladies (not young women, though) and I so want to lay my head upon their laps and kiss their hands. However, it's hard for me to express this.'[45]

The thrust of this argument is pragmatic and sentimental, very much in Tchaikovsky's style and fully in keeping with the occasion that provoked it. The desire to 'kiss the hands' of elderly women has little in common with the 'cruel suffering' postulated by some biographers.[46]

---

[43] For more on Tchaikovsky's psychosexuality see Poznansky, *Tchaikovsky*.

[44] *PSS* x. 244; cf. letter to Modest of 26 Sept. 1883 with the display of similar transient feelings caused by Nikolay von Meck's courtship of his niece Anna, *PSS* xii. 243; see also Poznansky, *Tchaikovsky*, 431.

[45] *PSS* xi. 55–6.

[46] Some biographers wish to read a homosexual innuendo in the entry of Tchaikovsky's diary of 23 April 1884 (i.e. Holden mistakenly dates this entry to the time of the scoring of the *Pathétique* in 1893; the diary for 1893 does not exist), where the composer exclaims: 'Oh, what a monster of a person I am!' This is misguided, this utterance has nothing to do with sexuality since it appears in the context of card playing, his addiction to which Tchaikovsky considered a shameful vice.

Tchaikovsky's correspondence with Modest in subsequent years, after his marriage, particularly from abroad, is full of graphic and uninhibited descriptions of erotic encounters with homosexual prostitutes which were hitherto censored in all publications. Their frequency and candour strongly speak against an assumption of perpetual torment of conscience that he must allegedly have suffered.

This is a characteristic passage from the letter to Modest of 26 February 1879, in which he described a one-night stand with a young male prostitute in Paris:

A bed, a pitiful little trunk, a dirty little table with a candle-end, a few shabby trousers and a jacket, a huge crystal glass, won in a lottery—those make the room's only decorations. Yet it did seem to me at that moment that this miserable cell is the centrepiece of the entire human happiness. . . . There occurred all kinds of *calinerie* [tenderness] as he put it, and then I turned frantic because of amorous happiness and experienced incredible pleasure. And I can say in confidence, that not only for a long time, but almost never have I felt so happy in this sense as yesterday.

The post-coital remorse which Tchaikovsky experienced the following morning did not relate, characteristically, to the matter of sexual perversion. Rather they betray the same traditional Russian sensibilities found in the characters of Tolstoy and Dostoevsky, namely, the compassion for a fallen woman (in this case, young man), who was forced or chose to become a prostitute, and a concurrent desire to attempt a rescue:

I woke with remorse and full understanding of the fraudulence and exaggerated quality of that happiness which I felt yesterday and which, in substance, is nothing but a strong sexual inclination based on the correspondence with the capricious demands of my taste and on the general charm of that youth. Be that as it may, this young man has *much good* at the roof of his soul. But, my God, how pitiable is he, how thoroughly debauched! And instead of helping him to better himself, I only contributed to his further going down.[47]

And Tchaikovsky felt prepared to part with 500 francs so that the young man could return to his family in Lyons.

As regards the fundamental impossibility of experiencing full satisfaction in love, Tchaikovsky saw it otherwise—one is tempted to say dialectically—in a letter to Mrs von Meck of 9 February 1878:

You ask my friend, whether I have ever known *non-Platonic love. Yes and no.* If the question is put in a slightly different way, i.e. by asking whether I've experienced full happiness in love, then the answer is: *no, no, and no again!!!* Moreover, I think there is an answer to the question in my music. But, if you ask me whether

---

[47] GDMC, A³, no. 1541; *PR* 548 (omitted); *PSS* viii. 139 (omitted).

I appreciate all the power, all the invincible force, of this emotion, then I'll answer *yes, yes and yes again*, and I would say yet again that I've repeatedly tried to express lovingly in my music the torments and bliss of love.[48]

These correspondents, to put it in modern terms, were employing the same semiotics, but had in mind different semantics: Mrs von Meck— heterosexual love, Tchaikovsky—homosexual love. But it follows that within his own framework, the composer had already experienced both the torment and the bliss, which means the complete satisfaction, since he had found himself able to understand and express them in music. Incidentally, when these letters to Modest and Mrs von Meck were written, Tchaikovsky had not yet experienced what was to became the most powerful and all-embracing passion of his life—his love for his nephew Bob Davydov.

III

There is every reason to think that by the end at 1893 Tchaikovsky's love life had assumed forms which were more than satisfactory. His relations with Bob Davydov were at an exceptionally high level, regardless of whether or not sexual intimacy was involved. His immediate company, the so called 'Fourth Suite', made up of bright and attractive youths who undoubtedly would have permitted at least a caress, must have filled his spare time with pleasure. His aura of world fame would have made him irresistible to those young men who shared his sexual orientation or needed his protection.

The dramatic tension of Tchaikovsky's amorous experiences in the latter years of his life must have been determined by the conflict of the spiritual and the carnal in his relations with Bob. For an exacting and sensitive artist such a conflict more than sufficed to enhance and to sharpen artistic inspiration and have a bearing on the artistic product—in this case, one is naturally reminded of the pessimistic tenor prevailing in the *Pathétique* Symphony. Such experiences in the realm of the spirit evolve, as a rule, independently of any mundane developments and by no means entail an eventual catastrophe. Otherwise Dante, Petrarch, Shakespeare, Goethe, and a multitude of outstanding creative individuals who suffered deeply from unreciprocated love, would have taken their own lives without hesitation, and while still young.

With the arrival of world renown, Tchaikovsky had to face the fact that he was now talked about and discussed in salons and musical circles

---

[48] Tchaikovsky, '*To my best friend*', 176.

from the capital to the farthest provinces of the Empire and that inevitably his personal life was being touched upon as well. It would not be an exaggeration to say that by 1893 most of society was aware of the composer's homosexuality.

Alexander Siloti, an eminent Russian pianist and Tchaikovsky's friend, insists 'that everybody knew about it. . . . His continuous urge for solitude, his reserve, his secretiveness, contrasted with his genuine love of people, we used to explain by this pathological abnormality of his. Thereby we pitied and loved him even more.'[49] One could respond to this situation, depending on one's measure of tolerance, with anger, curiosity, compassion (as Siloti), or, above all, with indifference as did Alexey Suvorin, editor-in-chief of the *New Times*. He wrote characteristically in his diary on 18 March 1893: 'Tchaikovsky and Apukhtin, both pederasts, used to live together like husband and wife in the same apartment; Apukhtin would be lying in bed, Tchaikovsky would go over to him and say he was going to sleep. Apukhtin would kiss his hand and say: "Go, my dear, I shall come to you presently." '[50]

I wonder whether music always stands in need of a biographical explanation. The Sixth Symphony is permeated with the sense of tragedy not because its author was homosexual, but because of his poignant recognition of mortality, the main feature of the human predicament.

There is no doubt that originally the *Pathétique* Symphony, which Tchaikovsky finished in February 1893, was linked to the plan of the E flat major symphony he thought to call simply *Life*. It was abandoned by the composer in September 1892. The early sketches of the *Life* symphony go back to May 1891, when he was on the return voyage from America. They actually mention that the symphony was to end with the Finale 'death—result of collapse'. Thus, the irreversible doom sounding in the symphony's last movement—which has been adduced in support of the suicide theory—goes back to at least two years before the symphony's première.

Periods of depression are habitual in the life of a creative artist. Tchaikovsky experienced them even when he felt at the peak of his abilities, as for instance, at the time when he worked on *The Queen of Spades*. No less unusual is an occasional presentiment of approaching death such as seized him, according to the recollection of the pianist Vasily Sapelnikov, during his visit to the Tyrol in June 1893. The same memoirist, however, made it clear that at the very same moment Tchaikovsky was full of creative projects.[51]

---

[49] GGTMMK, f. 286, no. 30, 5.
[50] RGALI, f. 459, op. 2, ed. kh. 140, l. 305; incorrectly published in Suvorin, *Dnevnik*, 29.
[51] Poznansky, *Samoubiistvo Chaikovskogo*, 63–4, 66.

This is supported by other documentary evidence. We know of several
opera projects and ideas which Tchaikovsky entertained specifically in
1893. One was Shakespeare's *Merchant of Venice*, which he ultimately
rejected, as he wanted 'something original and profoundly moving'.[52]
Similarly, he decided against another subject, proposed by Modest, Vasily
Zhukovsky's *Nal' and Damaianti* (a version of an episode from the
Mahabharata): 'It is too far removed from life, I need a subject like
Cavalleria Rusticana,' he wrote to his brother.[53] The very last project was
a plot borrowed from George Eliot's tale *Mr Gilfil's Love-Story*. According
to Herman Laroche, this idea 'enthralled him particularly with the pa-
thos of its content'.[54]

Nor was he lacking by this time in public recognition. In 1893 his status of national treasure was further enhanced by a series of highly successful concert tours to Odessa and Kharkov, and his international
reputation was confirmed by an honorary degree awarded to him at the
University of Cambridge. Involved in numerous projects, he was evidently
entering a new period of creative energy.

This is not, however, to deny that, especially late in his life, Tchaikovsky
was often possessed by the fear of death, which in itself speaks strongly
against any suicidal intent. Thus he wrote to his cousin Anna Merkling on
27 April 1884: 'And furthermore what is necessary is to do away with my
fear of death. In this particular regard I cannot boast. I am not so deeply
religious that I might see in death the beginning of new life, and I'm not a
philosopher, that I might reconcile myself to that abyss of non-existence
into which we must sink.'[55]

That he would respond with pain after learning about the deaths of his
acquaintances is, for instance, manifest from the following confession: 'As
a man who passionately loves life (in spite of all its calamities) and who
hates death just as passionately, I always feel deeply shaken when a crea-
ture whom I know and cherish dies.'[56] In this context one has to recall
that in the year 1893 alone Tchaikovsky lost no less than five old friends,
which could not but cause him deep melancholy.

The dedication of the *Pathétique* Symphony to Bob Davydov hints at
an erotic dimension to its content. A characteristic emotional confusion,
a mixture of pleasure and pain, is evidenced in Tchaikovsky's letter to
Bob of 17 May 1893, which is sometimes wrongly cited as proof of a psychological and physical crisis:

[52] *PSS* xvii. 35.
[53] Ibid. 79.
[54] *VC* (1980), 352.
[55] *PSS* xii. 363.
[56] *PSS* xvi. 231.

2. Tchaikovsky with the members of Kharkov Music Society, 14 March 1893

I write to you with a certain voluptuousness. The thought that this piece of paper will be in your hands, at home, fills me with joy and moves me to tears. Is it not curious, in fact, that I voluntarily subject myself to these tortures? What the devil do I need this for? Several times yesterday during the journey I had made up my mind to give it up and bolt, but it's somehow a shame to return with nothing. Yesterday my torments reached the point where I lost sleep and my appetite, and this is extremely rare with me. I suffer not only from an anguish defying verbal expression (in my new symphony there is a place, which seems to express it well), but also from an abhorrence of strange people, from a vague dread and the devil knows what else. Physically this condition manifests itself in a pain in the lower abdomen and an aching and weakness in the legs.[57]

The 1893/94 concert season was extremely full. Ivan Grekov had entreated Tchaikovsky to come to Odessa again. The composer had difficulty in finding the time: concerts were scheduled for 16 October and 27 November in St Petersburg, 4 December in Moscow, 15 and 29 January in St Petersburg again, in March Amsterdam, in April Helsinki, in May

---

[57] *PSS* xvii. 97.

London. He had invitations to Kharkov, Warsaw, Frankfurt am Main, and other cities as well.

So far as his physical condition was concerned, in the course of 1893 Tchaikovsky suffered from a series of indispositions, primarily stomach-related illnesses. The first indisposition occurred in February, when he was on his way from Kamenka to Moscow in a train compartment. He wrote to Modest a few days later: 'I was taken so ill in the carriage that I frightened my fellow passengers by becoming delirious, and had to stop at Kharkov. After taking my usual remedies of castor oil and long sleep, I awoke quite well in the morning. . . . I believe that it was an acute stomach fever.'[58]

Next, while Tchaikovsky was visiting his brother Nikolay at his home in Ukolovo near Kursk in July, there occurred a disorder which his contemporaries called 'cholerina' and considered the early stage or a mild case of cholera. Nikolay wrote about this incident to Modest on 28 July 1893: 'Pyotr left us a day after your departure. He was delayed by the onslaught of cholerine caused by the excessive consumption of cold water.'[59]

One should note that this already affected Tchaikovsky when a cholera epidemic was in progress in Russia and Tchaikovsky was himself aware of it: in one of his letters he enquired of his brother Anatoly, who was at the time the vice-governor of Nizhny Novgorod, as regards the spread of cholera in that area. None the less he continued the habit of drinking unboiled water at meals. Modest was probably correct when in his brother's biography he wrote that Tchaikovsky had little fear of contracting cholera. Another well-documented fact, prominent in his correspondence, is that Tchaikovsky had a particular predisposition to stomach problems. Five years after his death his nephew Bob Davydov went so far as to claim in a letter to Modest that Tchaikovsky for most of his life 'had awful stomach catarrh . . . which reached a crisis and finally became a cause of his mortal illness'.[60] Incidentally, the very fact that the two of them discussed the details of his last illness in their private correspondence altogether rules out the possibility that they could have knowingly participated in a cover-up of the alleged suicide of the composer.

In the latter part of July 1893 Tchaikovsky returned to Klin and set to work at once on scoring the Sixth Symphony. He even asked a few of his friends to come and assist him in the process. The violinist Jules Conus recalled those days in August: 'I must confess that I was really not in the

---

[58] *PSS* xvii. 34.
[59] GDMC, B¹⁰, no. 6670.
[60] GDMC, B¹⁰, no. 1723.

least attracted by the actual music of the Sixth Symphony since the author's performance was as bad as one may imagine. His red hands with thick and by no means supple fingers pounded out the most poignant passages crudely and hurriedly, as if they hastened to finish and rid themselves of that boring thing.'[61]

Undaunted by the slow progress of his work, Tchaikovsky felt none the less increasingly confident about the symphony. He told Bob in early August: 'I am very pleased with its content—although I am not satisfied, or rather, not completely satisfied, with the orchestration. . . . I shall not be surprised if this symphony is torn to pieces or little appreciated, for that will not be the first such case. But I absolutely believe it to be the best and, in particular, the sincerest of all my creations.'[62]

The *Pathétique* Symphony is often regarded as Tchaikovsky's last work, which is demonstrably wrong. Its drafts were completed in 24 March 1893, its score was done between 19 July and 19 August. If one discounts instrumentation, all the movements of the symphony up to the minutest detail were laid down by Tchaikovsky before his composition of eighteen pieces for piano, six songs, the Third Piano Concerto, the Andante and Finale for piano and orchestra, the vocal quartet *Night*, and, most probably, the unfinished duet of Romeo and Juliet. None of these pieces seems particularly tragic: those eighteen piano pieces seem to express the sense of contentment and peace of mind, while the songs after poems by Daniil Rathaus, even though not devoid of some passionate melancholy, do not strike one as at all morbidly pessimistic. The concerto, the Andante and the Finale, ultimately derived from the earlier unfinished E flat major symphony. The very fact that in the last weeks of his life Tchaikovsky returned to the principally vigorous motifs of that work suggest that his creative mood was far removed from black depression.

In a letter to the Russian poet Daniil Rathaus on 1 August 1893 Tchaikovsky thus described his psychological condition after completion of the Sixth Symphony: 'In my music I claim utter candour, and although I too have a predilection for songs of wistful sadness, yet, in recent years at least, I, like yourself, do not suffer from want and can in general consider myself a happy person!'[63] And there is no reason whatsoever to doubt the veracity of this statement.

Towards the end of August or the beginning of September Tchaikovsky finally came up with the title of his new symphony as shown by the unpublished letter of his publisher Pyotr Jurgenson to Tchaikovsky of 20

[61] GDMC, DM², no. 42; *PBC* 174.
[62] *PSS* xvii. 155.
[63] *PSS* xvii. 154.

September 1893.[64] Tchaikovsky decided to call it *Pateticheskaya simfoniya*
and probably around this time he wrote this title in French on the opening
page of the score. This certainly contradicts Modest's claim that he was
solely responsible for the invention of the title (promptly approved by his
brother) on the spur of the moment, the morning after the symphony's
first performance in St Petersburg on 16 October. In Russian *Pateticheskaia
simfonia* means roughly the same thing that Beethoven meant when he
called his Sonata in F minor, Op. 57, the *Appassionata*, that is, 'impas-
sioned', and it does not possess the connotations of its better-known French
equivalent—*Symphonie Pathétique*, 'a symphony of suffering'. Note, for
instance, the title of Mikhail Glinka's *Pateticheskoe trio*—*Trio pathétique*,
which is in fact a very cheerful piece.

Tchaikovsky had almost finished his work when he learned that one of
his oldest friends, the poet Alexey Apukhtin, had died in St Petersburg.
In September he wrote to the Grand Duke Konstantin about his new
symphony: 'Without exaggeration I have put my whole soul into this
work.' He also discussed in this letter the Grand Duke's suggestion to
write a *Requiem* to the poem by Apukhtin; one finds some important
reflections, which are liable to misconstruction:

I am somewhat troubled by the fact that my latest symphony, which has just
been written and is scheduled to be performed on 16 October (I should awfully
like Your Highness to hear it), is imbued with a mood very close to that which
also fills the *Requiem*. I believe that this symphony has turned out well, and I am
afraid of repeating myself, by taking on just now a composition akin in spirit and
character to this one.[65]

Does it follow from this, as some authors would have it, that in creating
the *Pathétique* Symphony Tchaikovsky intentionally wrote a requiem for
himself? Most unlikely. In the letter to the Grand Duke of 26 September,
he clarifies the point, by conclusively rejecting the latter's idea concerning a *Requiem* to a text by Apukhtin:

For the music to be worthy of the poem you like, that poem would have to warm
my creative feelings, to touch and agitate my heart, to awaken my imagination.
The general mood of this piece does, of course, call for musical reproduction, and
my last symphony (particularly the Finale) is permeated with a similar mood.
But if one turns to the details, there is a great deal in this poem of Apukhtin's
that, though expressed in excellent verse, does not call for music—is in fact, even

---

[64] Jurgenson enquired of Tchaikovsky: 'About this *Pathétique* Symphony of yours. It should
be styled *not* Sixth *Pathétique* Symphony but: Symphony No. 6, Pathétique. Do you agree?' This
letter will be published in full by Thomas Kohlhase and Polina Vaidman in Tchaikovsky's *New
Edition of the Complete Works*, 76 vols. (Mainz/Moscow, 1993–).

[65] *PSS* xvii. 186.

antimusical. . . . There is a . . . reason why I am reluctant to compose music for any sort of requiem at all, but I fear to touch indelicately upon your religious sentiment. In the *Requiem* much is said about God the Judge, God the Chastiser, God the Avenger (!!!). Forgive me, Your Highness—but I shall dare to hint that I do not believe in such a God, or at least such a God cannot arouse in me those tears, that rapture, that worship for the creator and source of all blessings, which should inspire me.[66]

In September Tchaikovsky wrote a letter to the Polish composer and pianist Sigismund Stojowski, whom he met in June 1893 in London. He communicated to him the decision to include Stojowski's suite in one of his four concerts he intended to conduct that season in St Petersburg. It was indeed a great favour on the part of the world-famous composer in regard to the young man of 24, and Tchaikovsky hastened to inform him that the actual event was planned for 15 January 1894. He also looked forward to seeing his correspondent at that time in the Russian capital. Telling him of his own news Tchaikovsky remarked in passing that at the moment he felt 'very well, pleased with the completion of the new symphony'.[67]

---

[66] *PSS* xvii. 193–4.
[67] *PSS* xvii. 181.

1

At Home

5 October–9 October 1893

———

5 October

PYOTR TCHAIKOVSKY

Letter to Anatoly Brandukov—cellist, Tchaikovsky's student at the Moscow Conservatoire, and a close friend of the composer; he was the first to perform the *Pezzo capriccioso* (1887), which Tchaikovsky also dedicated to him.

I expect you and Poplavsky tomorrow by the mail train; bring the Saint-Saëns concerto.

PSS xvii. 200

6 October

PYOTR TCHAIKOVSKY

Letter to Sigismund Stojowski—a young Paris-trained Polish pianist and composer, whom Tchaikovsky met for the first time in March 1889 in Paris and later in June 1893 in London. His *Suite for Orchestra*, Op. 9, Tchaikovsky planned to include in one of his four concerts that season in St Petersburg.

As I wrote to you, my new symphony is completed. I am now working on the scoring of the (third) concerto for our dear Diémer.[1] When you see

---

[1] Louis Diémer, French pianist and professor at the Paris Conservatoire. Tchaikovsky dedicated his Third Piano Concerto, Op. 75, to him.

him please tell him that when I proceeded to work on it, I realized that
this concerto is of depressing and threatening length. Consequently I
decided to leave only part one which in itself will constitute an entire
concerto. The work will only improve the more since the last two parts
were nothing very much.

PSS xvii. 201–2 (original in French)

YULIAN POPLAVSKY

A young cellist, graduate of the Moscow Conservatoire, whom
Tchaikovsky had met earlier that year in Moscow. His lively
memoir is the most detailed description of Tchaikovsky's life in
Klin during his last years and is therefore worth quoting *in extenso*.

[On 6 October] Anatoly Brandukov and I were met [at Klin] by a
sprightly, curly-haired coachman, who brought us to the entrance of a
two-storeyed wooden house with a glass-roofed balcony, the last along
the Moscow highway.

Pyotr Ilyich occupied the upper floor. A large room with shelves of
music along the walls and a piano in the middle, a dining-room, and a
bedroom—this was all that was necessary for the solitary musician; all
the remaining rooms of the large house, besides two or three for guests,
were left at the disposal of Alexey, his devoted manservant. Apart from
the main room, none of the other rooms resembled the abode of the most
popular Russian composer, the creator of the opera *Eugene Onegin*. In the
dining-room, in a prominent spot, were displayed memorabilia from *Niva*
[a popular magazine]—Alexey's property. In the bedroom, besides the
bed, a washstand, and a little dressing-table, were an unpainted pine table
near the window and a simple armchair. On the table stood a simple
crystal inkstand, a marvellously crafted china Pierrot head, and a few
small knick-knacks of quite crude workmanship. There too lay some music
paper, a pen, and the manuscript of his last [E flat] piano concerto, which
Pyotr Ilyich had been looking through when we arrived—the concerto,
dedicated to Louis Diémer, who played under the direction of Pyotr Ilyich
in Cambridge, where Tchaikovsky was awarded an honorary doctorate of
music.[2]

This bedroom was also Pyotr Ilyich's study. Its window looks out on a
small, fenced garden with beds of flowers planted by Pyotr Ilyich himself.
If one sat in the chair and looked straight ahead there was nothing apart
from the clouds above, the monotonous fields stretching to the horizon,

---

[2] In fact, Tchaikovsky did not conduct on that occasion but was merely attending Diémer's
concert.

3. Tchaikovsky's house at Klin, near Moscow

and Pierrot's enigmatic smile, to distract one's gaze. It was at this pine table that Pyotr Ilyich worked, rising every morning at seven o'clock. Neither in the mountains of Switzerland, nor on the shores of the Adriatic, nor in America did Pyotr Ilyich write with such willingness as in his own house—in Klin. In the main room, not far from the fireplace, stands a large writing-desk on a pedestal with a beautiful, expensive desk-set and a proliferation of no less costly, elegant knick-knacks. This desk was designated exclusively for correspondence.

As this last visit to Pyotr Ilyich was at the same time my first visit to his house in Klin, I gladly took advantage of my host's hospitality and conscientiously occupied myself with studying the contents of his shelves and albums.

Pyotr Ilyich's music library was unusually diverse. First and foremost was a bookcase with a magnificent Leipzig edition of all the works of Mozart. The works by composers of modern times nearly all included cordial inscriptions from the authors. A place of honour was occupied by the scores of Glinka. Some works by younger composers contained numerous corrections and notes, and frequently suggestions written in the margin in Pyotr Ilyich's hand. He took an interest in every new published score and examined each one carefully.

One of the bookcases was devoted to masters of word and thought. Here, alongside Pushkin, Heine, Alexey Tolstoy,[3] Hugo, were prominently housed weighty volumes, the spines of which were inscribed with the names of Wundt, Schopenhauer, Mill, Spencer, and other philosophers whom artists tend usually to respect rather than read. There, too, stood a small bookcase with artistic, primarily English, editions of world poets—Dante, Shakespeare, Byron, Milton. In the corner was a cabinet with costly gifts. The most striking of these were a gold pen, some goblets and wine bowls, and a little silver Statue of Liberty, brought back from America.

Next I turned to the photographs. The collections went far beyond a fancier's most fervid imagination. Wall portraits of Bach, Handel, Mozart, Beethoven, Glinka, Nikolay Rubinstein, and other musicians, many of them signed 'à mon ami', 'to a great artist', or 'to my colleague', alternated with silver wreaths and family portraits. In a cosy corner with upholstered furniture, on a small oval table, lay artistically executed files with the addresses of Russian and foreign institutions and academic and musical societies. There too stood some lovely morocco boxes filled with photographs, which were divided into sections according to format and size. Here, among artists, singers, poets, composers, and virtuosos from all over the world, I was, I admit, not unpleasantly surprised to see my own signature beneath my own familiar beardless face.

Pyotr Ilyich finished looking over his manuscript, and we proceeded into the dining-room. That evening he spoke to us at length about virtuosos and the demands made upon them by the public. As always, Pyotr Ilyich's conversation was adorned with striking examples from the lives of now celebrated artists whose first steps towards fame Pyotr Ilyich had not only witnessed but quite often directed. . . .

Recalling the start of his musical career, Pyotr Ilyich told us the story of his first honorarium for music. 'When I was at the Conservatoire I was considered a born accompanist. Around this time a young violinist who is now well known in Moscow, Vasily Bezekirsky, arrived in Petersburg and was invited to play at a soirée at the home of the Grand Duchess Elena Pavlovna.[4] I accompanied him at this soirée and received from Bezekirsky a present of a nocturne he had composed. Imagine my surprise the following day when a package arrived from the office of Her Highness and in it were twenty roubles.'

It was about ten in the evening; Klin was already asleep. The family of the servant Alexey had apparently gone to bed as well. Suddenly, in the midst of the almost perfect silence, clear chords like the sounds of

---

[3] Alexey Konstantinovich Tolstoy, Russian poet and writer. Tchaikovsky set a few of his poems to music.
[4] Patroness of the RMS.

4. Yulian Poplavsky, cellist

a tuning fork rang out, and the striking of silver bells began to peal and resound through the entire house. The thirds and sixths of the lesser ones merrily ran through an octave, sometimes lingering over the transitional notes, while the two bells with the clearest and lowest tones carried on an angry exchange into a fourth and, like a bass mainspring, vibrated long and resonantly in the air. It was the chimes of the mantel clock, which Pyotr Ilyich had acquired in Prague. The clockmaker, recognizing his buyer as the conductor of the concert the night before, barely agreed to accept the cost of materials and labour for the clock.

After supper the conversation became quite jolly thanks to one or two jokes of Pyotr Ilyich's concerning his guests and which he delivered *à part*, turning aside from us, as actors do on the stage.

Pyotr Ilyich proposed that we take a look together at a cello concerto by Saint-Saëns with which he was unfamiliar and which Anatoly [Brandukov] intended to play in Petersburg under Pyotr Ilyich's direction, and we got up from the table. Not without some nervousness did I sit at the piano and open the orchestral score, though I had already studied it earlier. When I struck the first chord, I involuntarily jerked my hands back from the keys—never before had I encountered a piano so out of tune. I recalled the assurances of some 'shrewd' people that Pyotr Ilyich wrote exclusively at the piano. One could hardly find more graphic refutation of these absurd conjectures. After testing together the most unsuitable keys, we managed to play: Pyotr Ilyich followed and played the wind part with his left hand, Anatoly [Brandukov] sang the cello theme. This improvised trio with the participation of Pyotr Ilyich Tchaikovsky will always remain in my memory.

Until eleven o'clock, when Pyotr Ilyich usually went to bed, the time passed imperceptibly. Our cordial host personally inspected the rooms prepared for us to make certain that Alexey had provided everything we might need; he went himself to bring us extra blankets, fearful lest we catch a chill during the night, and only then did he wish us good night.

7 October

YULIAN POPLAVSKY

The next morning, at half past eight, I found Pyotr Ilyich having his tea. He was reading the newspapers and sitting by a small table near the window in the main room. Every morning he would drink two cups of hot tea while glancing at the newspapers and reading the dozens of letters which were sent up from the station once a day. Then he would cross over to his writing-desk and write a reply to nearly every letter. All the letters were preserved in the lower drawers of the desk; at the end of the year the drawers were emptied out, and all the correspondence, bundled into folders with the year marked on them, was handed over to Alexey for storage. Pyotr Ilyich was always meaning to sort through this enormous archive—of some twenty years—and single out only the more interesting letters.

Pyotr Ilyich showed me and Anatoly [Brandukov], who had come in, several amusing letters, translating some (he conducted correspondence in five languages). In one, for example, he was invited to participate in a concert somewhere in the south of Germany, being also asked 'to bring along Anton Rubinstein and Glinka (?!)'. It appeared, moreover, that nearly every celebrity pursuing his occupation on the concert platforms of our capital had been invited on Pyotr Ilyich's advice or through his mediation.

A third cup of already cold tea Pyotr Ilyich, as always, took with him to his work-table in the bedroom.

That morning, explaining his view on emotion and expression in music, Pyotr Ilyich said roughly the following:

'The chief goal in performing a work of music must be the task of fathoming and understanding—to the best of one's talent and knowledge—the composer's hidden idea, which, properly speaking, is the content of his music, its meaning. How diversely and richly gifted must a musician's nature be, to express even the main features of a national character: the vivacity and refinement of the Frenchman, the passion of the Italian, the furious gaiety of the Spaniard. The great musicians have created for the entire world, but every one of their works reflects their national character, their epoch. These last two qualities sharply distinguish one work from another and constitute its style. Just as unruffled waters reflect the clouds above, so the soul of an artist reflects what he sees and hears. The ability to convey one's feelings to others is what makes up talent. The greater this talent, the more it reflects the world and the more clearly and comprehensibly it will convey it. A musician before a work of art, like a man deprived of sight before precious jewels he has once seen and now forgotten, can only find a diamond if his hands are capable of sensing the shape, facet, and density of that stone—and the more subtle his touch, the more quickly he will attain his goal. That is why only a genius can comprehend a genius, as Schumann said. One contains an entire treasure-house of diamonds, the other scoops a handful from this treasure-house. Performers of just one type of musical work are blind from birth.'

After ten o'clock we headed out to the forest, which was less than a mile away. If Pyotr Ilyich's home outfit was plainer than plain, the coat in which he appeared on the streets of Klin could safely compete in an exhibition of antique fashions. It had been bought in Vienna a very long time ago. Winter and summer, whatever the weather, Pyotr Ilyich went walking for two hours. Every tree was familiar to our guide. We came to a ditch—the remains of an effort to dig a canal during the reign of Nicholas I, which had been projected to join the Volga with the River Sestra. Well acquainted with the district, Pyotr Ilyich told us about the sad plight of the serfs who had worked on this project. He also expressed regret that he had not had time that summer to accomplish a plan he had conceived with Nikolay Kashkin [a professor at the Moscow Conservatoire] to travel along this canal on foot straight to the banks of the Volga, and hoped to carry out this project the following spring. Dear Pyotr Ilyich, I too had hoped to accompany you!

Imperceptibly we came upon a marvellous spot. A small clearing climbed steeply towards the forest; on the right meandered the Sestra, to the left lay flat fields as far as the eye could see; and if one stood with one's back to the forest, one saw on both sides the bed and embankment of the Nikolaev railway. In the distance could be seen Frolovskoe. Indicating the beauty of this spot, Pyotr Ilyich told us that he would be buried here, 'according to his will'. 'As they pass by on the railway,' he said, 'my friends will point to my grave.' I was somewhat struck by these words. Some five years earlier, when the doctors predicted the death of my late professor Wilhelm Fitzenhagen, and in the spring of 1893, when once again one of Pyotr Ilyich's friends was expected to die any day, he had constantly avoided any discussion about the illness of these people close to him, from which I had concluded that Pyotr Ilyich disliked talking about death.[5]

A strong wind blew up; chilled through, we chose a post or stump some fifty yards off and ran races to warm up. A single yellow mushroom, discovered by Pyotr Ilyich, was deemed the prize of this contest and awarded to the most fleet of foot.

We then decided to return home. Alexey announced with a displeased expression that dinner was not yet ready, and, to fill the time, Pyotr Ilyich suggested that we look over [Herman] Laroche's *Karmozina* Overture.

During dinner Pyotr Ilyich spoke about his latest symphony. Noting his particularly good spirits, we pestered him with our constant request —to write a concerto for cello. 'Why don't you just play some of my

---

[5] Poplavsky probably learned of Tchaikovsky's reaction to the predicted death of Fitzenhagen from Brandukov.

Variations [on a Rococo Theme]?' was his unvarying reply. I started to complain about the inconvenience of several of the variations for cello, and that on the whole they contained very little singing. 'They don't know how to play, but still they pester me,' joked Pyotr Ilyich. 'I've always said that the best work of Tchaikovsky's is sung by [Alexandra] Krutikova in *The Queen of Spades* [the Countess's song in *The Queen of Spades* is borrowed from Grétry's *Richard Cœur-de-lion*]—one of us is not indebted'—and we all laughed.

Pyotr Ilyich was then awaiting a libretto in order to begin an opera (what it was, he did not say), in October he expected to write a concerto for flute which he had already conceived (he intended it for [Paul] Taffanel, the well-known Parisian virtuoso), then several small pieces for piano, and then after that he promised to tackle a cello concerto.

After dinner we stopped at one of the finest grocer's shops in Klin; the owner met us at the door—a tall and thick-set local merchant in a soiled, warm peaked cap. On seeing him, Pyotr Ilyich stretched out his hand. Being remote from music in general and from the works of the composer standing before him in particular, the honourable tradesman showed his respect for Pyotr Ilyich merely by calling him 'your excellency'. From the many 'victuals' proposed we selected an apple fudge. Before it got dark, Pyotr Ilyich showed us his simple housekeeping: hot-air heating, supplies of wood for the winter, stores of cabbage that needed to be chopped up [for canning], in which Pyotr Ilyich himself quite often took part.

Towards five o'clock we began preparing for the trip to Moscow. The contents of the two bags, Pyotr Ilyich's inevitable travelling companions, which I knew well, were gone through and supplemented by Alexey. Egorka appeared, Alexey's two-year-old son and our host's godson. Taking leave of them, Pyotr Ilyich exchanged kisses with both son and father. Alexey, handing his master sixty roubles, bade him buy in Moscow cloth for a coat and some other articles for his wardrobe. We hopped into the cab and twenty minutes later were cheerfully boarding a carriage on the evening train.

VC (1980), 318–24

NIKOLAY KASHKIN

Teacher and music critic; one of Tchaikovsky's professional friends from the Moscow Conservatoire.

Tchaikovsky spent, if I am not mistaken, three days in Moscow, from the seventh to the ninth of October. One day we met at the requiem mass for

[Nikolay Zverev, a pianist and professor at the Moscow Conservatoire] at the church in Gnezdniki [a district of Moscow], and from there Pyotr Ilyich went to the Danilov Monastery to visit Zverev's grave.

N. D. Kashkin, *Vospominaniia o P. I. Chaikovskom*
(Moscow, 1954), 179

8 October

LEONID SABANEYEV

Russian writer on music and composer, who studied with Taneyev at the Moscow Conservatoire.

I remember a solemn funeral mass (in honour of Nikolay Zverev) at the Boris and Gleb Church which was filled with that same public that I used to see at the rehearsals and concerts. I remember the shapely and mobile figure of Tchaikovsky who looked distractedly around and appeared as if he was almost dancing. My mother, who stood side by side with him, addressed him directly, resorting to her right of a lady:
   'Why are you dancing here, Pyotr Ilyich, this is a church . . .'
And, smiling, he straightened up and stood thoughtfully.

Leonid Sabaneev, S. I. Taneev: *Mysli o tvorchestve i
vospominaniia o zhizni* (Paris, 1930), 111

PYOTR TCHAIKOVSKY

Letter to Sergey Taneyev.

May I visit you tonight at seven o'clock? I need your advice on my work (a concerto).

PSS xvii, 202

SERGEY TANEYEV

Russian composer, professor at the Moscow Conservatoire. Studied composition with Tchaikovsky. The following is a short note.

Note from P[yotr] I[lyich] about his E flat major concerto. That day he and Brandukov came to see me. I accompanied him to the Moscow Hotel, had supper with him and [Sergey] Remizov [a Moscow Conservatoire professor]. The last time I saw P[yotr] I[lyich]. No! The next day I saw him at the Conservatoire, where they performed [Tchaikovsky's] *Night*.

RGALI, f. 880, op. 1, ed. kh. 55, l. 3

VASILY YASTREBTSEV

Musical writer and memoirist; biographer of Nikolay Rimsky-Korsakov. The following is from Yastrebtsev's diary.

I learned (from Rimsky-Korsakov) that in the course of this season . . . Tchaikovsky will conduct four concerts, and in the very first one he will perform the newly rewritten Sixth Symphony with the conceptually original Adagio instead of a Finale.[6]

V. V. Iastrebtsev, *N. A. Rimskii-Korsakov: Vospominaniia*
(2 vols., Leningrad, 1959–60), i. 119

9 October

NIKOLAY KASHKIN

On the morning of 9 October he had promised to be at the Conservatoire to hear a performance of his vocal quartet [*Night*] based on a passage from Mozart's piano Fantasia [in C minor, K 475]. Mozart's music remained virtually unchanged, but Tchaikovsky had written the words himself. The quartet had been completed in March 1893, and Pyotr Ilyich at the time had expressed a desire to hear it. Elizaveta Lavrovskaya [a singer (contralto) and also a professor at the Moscow Conservatoire] had promised him to give the quartet to the students in her conservatoire class to learn, and during this visit she told him that the quartet was ready and on the morning of 9 October a number of people gathered in the conservatoire hall to hear it. Tchaikovsky and I sat next to one another in the middle of the hall, the quartet was sung very well and Pyotr Ilyich asked them to repeat it, which they did. He told me that this piece of music held an indescribable charm for him and that he himself could not properly account for why this uncommonly simply melody pleased

---

[6] Yastrebtsev must have been aware of Tchaikovsky's earlier aborted attempt to write the Symphony in E flat.

him so much. Having thanked the performers and Elizaveta Lavrovskaya, Pyotr Ilyich left the Conservatoire, inviting me to dine with him that evening at the Moscow Hotel.

Kashkin, Vospominaniia, 179–80

JULES CONUS

A young violinist and later composer and professor at the Moscow Conservatoire, who helped Tchaikovsky in the scoring of the Sixth Symphony.

Having approached the door (of the room in Grand Moscow Hotel) I still do not dare to enter since I hear that inside Tchaikovsky is angrily scolding someone. Still, having knocked I enquire, 'May I come in?' to which there was a stern response: 'Come in!' To my amazement I see that P[yotr] I[lyich] is moving in the room fiercely and in utter solitude, red in the face: 'What a rascal, what a villain!—that is how he addresses me. 'Can you imagine, I have just visited Jurgenson[7] and he gave me in advance 300 roubles to cover travel expenses, and back here I found the Conservatoire student Abezgauz—you know, the one who plays the bassoon very badly—and he managed to extract from me those 300 roubles, so now I am again without a penny in my pocket, and I have not even money to pay for the hotel!' I immediately offered to provide him with that modest sum. Looking at me with some bewilderment, and after a little thought, he told me laughing: 'Well, find it and come here to have breakfast!'

GDMC, DM[2], no. 43; PBC 174–5

IVAN LIPAEV

Musician, founder of the Society for Musicians' Mutual Aid in 1903.

Only in the autumn of 1893 did I meet Tchaikovsky again in Moscow. . . . I brought him the prepared copy of the statute of the projected Society for Musicians' Mutual Aid. Pyotr Ilyich was incredibly well pleased with this.
    'Pour yourself some tea, while I. . . .'
With those words he snatched the bunch of papers from me and, with a shining expression on his face, became fully engrossed in reading. He started to read silently and quietly, but then became agitated, jumped

---

[7] Pyotr Jurgenson, Tchaikovsky's publisher.

from his chair, went to his desk and began hurriedly to work with a pencil. He would put either question or exclamation marks. I stood behind him and followed his corrections. . . . Tchaikovsky energetically underlined what he considered inaccuracies. My God!—an hour later the entire statute was covered with his pencil notes. From them all one could see that the kindness and humanity of that man knew no limits. . . .

This was late in the autumn. It drizzled, there was noisy wind and slush. I visited Tchaikovsky, contrary to my custom, at six in the evening, and found him at home. He was very happy to see me and, it seems, largely because I introduced a certain variety in his solitude. He was somewhat dispirited and the conversation did not flow. While showing me out, Pyotr Ilyich said with somewhat forced animation:

'Perhaps, we will not see each other soon. . . . I go to St Petersburg for a time. On the other hand, I will be back in a month. When you finish with the statute, send it to me. I will take care of it. . . .'

We said good-bye to each other.

VC (1980), 275–6

NIKOLAY KASHKIN

Visiting Moscow at this time was the manager of the Hamburg Opera, [Bernhard] Pollini, who was an ardent admirer of Tchaikovsky's talent and whose operas he had staged at his theatre in Hamburg. Arriving at the Moscow Hotel that evening for dinner, I found there Pollini, Vasily Safonov [a pianist and conductor, professor at the Moscow Conservatoire, late director of the National Conservatory in New York from 1906 to 1909], and two other foreign guests. The dinner turned out to be of a semi-business character, as we discussed Pollini's suggestion of a grand concert tour through Russia with a German orchestra under the direction of Russian conductors. Pollini proposed to assemble an excellent orchestra in Germany and during the summer season, beginning in June, to travel with this orchestra through central and southern Russia, along the coast of the Black Sea and through the Caucasus, down the Volga, and so on. The conductors were to be Tchaikovsky for his own compositions and Vasily Safonov for the rest of the programme. The orchestra would arrive in Moscow in May and thoroughly rehearse two symphonic concerts—no more than that were planned for any one city—and the tour was proposed to begin in June, with only one concert being given in most cities. The project was enticing in that, given Pollini's resources and his knowledge of business, he could solve any possible problems, and that such concerts for the provinces would be quite unprecedented as far as standards of performance and care of preparation were concerned. In principle

Pollini's project was warmly greeted by all present, and they decided to work out the details, draw up precise estimates, and, if possible, carry out the plan the following summer. Pollini, Safonov, and one of the foreigners went off to an adjoining room where they busied themselves with various preliminary deliberations concerning the general organization of the business; the foreign singer who was with us left for her hotel or the theatre, and Pyotr Ilyich and I were left alone.

We had not seen each other all summer, and therefore had much to talk about. He told me about Cambridge, speaking with great warmth of the professor [Maitland] at the university there, who had put him up in his own house, and of one of his fellow degree recipients, Arrigo Boito, who had charmed him with his wit and culture. I told him about a trip I had made to Sweden and Denmark, and he asked me all sorts of details, showing great interest, for he himself had long wished to travel there but for some reason had never managed to do so. Learning that I had been not far from Bergen, he at once reproached me roundly for not going to meet Edvard Grieg, who lived near Bergen. Pyotr Ilyich not only valued his talent as a composer, he was also personally very fond of both Grieg and his wife, who was, in his words, a guardian angel to her husband, whose health was delicate. Unconsciously the talk turned to our recent losses: the death of Albrecht [Konstantin (Karl) Albrecht, a cellist and professor at the Moscow Conservatoire] and Zverev. We thought of the gaps time had made in our circle of old friends and how few now remained. Involuntarily the question arose: who would be the next to depart forever? With complete conviction I told Pyotr Ilyich that he would no doubt outlive us all; he disputed the probability, but in the end admitted that he had never felt as healthy or as happy as he did now. Pyotr Ilyich had to catch the express to Petersburg that same evening, and it was already time to leave for the station. He was going to Petersburg to conduct his new symphony, the Sixth, with which I was quite unfamiliar. The composer told me that he had no doubts whatever concerning the first three movements, but that he was still uncertain about the final movement, and perhaps after the Petersburg performance he would destroy that movement and replace it with something new. The Musical Society in Moscow had scheduled a concert for 23 October. Tchaikovsky intended to return to Klin a few days earlier, and to arrive in Moscow on the day of the concert. In case we did not see one another at the concert, we arranged to meet after the concert at the [Grand] Moscow Hotel, where he wanted to take several people to supper, including the singer Eugène Oudin, who had been invited to the Musical Society at his instruction. With this our conversation ended, we parted, and Tchaikovsky left for the station, where his luggage had already been taken from the hotel. Neither Pyotr Ilyich nor I were fond of farewells, so it did not occur to me to go with him to the station, especially as we expected to see each other again in two weeks' time, while the possibility of eternal separation, of course, never entered our heads. . . .

Let me mention that, in my opinion, people are quite wrong to perceive some connection between the Sixth (*Pathétique*) Symphony in B minor and the death of its composer; they strive to find in it an expression of presentiment of death, some sort of final testament to the living. I was left with nothing at all resembling such an impression after my final meeting with Tchaikovsky; he mentioned in passing his original intention, later abandoned, to write an entire programme for this symphony, generally speaking about it like any other composition, and, having completed the symphony in August, he had immediately set to work on other projects. During the last days he spent in Moscow, he reminded me of his plans to embark on an enormous ocean voyage, such as a trip to South America or Australia, with me accompanying him. When we discussed my trip to Sweden, he mentioned that the coming winter he would finally be visiting Stockholm, where he intended to conduct one or two concerts and where he was already expected, as I was told, in Stockholm itself. The composer Svendsen from Copenhagen recently informed me that he had received a letter from Tchaikovsky, announcing his impending arrival in Denmark. . . . This serves as still further evidence that he was full of plans for the future. At the same time he had already plotted his next big project: a major revision of his opera *The Oprichnik*, in which nearly half the opera was to be completely rewritten and the libretto itself significantly altered. In short, he was preoccupied with thoughts and plans concerning life, not death; for the past several years we had spoken of death as the approaching inevitable end to our existence, and in those final days we did not speak of it any more than before. In the days of his youth Tchaikovsky feared the very idea of death, but as he approached old age this fear vanished completely, though he never lost his desire to prolong his earthly existence as long as possible, whose greatest fascination for him lay in his own inner life and his delight in nature, which he loved to the point of worship.

Kashkin, *Vospominaniia*, 179–85

PYOTR TCHAIKOVSKY

Letter to Frederic Lamond, young Scottish pianist and composer. Tchaikovsky met him in Germany in February 1889.

Dear Fellow Artist, I understand with joy from your letter that you play my pianoforte concertos. Perhaps an opportunity may be found to play here in Moscow, and I have spoken warmly about it to Monsieur Safonov [principal conductor of Moscow Branch of the RMS]: tout à vous, Tchaikovsky.

Frederic Lamond, *The Memoirs of Frederic Lamond*
(Glasgow, 1949), 95; *PSS* xvii. 202–3 (original in French)

Clearly, the material presented in this chapter refutes the contention by some biographers that shortly before his death Tchaikovsky was experiencing a severe psychological and spiritual crisis which led ultimately to catastrophe. It has been argued that Modest manipulated or suppressed pertinent evidence in his narrative in order to create a false impression that no crisis had existed—a somewhat preposterous claim, given that no clear or persuasive evidence has yet come to light supporting the existence of such a crisis. In fact, Tchaikovsky's correspondence of the period bears no trace of any unusual strain, but rather reveals his habitual mixture of high and low moods, of creative inspiration and dissatisfaction, with occasional complaints about numerous stomach problems, which were a characteristic feature of what may probably be termed Tchaikovsky's lifelong somatic neurosis.

Those who hold to the prejudiced view in regard to Modest's chronicle have, however, gone so far as to disclaim his statement that his brother was in excellent spirits during his last residence in Klin in October 1893. For this reason Modest's account is here replaced by the memoir of Yulian Poplavsky, who visited the composer in Klin at precisely this time and published his testimony just a year after the events he described and long before Modest's biography of Tchaikovsky saw the light of day. What Poplavsky recalls, however, supports unequivocally and further amplifies Modest's assertion. The man who emerges from these reminiscences is well content with life, strictly following his established work routine and preoccupied with his professional interests. He is not averse to a joke, sharing with his guests not only meditations on loftier matters but also amusing stories and anecdotes. He also confided in them thoughts about his creative projects for the near future—a new opera, a concerto for flute, several pieces for piano, a cello concerto—as well as his plans for making a journey to the banks of the Volga on foot the following summer with his friend Kashkin.

Poplavsky has an eye for detail, and he lovingly portrays Tchaikovsky's personality and his surroundings. The only melancholy note in his account is the composer's mention of his wish to be buried in Klin. The remark sounds authentic enough and in fact accords with Tchaikovsky's known taste for sentimentality. It was a subject, moreover, that must have loomed fairly large in his mind at that moment for the simple reason that the year 1893 had witnessed the deaths of several of his close friends, no less than five of whom had died within a short space of time. Just a few days before Poplavsky's arrival he learned of the death of the professor at the Moscow Conservatoire Nikolay Zverev. As we already know, Tchaikovsky's fear of death, particularly in his earlier years, is well documented. Still, an anecdote found in the Sabaneyev reminiscences, which rings true for the very reason of its contrast with the behaviour expected under the circumstances, indicates that even in the course of the solemn funeral mass Tchaikovsky was moved by things which were evidently far from morbid.

It is true that the theme of health and foreboding also—but only to be dismissed as of no consequence—stands out in Nikolay Kashkin's account of his last meeting with Tchaikovsky in Moscow on 9 October—a memoir published, like that of Poplavsky, before the appearance of Modest's work. That the composer's remarks as reported—given their context—could hardly have been invented by Kashkin, makes the latter's statement particularly valuable. According to Kashkin, when their conversation touched upon the dwindling of their circle owing to the recent deaths of friends, Tchaikovsky nevertheless admitted that 'he had never felt as healthy or as happy as he did now'. Also worth noting is Kashkin's testimony regarding the composer's uncertainty about the last movement of his Sixth Symphony, the *Pathétique*. Apparently Tchaikovsky was hesitating over whether to leave the movement as it was or to replace it with something new. It is, of course, this very movement, the famous *Adagio lamentoso*, which has led so many later critics and admirers to believe, in retrospect, that it is a poignant expression of some mysterious private torment plaguing the composer, a kind of presentiment of his own death or even of some suicidal intent. Finally, Kashkin's text allows another glimpse of Tchaikovsky's plans for both the immediate and the more distant future, ranging from a concert of the Moscow Musical Society scheduled for 23 October to participation in a grand concert tour across Russia by a German orchestra the following June. The entry from Sergey Taneyev's notes provides further confirmation of the composer's chiefly professional preoccupations during his last brief stay in Moscow, and a little vignette provided by Jules Conus offers a vivid snapshot of a man in high spirits, and full of generosity despite mundane concerns he might have had. Ivan Lipaev's reminiscences portray Tchaikovsky in two different moods, which is by no means unusual: moodiness was a prominent trait of Tchaikovsky's character. Nothing justifies the attempts of some biographers to read into this account a hint of some impending trouble or premonition of death. On the contrary: the composer is shown as busily engaged in important social and professional matters, and looking forward to resuming the same activities upon his return from St Petersburg. The letters to the young pianists Sigismund Stojowski and Frederic Lamond demonstrate strongly that Tchaikovsky had plans to help both of them in their musical careers and was looking forward to seeing each in the near future.

2

The *Pathétique*

10 October–17 October

10–15 October

MODEST TCHAIKOVSKY

The composer's younger brother, a playwright, translator of Shakespeare, and Tchaikovsky's biographer. Modest's account is quoted from his three-volume biography, *Zhizn' Petra Ilicha Chaikovskogo* [*The Life of Pyotr Ilyich Tchaikovsky*], published in Moscow between 1900 and 1902, with occasional verification against its first publication in St Petersburg's newspapers on 1 November 1893.

Pyotr Ilyich arrived in St Petersburg on 10 October. As usual, our nephew and I met him, and I found him as hale and hearty as when I had last seen him in Moscow. He liked everything about our new apartment, and his good mood stayed with him, especially during the first few days, while his arrival was not yet known in the city and he could still dispose of his time freely.

Only one thing disturbed him: the musicians at the rehearsals were little impressed with his Sixth Symphony. Besides the fact that he valued their opinion, he was worried that their indifference might affect the actual performance of the piece. Pyotr Ilyich conducted well only those of his works which he knew the orchestra liked. In order to achieve subtlety of shading, overall harmony, it was essential for him to feel sympathy and pleasure from those around him. A cold expression, an indifferent gaze, the yawn of an orchestra member, all understandable when a piece was as yet unfamiliar, constrained and flustered him, and he paid scant attention to polishing up details, but tried to get the rehearsal over with as quickly as possible in order to release the musicians from their boring chore. Thus whenever he was conducting a new composition for the first time, his performance showed an uncertainty, even carelessness, in his communication of details—a lack of determination and strength in communicating the whole. That is why the Fifth Symphony and *Hamlet*, given such a pallid showing by their composer, had so bad a time winning a true appraisal, and also why the *Voyevoda* ballad perished.

ZC 642–3

NIKOLAY KASHKIN

During his last visit to Petersburg, at rehearsals for the première of his Sixth Symphony, he began to despair over his ineptitude and the day before the concert went to Eduard Nápravník to ask him to conduct the symphony in his stead, but Nápravník refused, as he could not possibly familiarize himself with a new and very difficult composition in the one rehearsal remaining—and Tchaikovsky had to conduct it himself. The performance was probably far from brilliant, and it must have cost the composer dearly to know that he himself had spoiled his work.

MV, 23 June 1903

WALTER NOUVEL

Music critic for the journal *World of Art* and friend of Sergey Diaghilev.

As with all the works of this great composer, we waited with impatience for the first performance of his latest symphony [the *Pathétique*], which he was to conduct himself at the symphonic concert of the Imperial Music Society.

The day before, at nine in the morning, Diaghileff and I went to the *répétition générale*. With what eager attention did we listen to his rehearsal of the symphony, and to his piano concerto! We drank in each note. I remember, also, that on the same programme were Mozart's *Danses d'Idoménée*. I shall never forget the expression of beatitude on Tchaikovsky's face while he played the work of the composer for whom he had an admiration amounting almost to worship.

Arnold L. Haskell, in collaboration with Walter Nouvel,
Diaghileff (New York, 1935), 48

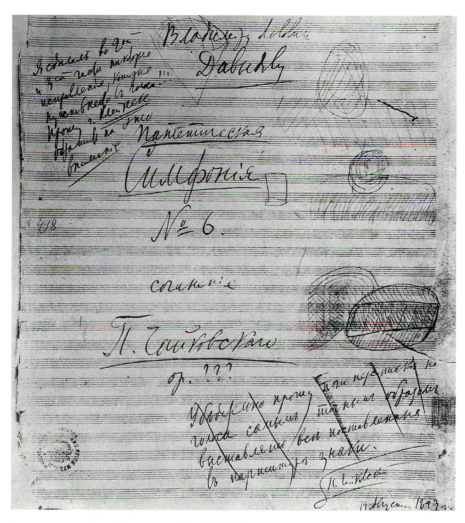

5. Title-page from the score of the Sixth Symphony

16 October

EDUARD NÁPRAVNÍK

Composer and chief conductor of the Maryinsky Theatre; throughout nearly his entire professional life Nápravník kept a meticulous
record of musical events at which he was present in his journal or
Pamiatnaia kniga.

At the first symphonic concert of the Imperial Russian Musical Society
under the direction of P[yotr] I[lyich] Tchaikovsky [was performed] his
new Sixth Symphony in B minor, the *Pathétique*(?!).

RIII, f. 21, op. 1, ed. kh. 227, ll. 57–8

MODEST TCHAIKOVSKY

Besides the Sixth Symphony the programme . . . of the concert directed
by Pyotr Ilyich included [after the interval] the Overture to Laroche's
unfinished opera *Karmozina*, Tchaikovsky's Piano Concerto in B flat Minor, Op. 23, performed by Miss Aus-der-Ohe, the dances from Mozart's
opera *Idomeneo*, and the piano solo from Liszt's *Spanish Rhapsody*, performed by [Adele] Aus-der-Ohe [a German pianist].

ZC 643

GRAND DUKE KONSTANTIN KONSTANTINOVICH

This entry and the subsequent quotations in the following chapters
are taken from the Grand Duke's unpublished private diary.

We went to the city to hear at the Hall of the Nobility the first symphonic concert with Tchaikovsky as conductor. The concert started with
Tchaikovsky's new Sixth Symphony in B minor. I liked it very much.
The introductory Adagio is very sombre and mysterious, and it sounds
charming. It transforms into an Allegro which has beautiful passages.
The second part *Allegro con grazia* is written in 5/8 or 5/4, and it is very
lucid and good. The third part, a kind of Scherzo has a loud march in the
end. And the Finale in the tempo Adagio; it has passages reminiscent of
a funeral service. I saw Tchaikovsky in the interval.

GARF, f. 660, op. 1, d. 40, l. 135

6. The Hall of the Nobility in St Petersburg, where the first performance of Tchaikovsky's Sixth Symphony was held

THE ST PETERSBURG REGISTER

The season of symphonic concerts organized by the Russian Musical Society opened in the Hall of the Nobility. The interest of the first concert lay in the fact that it was conducted by P[yotr] I[lyich] Tchaikovsky. The public extended a warm and heartfelt welcome to its beloved composer and every number on the programme was accompanied by friendly approval. The main piece of the evening was the first performance of Tchaikovsky's Sixth Symphony. In thematic respect this new large-scale work by the talented composer does not show particular originality. Its themes are neither novel nor terribly striking, but this shortcoming is compensated for by the highly effective and brilliant orchestration, in which Tchaikovsky has achieved great perfection. The finest movement in the symphony is the last: an *Adagio lamentoso*. This movement, thanks to the splendid qualities of the orchestra, makes a powerful impression. The two Allegros are less well developed by the composer. All in all, however, the symphony pleased the audience and was a success.

SPV, 18 Oct. 1893

WALTER NOUVEL

The performance took place before a packed and enthusiastic house. We were all especially impressed by the fact that the symphony was concluded by a melancholy *Adagio*, whose last bars diminished like a dying breath.

Haskell, *Diaghileff*, 48

SERGEY DIAGHILEV

Creator and director of the famous Ballets Russes.

The work had been passionately awaited. At the rehearsal opinions were greatly divided. . . . The concert's success was naturally overwhelming. . . . That evening the composer conducted in his usual nervous way. I heard afterwards that he had overlooked numerous mistakes in the scoring.

Richard Buckle, *Diaghilev* (New York, 1979), 23

NIKOLAY RIMSKY-KORSAKOV

Composer and member of the 'Five'.

During the interval, after the symphony had been performed, I asked whether he had any programme for this composition. He said that of course he had, but that he did not wish to reveal it. It was only at this concert that I saw him during this, his last visit.

N. A. Rimsky-Korsakov, 'Letopis'moei muzykal'noi zhizni', *Polnoe sobranie sochinenii* [Complete Works] (Moscow, 1955), i. 193

ANATOLY LYADOV

Composer, conductor, and professor at the St Petersburg Conservatoire.

Following the performance of the Sixth Symphony . . . I visited the dressing-room just as one of the directors of the RMS, Mr Klimenko, was attempting with various courtesies to disguise the fact that he had not liked the symphony. 'But Anatoly here likes it,' said Tchaikovsky, addressing me. He well perceived that despite their applause the public remained cool to his new composition. But I could express my genuine opinion, since I had been greatly impressed by the Sixth Symphony.

SR 44 (1913), 10

LEOPOLD AUER

Hungarian violinist and pedagogue; from 1868 he taught at the St Petersburg Conservatoire where he became one of the most famous violin teachers in Russia.

On [16] October Tchaikovsky had directed his swan-song, the *Symphony Pathétique*, for the first time in public, at a Philharmonic concert. The last movement of this famous symphony is an *Adagio lamentoso*, a kind of funeral song, and it almost seemed as though the composer had anticipated his sudden end, notwithstanding that he was in perfect health and full of vigour. All of us in the concert hall that night were not only impressed by the beauty of the work, but also profoundly moved by the dramatic poignancy of the final chords. When I went up to congratulate him, he appeared utterly happy and content with the success he had achieved, joked and laughed; and, at the same time—there was this strange finale, unique of its kind as the closing movement of a symphony!

Leopold Auer, *My Long Life in Music*
(London, 1924), 284

ANATOLY KOPTYAEV

Music critic.

I recall the performance of the *Pathétique*. . . . Afterwards, not yet a musician then myself, I met in the Hall of the Nobility a celebrity who proclaimed: 'Only the first movement is any good,' which served as an oblique reproach against the conductor-composer.

BV, 20 Oct. 1913

ALEXANDER GRECHANINOV

Composer and conductor.

The concert season that year began with Tchaikovsky's new Sixth Symphony, which was performed under the direction of the composer. . . .

Tchaikovsky, as everyone knows, was a poor conductor and his now celebrated *Pathétique* Symphony met with only modest success.

A. Grechaninov, *Moia muzykal'naia zhizn'*
(Paris, 1934), 41

VIKTOR KOLOMIYTSOV

Music critic.

When Tchaikovsky appeared on stage at the concert—as usual, somewhat embarrassed and concealing his anxiety with movements exaggeratedly assured—the entire Hall of the Nobility, full of people, greeted him with a long ecstatic ovation and the orchestra played him a flourish even though, it would seem, there was no specific reason for such festivity and joy: salutation spontaneously, involuntarily broke out. When everything had quietened down, Pyotr Ilyich put on his pince-nez, and with the same assured gesture opened the large manuscript score on the conductor's rostrum, knocked with his baton, and the sounds of *Pathétique* Symphony poured out for the first time. Apparently, it was liked, every part of it was heatedly applauded, but this new work still had not extraordinarily impressed the majority of the audience. The blame must be placed on the author himself whose talent as a conductor was by no means particularly brilliant.

V. Kolomiitsov, *Stat'i i pis'ma* (Leningrad, 1971), 64–5

HERMAN LAROCHE

Music critic and composer, and Tchaikovsky's classmate at the St Petersburg Conservatoire.

The principal work of the first concert of the RMS, given . . . under the direction of Pyotr Tchaikovsky before a packed house, was the conductor's new symphony (No. 6 in B minor, manuscript). . . .

One must first of all make a distinction in the new work between *material and form*. The material, that is, the melody and its contrapuntal development, is magnificent throughout. As far as the melody is concerned, we have begun to see in the last few years a particular richness in Tchaikovsky's work, an inexhaustible abundance and passionate thematic charm, and his new symphony in this respect deserves to stand with this whole period. The contrapuntal treatment, for its part, shines with compressed energy and unfailing beauty; like the fate of the main characters in a skilfully constructed novel, the fate of the themes in the contrapuntal passages of the B Minor Symphony constantly 'intrigues' you, and nowhere does the interest flag. But the form is somewhat mysterious. The 'secondary part', that is, the second theme of the first Allegro, has the character of a small independent *andante*, contained and separated from the continuation with unusual firmness, through the aid of a cadenza repeated several times; this is followed by a sort of dramatic seething, not unlike those rhythmical and orchestral devices which in opera are used to depict popular unrest, inrushing crowds, and so on. Only then does the development begin, that is, the contrapuntal elaborated middle section of the Allegro. The secondary part is more operatic in style than symphonic. I feel obliged to add that it seems to me personally that the mutually alien elements in the third part of the Allegro converge and flow together comparatively more, perhaps, simply because we have already had time to hear both themes. All the same, one is left with an impression of something alluring and uncommonly beautiful, but which goes beyond symphonic boundaries. The same is true of the final (fourth) movement of the symphony, an Adagio instead of the usual Allegro or Presto, which has a flowing melody in a major key and ends in a minor key, with a muffled morendo in the lowest register of the orchestra, as though an accompaniment to something occurring on stage, such as, for instance, the slow death of the hero; here too, with the extraordinary beauty of the melody, one senses not so much a symphonic as an operatic character. The same cannot be said of the two middle movements of the symphony, which in my view (for all the beauty of the first and final movements) constitute the pearls of the score. Here the music exists solely on its own terms and produces a fully aesthetic impression, without confusing the listener with some conception of a sphere merged with it or bordering on it. The second movement—a sort of intermezzo in 5/4 time, holding a median between a fast and a slow tempo—is based on a graceful, charming theme (constructed on an ascending major scale) and once again captivates us with the inexhaustible versatility and variety of its contrapuntal accompaniment. The third movement belongs to that type of fast Scherzo so popular nowadays, where the main theme is glimpsed fleetingly as it rushes by pianissimo and spiccato, the first example of which, if I am not mistaken, was offered by Beethoven in his *Eroica* Symphony. But here we are dealing with a completely new, original, and indivisible form of this kind of Scherzo. A fast, simple theme combines with that of a lighthearted and foppish march, the four fourths of which constitute the four bars of the first theme; as it progresses, lively, brisk, bold, the march becomes denser and more powerful, gaining increasing dominance, until finally, having overwhelmed the airy initial theme completely, it thunders forth in magnificent fortissimo. The purely elemental process of gradual *thickening* (like all processes of *mobile* elements, which are highly akin to music) is represented here in a corresponding musical picture which is not only technically brilliant but also full of genuine poetry. I cannot recall a single one of my favourite compositions by Tchaikovsky which combines to a greater degree originality of design and artistry of execution, the skill of a master and the inspiration of a creator, and I believe the time is not far off when the public too, who on the whole regarded the new score, including the Scherzo, with respectful reserve, will come to understand its beauties and place it alongside the composer's most valued pages. . . .

Let me say a few warm words about the audience. They behaved, as it were, in a *foreign* manner: without speaking or making noise, they listened with the greatest attention and applauded sparingly (though they greeted Tchaikovsky rapturously *at his first appearance*). . . . I felt a respect for the public which, to tell the truth, they have rarely inspired in me. If they did not get to the core of Tchaikovsky's *Sixth Symphony* today, then tomorrow or the day after tomorrow they will begin to appreciate it and, in the end, come to love it. In any event, they were preoccupied with what they had come for, that is, music.

TG, 22 Oct. 1893

VLADIMIR NÁPRAVNÍK

Son of the conductor Eduard Nápravník.

I attended all the rehearsals, beginning with the first play-through. The Maryinsky Theatre orchestra, which played at all the major concerts in Petersburg, felt sincere affection for Pyotr Ilyich as a composer and a person, and the musicians met all the composer's intentions—but nevertheless things definitely did not work out well at all. To Pyotr Ilyich's great chagrin, the symphony was not a genuine success. The ovations of the public were directed more to the person of the universally beloved composer than to the new work.

VC (1980), 222

MODEST TCHAIKOVSKY

We have seen . . . several times how easily Pyotr Ilyich was infected by other people's opinions of his works and how often under someone else's influence he might shift from an enthusiastic to a disdainful attitude towards a work, or the reverse. This time he remained unshakeable, and, despite the coolness of the musicians, continued to maintain that he 'had never written and never would write anything better than this symphony'. Nevertheless, he did not succeed in making either the performers or the public believe this at the concert of 16 October. The symphony was liked— it was applauded, and the composer called forth, but no more enthusiastically than after the performance of his other works.

ZC 643

ALEXANDER GLAZUNOV

Composer and conductor, director of the St Petersburg Conservatoire (1905–28).

I remember leaving the concert with him. . . . He complained bitterly to me that his latest composition had not been much of a success and that the musicians seemed to dislike it. At the same time he remarked that he always tended to be disappointed after the first performance of his works, but that this time he was pleased with his offspring.

VC (1980), 209

17 October

VLADIMIR NÁPRAVNÍK

The next day he came to have breakfast with my father. Stopping by my room, he said: 'You know, the symphony yesterday wasn't much of a success with the public; but what grieves me even more is that I feel the orchestra didn't like it.'

VC (1980), 222

ANATOLY KOPTYAEV

The following morning I visited Pyotr Ilyich (he was staying with his brother Modest Ilyich, on what was then Malaya Morskaya Street) at the hour he had appointed, and noticed how the composer responded to my praise of his symphony with a majestic nod of his head (ordinarily he was unaffected). This nervous and uncomfortable haughtiness demonstrated how pained Pyotr Ilyich had been by the chilly reception of his symphony on the part of our public.

BV, 25 Oct. 1913

ALEXANDER GRECHANINOV

About two days after the concert I saw N[ikolay] R[imsky]-Korsakov and we exchanged opinions concerning the new symphony we had just heard.

'Yes, it's not too bad. It sounds good enough. Ending with a slow movement is original, but all in all it's nothing new after the Fourth or the Fifth.'

That, roughly, is what was said.

Grechaninov, Moia muzykal'naia zhizn', 41

YURY YURYEV

Actor with the Alexandrinsky Theatre in St Petersburg.

Only in the last year of his life did I make the personal acquaintance of the composer.

Not long before this I had graduated from the Theatrical School in Moscow and had joined the company of Petersburg's Alexandrinsky Theatre.

One of the first plays in which I was to appear was *Prejudices*, which was written by Modest Tchaikovsky, the composer's brother, and later his biographer. In assigning the parts, the producer of the theatre could not decide which role to entrust to me: the choice was between two characters—a progressive-minded student and an aristocrat, who is ridiculed in the play. In order to reach a final decision, I was advised to consult directly with the author, asking him to listen to me perform some excerpts from the play.[1]

This I did. On the appointed day I presented myself at Modest's apartment on the corner of Malaya Morskaya and Gorokhovaya—the apartment where Pyotr Ilyich was then also staying and which was fated to become the composer's final dwelling.

Warmly welcomed by Modest, I explained to him the reason for my visit, and, at his invitation, began reading.

I had barely finished when the door opened and the so easily recognizable figure of Pyotr Ilyich appeared on the threshold, accompanied by a young man in military uniform. The young man was Vladimir Davydov, 'Bob' as he was called, Tchaikovsky's favourite nephew. We were introduced.

'But uncle Pyotr and I have been eavesdropping on you!'

---

[1] In the end, Yuryev did not receive either role.

Vladimir announced mischievously, 'My uncle got down on his knees and was looking through the keyhole.'

I was quite amazed by the unconstrained playfulness of the respected composer.

We began talking. Pyotr Ilyich asked me all about my work in the theatre and my first impressions of Petersburg.

'Look what a splendid view we have,' and with these words he took my arm and led me out to the balcony. Before us in the glow of the sunset loomed the magnificent building of St Isaac's Cathedral.

Both brothers began to urge me to stay for dinner. Because of my timidity I stubbornly declined. But their irresistible hospitality ultimately won, and I was compelled to acquiesce.

In the dining-room I met several people unknown to me. They included two young men, the Litke brothers [Alexander and Konstantin], nephews of Pyotr Ilyich, the then well-known pianist Sapelnikov[2] and his brother, the violinist; Pyotr Ilyich's close friend, the music critic Laroche, who charmed me with his animation and wit.

The conversation turned to an invitation for Pyotr Ilyich to travel abroad to conduct a concert of his works and his reluctance to go. 'I agree with you—you're not much of a conductor,' said Laroche, half-joking. 'But you must know', he continued more seriously, 'how important this is for our cause, for the propagation of Russian music. You are obliged to go, you do not have the right to refuse.'

After dinner, coffee was proposed, and we all made ourselves comfortable in the cosy drawing-room. Pyotr Ilyich's kindness knew no bounds. 'What shall I play for you?' he asked me and in response to my request performed my favourite piece—the waltz from *The Sleeping Beauty*. Then he played the funeral march from his music for *Hamlet*.

'Won't you come with us tonight to the Maryinsky?' Tchaikovsky asked me. 'We have a box. They're doing *Carmen*. You know, it's my favourite opera. What extraordinary talent, what lushness and brilliance! I could listen to that opera every day.'

I. M. Iur'ev, *Zapiski* (2 vols.; Moscow/Leningrad, 1939–45), ii. 75–8

KONSTANTIN DE LAZARI

Actor and a friend of Tchaikovsky's from the time of his early years in Moscow.

---

[2] Vasily Sapelnikov was not in St Petersburg at this time; Yuryev must be confusing him with somebody else.

It was Sunday, 17 October 1893. I was riding along Morskaya, when suddenly I heard a loud voice: 'Konstantin, where are you going?'

Seeing Tchaikovsky and Laroche standing near a shop, I jumped down from the cab. We embraced and kissed and began asking one another questions.

'You should be ashamed, Konstantin, not to be at the concert yesterday where I conducted my new symphony and Laroche's *Karmozina* Overture!'

'But why didn't you let me know that you'd arrived?' I asked.

'I didn't know your address, dear fellow, otherwise I'd have stopped by or written. I'm planning to settle in Petersburg permanently. Then we'll see each other often, and I hope to dine with you once a week without fail. Only with Laroche as well, of course.'

I was especially struck by his uncommon vim and vigour. Not for quite some time had he appeared so energetic and healthy. We all kissed and parted.

RO, 18 July 1900

As evidenced by these contemporary accounts, the first performance of Tchaikovsky's Sixth Symphony in St Petersburg on 16 October 1893 enjoyed, at best, what can only be described as a moderate success. Yet at the symphony's second performance on 6 November, shortly after the composer's death, the response would be overwhelming: not only was the composition acclaimed as a masterpiece, it was also universally believed to have been intended by Tchaikovsky to serve as a personal requiem of sorts. Such is the remarkable power of hindsight in our perception of events. Nothing like this later exaltation accompanied the symphony's première just three weeks earlier. Though the work was commanded by both audience and critics, this was a far cry from the enthusiasm felt for his creation by the composer himself. Despite his annoyance at the indifference of the orchestra and the rather cool reception on the part of the public—circumstances which in earlier years would have plunged him into depression and self-doubt—he stood his ground and persisted in maintaining that the symphony constituted his finest achievement. The critics viewed matters otherwise, with the distinguished Rimsky-Korsakov contending, in agreement with a newspaper reporter, that the music of the Sixth Symphony represented nothing new in Tchaikovsky's career as a composer.

Notably, the famous final movement—destined to be the source of so much speculation and rapture—was deemed impressive by some, but dismissed by others as of no consequence. Even Herman Laroche, who in a subtle and intelligent piece of criticism predicted the eventual recognition of the symphony's greatness, openly preferred its two central movements to the first and the last. The Grand Duke Konstantin Konstantinovich on the other hand appreciated all the Symphony's movements at that performance even thought he found that some sounded 'gloomy and mysterious.'

Much was made of Tchaikovsky's remark, reported by Rimsky-Korsakov, that the Sixth Symphony had a programme which he did not wish to reveal. Some writers have inflated his comment to the point of enigma, wondering what exactly this 'secret' programme could have been: a confession of homosexual anguish or a projection of suicide? The debate is both idle and naïve. There is evidence enough to assume that the programme in question is no mystery at all. In fact, Tchaikovsky developed the composition to a great extent from the sketches for an earlier work, a symphony in E flat major (1891–2) which he planned to entitle *Life* in his notebooks, but which he considered a failure and never completed.

As is clear from Eduard Nápravník's entry of 16 October in his diary (*Pamiatnaia kniga*), Tchaikovsky's last symphony had been already given the title *Pathétique*. This contradicts again Modest's claim in his biography that he was solely responsible for the title by having suggested it the day after. As it was noted, this title was decided upon by Tchaikovsky himself at least a month earlier.

One should, however, be aware that Yury Yuryev's memoirs are often unreliable and to some extent even fictional, but on the other hand he successfully reproduces many valuable details, which vividly recreate the atmosphere of the time.

3

St Petersburg

18 October–20 October

---

18 October

PYOTR TCHAIKOVSKY

Letter to Pyotr Jurgenson, Tchaikovsky's music publisher in Moscow.

Please, my dear, inscribe the following on the frontispiece:

To Vladimir L'vovich
Davydov
Symphonie Pathétique
(No. 6)
op. ???
by P. Tchai[kovsky]

I hope it is not too late! Something strange is going on with this symphony! It is not that it wasn't liked, but it has caused some bewilderment. As far as I am concerned, I am prouder of it than any of my other compositions. But we shall speak of this soon, for I will be in Moscow on Saturday.

I embrace you. P[yotr] Tchaikovsky

For God's sake, send the Finale of the suite by Conus to the St Petersburg Conservatoire as soon as possible. If it is not printed, let it be sent in manuscript.[1]

PSS xvii. 205

---

[1] Tchaikovsky included the suite of Jules Conus's brother Georgy in the programme of the second concert given by the RMS which had been scheduled for 27 Nov. 1893.

THE PETERSBURG LEAFLET

On Monday Tchaikovsky gave a dinner for the pianist Aus-der-Ohe, with whose talent he had become acquainted during his visit to America, and in the afternoon he was present at the hall of the Kononov opera company for a dress rehearsal of his *Eugene Onegin*.

PL, 26 Oct. 1893

THE NEW TIMES

[At eight in the evening] P[yotr] I[lyich] attended a production of his opera *Eugene Onegin* at the Maryinsky Theatre.

NV, 26 Oct. 1893

NIKOLAY FIGNER

Singer with the St Petersburg Opera.

I saw P[yotr] I[lyich] on Monday, at the Maryinsky Theatre. He was cheerful as usual and talked of the last symphonic concert and of our projected tour to Paris. (P[yotr] I[lyich] planned to go there with my wife and me for a series of concerts.)

NBG, 26 Oct. 1893

VLADIMIR POGOZHEV

Director of the Petersburg branch of the Imperial Theatres.

During what turned out to be our last meeting in this world, one that I remember especially clearly, I persisted in renewing a topic of conversation I had already raised repeatedly with Pyotr Ilyich concerning his opera *The Maid of Orleans*. The charming first two acts of this opera had been a great success in their time, but the second half of the opera was considerably inferior to them and even spoiled one's general impression of the opera. Neither Joan's scene with Dunois, nor the scene in the cathedral, nor the Finale with Joan's execution had been successful. All this I expressed frankly to Tchaikovsky, urging him to rework the second part of the opera. I spoke enthusiastically and warmly of the beauties of the beginning of the opera, and hummed for Pyotr Ilyich the melodies from my favourite passages, such as, for example: the marvellous hymn in the first scene; the lovely song of the minstrels in the second scene, 'In unbroken file we all hasten towards the grave'; the Cardinal's arioso during the peal of thunder after Joan's speech at court: 'One must keep silent before the Word of Heaven!' Tchaikovsky became interested in what I was saying.

'How well you remember all this!' he said, clearly flattered and pleased.

'I remember it because it's beautiful, and if you rework the second part the whole opera will be beautiful!'

'You think so?' asked Pyotr Ilyich with animation.

'I not only think so, I'm convinced of it! The ascending line of Joan's career—a virgin, an inspired, ecstatic patriot, with the whole surrounding historical situation—is perfectly realized in your music. But the zenith of her triumph and the subsequent picture of the drama of Joan the woman, with the horror of her tragic end, is relatively pale and uninteresting and fails to captivate the listener.'

'Yes,' said Tchaikovsky, 'you are not the first to tell me this. In essence, I don't dispute it. I agree: the music needs to be reworked. But, my God! You can't imagine how difficult, how unpleasant it is even to begin reworking and revising an old composition!'

'Do it, my dear Pyotr Ilyich,' I urged. 'Do it, and you will create a *Maid of Orleans* of which you will be proud, for the subject is indeed a noble one! The opera will be an enormous success not only in Russia but throughout Europe and will become, believe me, your favourite creation.'

'I'll have to think about it,' he said, this time with a somewhat depressed indecisiveness.

'What's there to think about? Let me send an order to the music office straight away to send the score of *The Maid of Orleans* to your apartment!'

'Stop, stop! Why so quickly?'

'It's best to do it quickly! Get the score and give your word that you'll start reworking it!'

Several minutes passed as Pyotr Ilyich clearly wavered back and forth. I kept fanning the fire, even entreating him with various endearments, like a child.

Finally Tchaikovsky, having made his decision, rose form his place and, with an affectionate smile, said:

'Well, all right! Send for the score!'

'And do you promise to begin working on *The Maid of Orleans* at once?'

'I promise,' said Tchaikovsky.

VC (1980), 196–7

IGOR STRAVINSKY

Russian composer, 11 years old in 1893.

In the first interval we stepped from our lodge into the small foyer behind. A few people were already walking there. Suddenly my mother said
to me: 'Igor, look, there is Tchaikovsky.' I looked and saw a big man with
white hair, large shoulders, a corpulent back, and this image has retained
in the retina of my memory all my life.

Igor Stravinsky and Robert Craft, *Expositions and*
Developments (London, 1962), 86

VASILY BESSEL

Music publisher and a friend of Tchaikovsky's from the St Petersburg Conservatoire.

On 18 October 1893 Tchaikovsky informed our mutual friend, Senator
Aug[ust] Gerke, of his final decision to revise his opera *The Oprichnik*,
and to replace his agreement with our firm of 8 April 1874 with a new one.
The following day the draft of a new agreement, according to which we
returned to him the royalty rights with respect to the Imperial Theatres,
was drawn up by us, and then delivered by Mr Gerke himself, on the
morning of Wednesday, 20 October, to Tchaikovsky's apartment, where
it remained unsigned.[2] He had had the manuscript score of the first act of
The Oprichnik since Monday, having personally taken it from the library
of the Imperial Theatres. For the moment he had no need of the remaining portions of the manuscript (it takes up four volumes); he had changed
his mind about the revisions that were necessary in the opera, such that
he had decided to revise only a little: 'two or three days' work', he told
Dmitry Dudyshkin, the conductor of the private Russian opera company
then playing in the Kononov hall, promising that Dudyshkin would be the
first to receive the manuscript after the revisions, and also that he would
personally attend the rehearsals and even conduct the first performance.

RMG 12 (1897), 1720

---

[2] There is reason to believe that Tchaikovsky visited August Gerke in person on 20 October.
In GDMC there exists Gerke's note to the composer of 21 October (A⁴, no. 592) concerning a
cigarette-case which Tchaikovsky left at his apartment. That the contract remained unsigned
must not be taken as evidence of foul play, as some biographers suggest; Tchaikovsky may have
hesitated to finalize the contract owing to his doubts about whether he should continue his business relationship with the Bessel firm, and next morning he fell ill.

MODEST TCHAIKOVSKY

Throughout his final days, Pyotr Ilyich was terribly preoccupied with the thought of [the young conductor] Georgy Conus [*Suite from Childhood*]; several times he mentioned that he was eagerly looking forward to the pleasure he would derive from conducting it at the next symphonic concert, and he praised it everywhere, calling its appearance an 'event' in Russian musical life.

During these same days he also spoke to me a great deal about the revisions to *The Oprichnik* and *The Maid of Orleans*, which he intended to work on in the near future. For this purpose he borrowed the score of *The Oprichnik* from the library of the Imperial Theatres and acquired the complete works of [Vasily] Zhukovsky [Russian poet]. He never told me of his intentions concerning the first of these operas, but we did discuss the revision of the final scene in *The Maid of Orleans*, where I urged him, since he had already made wide use of Schiller's scenario, to follow Schiller's ending as well.[3] This appeared to interest him, but he was not destined to come to a final decision.

His mood during these final days was not exclusively cheerful, yet neither was it at all depressed. In the company of the people closest to him he was content and jolly, but then with strangers he was, as always, nervous and agitated, and afterwards tired and sluggish.

ZC 646

19 October

PYOTR TCHAIKOVSKY

Letter to Willem Kes, Dutch violinist and conductor.

Various reasons have until now prevented me from giving you any sort of precise answer. Now I believe that I can promise to come to Amsterdam towards early March. You will advise me, sir, will you not, of the exact date of the concert some weeks in advance?

PSS xvii. 206

---

[3] Schiller's lyric drama has Joan of Arc dying from wounds on the battlefield instead of being burnt at the stake in Rouen.

7. Modest Tchaikovsky, Tchaikovsky's younger brother

MODEST TCHAIKOVSKY

On Tuesday the nineteenth, at the request of the opera company which performed in the former Kononov Theatre, [Pyotr Ilyich] attended a production of Anton Rubinstein's *Die Makkabäer*.

ZC 647

THE PETERSBURG LEAFLET

On Tuesday P[yotr] I[lyich] attended a performance of Rubinstein's *Die Makkabäer* at the Kononov Theatre.

PL, 26 Oct. 1893

VLADIMIR TRAVSKY

Producer at Kononov's Theatre in St Petersburg.

I have a very interesting reminiscence related to Tchaikovsky. It happened when there was an opera company presided over by Beznosov and Dudyshkin, in the Kononov Theatre. I was that company's director. Things did not go well. We barely managed to balance our budget. To improve the profits we decided to approach Tchaikovsky and ask his permission to produce his opera *The Oprichnik*, which he had not allowed before. Thus, Beznosov, Dudyshkin, and myself proceeded to visit Tchaikovsky in his apartment. The famous composer welcomed us cordially. After learning the cause of our visit, Tchaikovsky told us that he would be pleased to help us, but that he was not happy with *The Oprichnik* since it is heavily influenced by Italian music and he did not want to see this work on stage. We began to implore Tchaikovsky and tell him about our critical situation. 'Well,' Tchaikovsky agreed, 'I will correct it and you will be able to perform *The Oprichnik* in two weeks.' Next Tchaikovsky asked us what was being performed in our theatre that very night. On hearing that it would be Rubinstein's opera *Die Makkabäer* he said that this was his favourite opera and that he would attend the performance with great pleasure. That evening Tchaikovsky came to the theatre and visited backstage.

TZ 170 (1913), 35

20 October

MODEST TCHAIKOVSKY

On Wednesday the twentieth, [Pyotr Ilyich] was perfectly healthy. Out on a stroll with one of our nephews, Count Alexander Litke, he told him many stories about [his eccentric friend Nikolay] Bochechkarov, about his oddities, sayings, and jokes, and spoke of how he missed him almost as badly now as just after his death in 1876.

That day he dined with his old friend Vera Butakova, née Davydova. For the evening he had a box at the Alexandrinsky Theatre, where Alexander Ostrovsky's *The Ardent Heart* was being performed. During the interval he and I visited the dressing-room of Konstantin Varlamov. He had always appreciated the latter's amazing talent, and in the 1890s, having made his acquaintance, he grew fond of him as a person. The conversation turned to spiritualism. Varlamov, with his characteristic humour, impossible to convey on paper, expressed his distaste for all 'that fakery', and for anything that reminded him of death in general. Nothing could have pleased Pyotr Ilyich better; he agreed with delight and laughed heartily at the original manner in which this had been said. 'We shall yet make the acquaintance of that repulsive snub-nosed monster,' he said and then, as he was leaving, he turned back to Varlamov: 'But you and I have a long way to go till then! I feel I shall live a long time.'

From the theatre Pyotr Ilyich went with our nephews the Counts Litke, and Baron [Rudi] Buchshoevden, to Leiner's restaurant. I was to join them there later, and when I arrived about an hour later I found all the persons mentioned above in the company of Ivan Gorbunov, Alexander Glazunov, and Fyodor Mülbach. They had all finished dining, but I learned that my brother had eaten macaroni and washed it down with his customary white wine and mineral water. The supper lasted only a short time, and soon after one o'clock the two of us returned home on foot. Pyotr Ilyich was quite healthy and calm.

ZC 647

THE PETERSBURG LEAFLET

On the evening of Wednesday [the twentieth] Pyotr Ilyich was seen in the company of friends, cheerfully discussing various musical matters. Tchaikovsky was all this time in good spirits, saying that he planned to

rest a bit longer in the country in order to renew his strength for continuing his composing activities. [Pyotr Ilyich] felt the need for this rest and
was making various plans concerning the future.

PL, 26 Oct. 1893

YURY YURYEV

The Alexandrinsky Theatre was presenting a new performance of Ostrovsky's *The Ardent Heart*. . . . At the theatre I saw Pyotr Ilyich, with his
entire 'suite' of relatives and friends. Everyone was in raptures over the
performance. 'And what a play!' exclaimed Pyotr Ilyich. 'Each word is
like gold.'

VC (1962), 363

[NIKOLAY TCHAIKOVSKY][4]

The composer's elder brother.

P[yotr] I[lyich] had appeared quite hale and hearty of late, and did not
complain of any illness. On Monday he attended *Eugene Onegin*, on Tuesday, 19 October, he was at the Kononov Theatre for a production of the
opera *Die Makkabäer*, on Wednesday he dined with an old relative, then
saw *The Ardent Heart*, and that night he was taken ill.

NBG, 26 Oct. 1893

THE STOCK-EXCHANGE REGISTER

On Wednesday evening, 20 October [Tchaikovsky] attended the performance of Ostrovsky's *The Ardent Heart* at the Alexandrinsky Theatre and
thereafter, together with several friends, his brother, and nephew, he
visited a restaurant where he was served a dish of spaghetti.

BV, 27 Oct. 1893

THE PETERSBURG GAZETTE

Following a concert on Wednesday evening Pyotr Ilyich stopped by
Leiner's restaurant with a few friends and his brother and nephews, where

---

[4] In the newspaper article Nikolay is called simply 'one of the relatives'. Closer scrutiny of this
account, where he refers to Modest as 'my brother', suggests the identification.

he had an order of macaroni but nothing to wash down this light supper, and on returning home asked that a glass of water be placed on the nightstand by the bed, which he drained during the night.

PG, 26 Oct. 1893

NIKOLAY FIGNER

The evening of Wednesday, 20 October, at Leiner's restaurant, [Pyotr Ilyich] had macaroni. Before bed he was supplied with a carafe of water as usual, since he had a habit of sleeping with his mouth open.

NBG, 26 Oct, 1893

YURY DAVYDOV

The youngest nephew of Tchaikovsky, brother of Bob Davydov.

We [Tchaikovsky and the author] arrived at the [Alexandrinsky] Theatre [after the dinner at Vera Butakova's] at the moment when the curtain was raised. In the box there were already my uncle Modest, my brother Vladimir [Bob], the two Litke brothers, Bob's friend Rudolf [Rudi] Buchshoevden, and my cousin Grigory Davydov. After the performance, which was acted brilliantly, all of us left, with the exception of Uncle Modest, who stayed to talk with Mariya Savina [a famous actress]. He promised to catch up with us if we went on foot. At the moment of our exit we encountered the most talented artist-comedian Ivan Gorbunov, and all together, as a crowd, we walked up Nevsky [Prospect], in the direction of the Admiralty. On the way . . . Pyotr Ilyich suggested that we should go to the Leiner restaurant, which I often visited with him, since it was one of the few that would let in us students through the back door, naturally not without a bribe to the doorman. That evening there was quite a number of us who were not allowed to enter. My brother, Buchshoevden, and Alexander Litke were army volunteers in military uniform, while Konstantin Litke and myself were cadets, and to all of us legitimate entrance to the restaurant was prohibited. Consequently, we all went to the courtyard and were waiting until Pyotr Ilyich negotiated the matter with the owner, and were then called in. We did not have long to wait. We were taken to a large separate room and met up with the others, with the addition of Fyodor Mülbach, the great friend of the Tchaikovsky brothers. At the very moment of our arrival Pyotr Ilyich was occupied with ordering supper for us. After completing his order,

8. Vladimir (Bob) Davydov, Tchaikovsky's nephew in 1893

Pyotr Ilyich proceeded to ask the waiter to bring him a glass of water. A few minutes later the waiter came back and reported that the boiled water had run out. Thereupon Pyotr Ilyich, not without certain irritation in his voice, said: 'bring me then some unboiled and as cold as possible.' Everyone tried to talk him out of drinking unboiled water, given the fact of the cholera epidemic in the city, but Pyotr Ilyich said that all this was prejudice, which he did not believe in. The waiter left to have his order carried out. At this point the door opened, and Modest entered the room accompanied by the actor Yury Yuryev, and exclaimed:

'Ah-ha, how well have I guessed! Passing by I thought it worth dropping in and asking whether by chance you could be here.'

'And where else could we be?' answered Pyotr Ilyich.

Almost following on Modest's heels the waiter entered with a glass of water on a tray. Having learned what was happening and about the matter of our continuous dispute with Pyotr Ilyich, Modest became truly angry with his brother and cried:

'I categorically forbid you to drink unboiled water!'

Laughing, Pyotr Ilyich jumped up and went to meet the waiter, and Modest rushed after him. But Pyotr Ilyich forestalled him and, pushing his brother aside with his elbow, succeeded in drinking in one gulp the fateful glass. Modest once again scolded him, and the merriment began. I say that merriment began because in Pyotr Ilyich's presence it was always merry. He beamed merriment as the sun beams rays. One must, however, emphasize that it occurred only in the company of people who were close to him, that is to say, those whom he was not shy of. One single unfamiliar person would suffice to make his whole mood of merriment disappear.

Thus in lively chattering over a glass of wine or a mug of beer we stayed there until two in the morning. I accompanied my uncles and my brother to their apartment and went home in bright and cheerful mood, recalling everything I had experienced in the last few hours and little concerned with the problem of how I could creep into the dormitory unnoticed by the officer on duty.

VC (1980), 332–3

YURY YURYEV

After the show the Tchaikovsky brothers invited me to the Leiner restaurant. Pyotr Ilyich, Modest, their sister-in-law—the wife of his brother Anatoly—Praskoviya, the two brothers Litke, Fyodor Mülbach, the owner of a piano factory, myself, and the Legat brothers—Nikolay and Sergey—

talented ballet dancers. . . . Since the company gathered was rather numerous, it was decided to occupy a separate room. All shared their impressions of the production. Pyotr Ilyich felt a slight indisposition, complained
about his stomach, and refused to eat meaty dishes. He limited himself to
oysters, washing them down with Chablis. Nobody ascribed any significance to his indisposition, and he himself did not in fact complain too
much, but rather to the contrary, exhibited high spirits: he was talkative
and made jokes. . . . We did not stay long at Leiner's. After we had left
the restaurant and parted at its gates, not one of us could ever imagine
that we were seeing Pyotr Ilyich for the very last time.

Iur'ev, *Zapiski*, ii. 81–2

Several eyewitnesses concur that Tchaikovsky was in exceptionally fine
form during the days immediately preceding his illness. He saw to various
business and professional obligations, wrote letters, made the society
round, attended musical recitals and rehearsals, and discussed his creative plans, among them the revision of two operas, *The Oprichnik* and *The
Maid of Orleans*. On 20 October he visited the theatre to see a performance of a play by an old acquaintance, Alexander Ostrovsky, and during
the interval chatted with another old friend, Konstantin Varlamov, spic-
ing the conversation with jokes about mortality and ridiculing the doc-
trine of spiritualism. Tchaikovsky ended this day with a late supper at
Leiner's restaurant. According to Modest, here were present his nephews
with some of their friends, as well as Ivan Gorbunov, Alexander Glazunov,
and Fyodor Mülbach. Some confusion arises from possible typographical
errors and Modest's use of the word nephews: his newspaper article gives
the impression that he considers 'the Counts Litke and Baron Buchshoevden' as such, which makes no sense since Baron Buchshoevden
was not related to the Tchaikovsky family. From the passage in his biography of Tchaikovsky, where he used the newspaper account almost in
full, however, it clearly follows that by the plural 'nephews' he had in
mind the two Litke brothers, who were his nephews once removed, and
Bob Davydov. The plural may or may not imply the presence of two
others nephews, Yury Davydov and his cousin Grigory Davydov, never
mentioned in any other testimony.

It is evident that Modest's account of that evening, written shortly
after the event and published when all the participants of the supper at
Leiner's were alive and well and could contest his report if it were in-
accurate, should be taken at face value. The same cannot be said, however, of the recollections of Yury Davydov and Yury Yuryev, which were

written almost simultaneously half a century later, in the mid-1940s. A careful analysis inevitably leads to the conclusion of their unreliability, starting with the fact that Modest does not mention the attendance of either. One is struck by the number of contradictions and inconsistencies between the two narratives, and the more so, if one compares them with that of Modest. Thus, for instance, they describe differently Tchaikovsky's state of health, the length of their stay in the restaurant, and cannot even agree on those who were present: for example Yuryev mentions Praskoviya, the wife of the composer's brother Anatoly, who most certainly was not even in St Petersburg at the time. There are additional reasons to believe that the entire account is made up by Yuryev who in fact did not attend the supper in question. Tchaikovsky's archives at Klin possess the typescript (and lengthier) draft of Yury Davydov's memoirs in which Yury Yuryev's name is added by hand, apparently later and in order not to impinge on the latter's own reminiscences. Yuryev's close friendship with Modest and Tchaikovsky's nephews is well documented, but only beginning with the period *after* the death of the composer.

No less questionable seems the veracity of Yury Davydov's memoir. At the time of its dramatic action he was, aged 17, a junior student in the military school and would hardly have dared to defy the strict regulations by attending both the theatre and the restaurant on the ordinary school day (unlike his cousin Konstantin Litke who by then was a senior and could afford to). Furthermore, the longer draft of his recollections, mentioned above, contains some demonstrable fictions which the author must have eventually removed to avoid embarrassment. Close reading reveals that Yury Davydov composed his recollections using the already existing biographical material on Tchaikovsky and claiming to witness only the episodes he would have known from other primary sources. All this casts very serious doubt on the important piece of evidence from his narrative which is otherwise unrecorded, namely, a rather theatrical episode with a glass of unboiled water. (Modest mentions nothing of the sort, although if it had indeed happened, this detail would have shown him in a favourable light as anxiously concerned with his brother's well-being, a notion he eagerly sought to impress upon the reader.) During my visit to Klin in 1992 when I met Xeniya Davydova, Yury Davydov's daughter, and discussed with her a wide range of events pertaining to Tchaikovsky's life, I chose to express my doubts as regards the reality of the glass of water episode. Visibly upset, she admitted none the less, somewhat to my surprise, that the whole story was indeed fiction. By way of explanation, she suggested that her father was perturbed by the continuous suicide rumours intimately linked to the fact of the composer's homosexuality.

Since under the Soviets the latter could not even be mentioned in print, he thought it expedient to include himself among the diners at Leiner's restaurant so that he could claim to have witnessed precisely the very moment of Tchaikovsky infecting himself with cholera by drinking the fateful glass of the allegedly contaminated water, and thus to refute the suicide theory for good.

Anyway there is no reason to doubt that Tchaikovsky remained in excellent spirits late into the night, as we are told by several of those present at the supper at Leiner's restaurant, where it seems the composer and his friends all had a jolly time.

4

Illness

21 October–22 October

---

21 October

NIKOLAY FIGNER

[Tchaikovsky] spent a troubled night: he had developed a severe stomach upset. Attaching little significance to this, as such things had happened to him before, in the morning Pyotr Ilyich, without telling anyone, took some Hunyadi-János water instead of the castor oil that he usually took in such cases. As a result he experienced increased diarrhoea, soon accompanied by vomiting.

NBG, 26 Oct. 1893

THE PETERSBURG LEAFLET

Upon returning home early on Thursday morning, Tchaikovsky felt the first signs of a stomach disorder, which continued throughout the night. Not suspecting anything dangerous in the developing illness, which Pyotr Ilyich put down to a simple upset stomach, he took the notorious purgative Hunyadi-János, which, according to the doctor, can have an extremely bad effect on the stomach during cholera; this remedy, as it turned out, only added fat to the fire. By morning Tchaikovsky still felt well enough to set out to visit Eduard Nápravník; but before reaching the home of the latter he was compelled to return home in a cab, having begun to feel ill. This was at twelve noon. Going up to the apartment of his brother Modest Tchaikovsky, [he] seemed in good spirits, even joking with the doorman, telling him of his absentmindedness in always misplacing his galoshes. But suddenly around four o'clock in the afternoon

Tchaikovsky was showing all the signs of cholera: continuous nausea, diarrhoea, vomiting, and general weakness, all of which naturally caused alarm in those around him. It was only then that the doctors were sent for, when many long hours had already passed since the onset of the illness.

PL, 26 Oct. 1893

PYOTR TCHAIKOVSKY

Letter to Ivan Grekov, manager of the Odessa Opera Theatre.

Forgive me for taking so long to answer your last letter. In part the reason has been the fuss surrounding the Musical Society concert which I conducted, and the preparation of the orchestral parts for my new symphony, and in part my hesitation in deciding about the trip to Odessa.

Ah, if only you knew how inconvenient this trip is for me and how difficult for so many reasons! I am uncomfortable enlarging on this, as it may seem that I am, as it were, trying to magnify in your eyes the size and significance of the sacrifice which I shall make on the altar of our friendship! And I am not even sure that this sacrifice will in fact be of any benefit to you. But let us assume that it will. Now the question arises: what is the least difficult and inconvenient time to come to you? After weighing and considering all the circumstances, I have come to the conclusion that I should not be in Odessa in February, if only because the Musical Society in Odessa has invited Nikolay Rimsky-Korsakov for February, and I might seem to be showing up in order to divert the attention of the Odessans from his highly attractive personality. So from the entire period the only two weeks or so I have free fall at the end of December and the beginning of January. If I am to do it that way, bear in mind that I must be in Petersburg no later than 8 January, as I am conducting a concert on the fifteenth. Therefore, kindly fix a time for my visit to you between 15 December and 5 January, bearing in mind that I cannot stay more than a week in Odessa. In your last letter you write of distributing roles, but I did not understand: In *Mazeppa* or *Yolanta*? This is difficult for me; I leave the distribution to you, the conductor, and the producer.[1]

OL, 27 Oct. 1893; *PSS* xvii. 207

---

[1] There is little doubt that this letter dates from 21 Oct. 1893, as is definitely stated by its first publishers in *Odesskii listok*, who were in possession of the original.

NIKOLAY FIGNER

P[yotr] I[lyich] intended to leave for his Klin estate on Thursday, [21] October,[2] in order to get down to work (he could never work here). He was generally reluctant to talk about planned or unfinished projects even with his closest friends. I only know that he was planning to write a new opera.

NBG, 26 Oct. 1893

MODEST TCHAIKOVSKY

When I came out of my bedroom on Thursday morning, 21 October, Pyotr Ilyich was not in the sitting-room taking tea as usual but in his own room, and complained of having spent a bad night because of a stomach upset. This did not particularly disturb me, because he quite often had such upsets, which were always very acute and passed very quickly. At eleven o'clock he changed and set off to visit Nápravník, but in half an hour he returned without having got there, and decided to take further measures in addition to the flannel that he had put on earlier. I suggested sending for Vasily Bertenson, his favourite doctor, but he flatly refused. I did not insist, knowing that he was accustomed to illnesses of this sort and that he always managed to get over them without anyone's help. Usually castor oil would help him in these cases. Convinced that he would resort to it this time as well and knowing that in any event it could do him no harm, I was quite unworried about his condition and, going about my own affairs, did not see him again until one in the afternoon. At lunch-time he had a business meeting with Fyodor Mülbach. In any event, during the period from eleven until one Pyotr Ilyich was in good enough shape to manage to write two letters, though by the third he had no patience to write a detailed letter and limited himself to a short note.[3] During lunch he showed no aversion to food.

He sat with us but did not eat, though only, it seems, because he realized it might be harmful. It was then that he told us that instead of castor oil he had taken Hunyadi water. It seems to me that lunch has a fateful significance, since it was right in the middle of our conversation about the medication he had taken that he poured a glass of water and took a sip from it. The water was unboiled. We were all frightened: he alone was

---

[2] In the newspaper interview: 22 Oct., but Thursday in Oct. 1893 fell on the 21st.

[3] There are serious reasons to believe that the short note to Olga Nápravník, wife of Eduard Nápravník: 'I shall not depart today. I kiss your hands' (*PSS* xvii. 206) was actually written in Nov. 1890, not 1893.

9. The house on the corner of Malaya Morskaya and Gorokhovaya Streets in St Petersburg, where Tchaikovsky stayed in the apartment on the top floor

indifferent to it and told us not to worry. Of all illnesses cholera was always the one he least feared. Immediately after this he had to leave because he began to feel nauseated. He did not return to the sitting-room, but lay down in his own room so that he might warm his stomach. All the same, neither he nor those of us around him were at all anxious. All this had happened often enough before. Although his indisposition grew worse, we attributed this to the action of the mineral water. I again suggested sending for Vasily Bertenson, but again was forbidden to do so: moreover, a little while later he felt better and, asking to be allowed to sleep, he remained alone in his room and, so I assumed, went to sleep. Satisfying myself that all was quiet in his bedroom, I went out on my own affairs and did not get back home until five o'clock. When I returned the illness had so much worsened that, despite his protests, I sent for Vasily Bertenson. However, there were still no alarming signs of mortal illness.

ZC 648–9

ALEXANDER GLAZUNOV

I saw Tchaikovsky for the last time on [Thursday], four days before his death.[4] I stopped in to see him, at his invitation, at the apartment on [Malaya Morskaya] Street around five o'clock in the afternoon. He felt very ill and asked to be left alone, saying that perhaps he actually had cholera, though he did not believe so, since he had experienced similar attacks many times.

VC (1980), 209–10

MODEST TCHAIKOVSKY

Around six in the evening I again left Pyotr Ilyich, after placing a hot compress on his stomach. At eight o'clock, when I returned, my servant, Nazar Litrov, was tending him and had managed to move him from his small bedroom into the spacious drawing-room, because during this time, that is, between six and eight o'clock, the vomiting and diarrhoea had quickly become so severe that Litrov gave up waiting for the doctor and sent for the first one who could be found, but still nobody was thinking about cholera.

ZC 649

---

[4] The original has 'Wednesday', which is obviously wrong; Tchaikovsky died on Monday, 25 October, and four days before this would of course be Thursday. Confusion regarding days of the week is one of the most common errors made by memoirists.

ALINA BRYULLOVA

Mother of Modest's deaf-mute pupil, Nikolay Konradi. She was
not present at Modest's apartment and probably learned this story
from her son.

As usual in a bachelor's apartment, everyone had dispersed and no one
was at home except a servant who began to employ all the home remedies
known to him. The patient grew steadily worse. Finally, at about seven
o'clock, Nazar ran to get Dr Bertenson, an old acquaintance of Tchaikovsky's. He immediately came and diagnosed cholera in its most acute form.
He sent for his brother, Professor Bertenson, and Modest Tchaikovsky
was found in the theatre.

VC (1980), 119

VASILY BERTENSON

Tchaikovsky's physician.

During Pyotr Ilyich's first visits from Moscow I was almost constantly
treating him for his famous stomach catarrh. In the end he grew so accustomed to his continuous ailment that he would treat himself without
resorting to my help, even when the attacks were more acute, according
to the routine I had already prescribed. But on the unforgettable day of
21 October 1893, arriving home around eight o'clock in the evening, I
found on the table a note from Modest with the following message:
    'Pyotr doesn't feel well. He has continuous nausea and diarrhoea. For
God's sake, come see what this means.'
    I went at once to see the patient.
    One should know that Pyotr Ilyich's delicacy towards those around
him knew no bounds. This was the main reason why Pyotr Ilyich, according to his brother, had so long refused to allow him to send for me.
    When I entered Modest Ilyich's small apartment, where he lived with
Pyotr Ilyich's favourite nephew—Bob Davydov—and where Pyotr Ilyich
was staying, I found the patient in bed. It was half-past eight in the
evening. Pyotr Ilyich, despite the fact that the attacks of his dreadful
illness were already troubling him incessantly, greeted me with words
characteristic of his sincere kindness and his surprising delicacy.
    'Poor Vasily,' he said to me, 'you're such a music lover and no doubt
you were longing to go to the opera; and today they're even performing
Tannhäuser. But instead you've had to come to see me, boring, nasty
Tchaikovsky, who's sick, and with such an uninteresting ailment . . .'

After hearing an account of the course of the illness and examining Pyotr Ilyich, I was convinced at once, to my horror, that he did not have an acute catarrh of the stomach, as all the members of the household as well as Pyotr Ilyich himself had assumed, but something worse. . . .

In Petersburg at this time (October 1893) cholera had already begun to build itself a solid nest, but the educated classes were rarely touched by it. Only the poor, as usual, died from it. I have to admit that I myself had not had occasion before this time to witness an actual cholera case. Nevertheless, upon examining the patient's excretions I was left with no doubt that Pyotr Ilyich had a classic case of cholera.[5] When I went into the next room and told Pyotr Ilyich's brother and nephews of the seriousness of the illness, and that I was unable and unwilling to undertake the treatment of such an illness alone, citing my moral responsibility, my dear friends would not at first believe me.

But in the end they had to believe. . . .

The most difficult thing (knowing Pyotr Ilyich's dislike of doctors) was to get him to agree to a consultation.

Finally we persuaded the patient of the necessity of this, difficult though it was for him. At the request of Pyotr Ilyich himself, the choice of a consulting doctor fell on my brother.

Thereupon, having prescribed all that was necessary, I rushed off at once to get my brother.

IV 128 (1912), 813

MODEST TCHAIKOVSKY

At a quarter past eight Vasily Bertenson arrived. The diarrhoea and vomiting were becoming ever more frequent, but the patient was still strong enough to get up every time he needed to. As none of his excretions had been preserved, the doctor could not at first establish that it was cholera, but he was convinced at once of the extreme seriousness and gravity of the illness. Prescribing all that was necessary in such circumstances, the doctor immediately judged it essential to call in his brother, Lev Bertenson. The situation was growing more alarming. The excretions were becoming more frequent and very copious. The weakening so increased that the patient was now unable to move by himself. The vomiting was especially unbearable; while vomiting and for several moments afterwards he would become quite frenzied and cry out at the top of his

---

[5] This claim contradicts Modest's account of Vasily Bertenson's visit which—since it was written straight after the events it described—should be preferred to the physicians's own recollections, which were published almost two decades later.

voice, never once complaining about the ache in his abdominal cavity, but only about the unbearably terrible state of his chest, and at one point he turned to me and said: 'I think I'm dying. Farewell, Modest!' He later repeated these words several times. After every excretion he sank back on the bed utterly exhausted. However, there was as yet no lividity or spasms.

ZC 649–50

[NIKOLAY TCHAIKOVSKY]

Towards noon on Thursday he showed signs of cholera in its most acute form: his vomiting and diarrhoea continued without ceasing for several hours.

NBG, 26 Oct. 1893

LEV BERTENSON

Court physician from 1897, who practised in St Petersburg high society.

I was called to see Pyotr Ilyich on Thursday evening, 21 October, by my brother, Dr Vasily Bertenson, who was a close friend of Tchaikovsky's family and always attended all the members of the family. Arriving at Modest Tchaikovsky's apartment, where Pyotr Ilyich was staying, at about ten in the evening, I found [him] in the so-called algid stage of cholera. The picture of the illness was indisputably characteristic, and I had immediately to recognize a very serious case of cholera. We began employing all the scientific measures prescribed for such a situation. Towards two o'clock we had almost succeeded in stemming the spasms, which by the time of my arrival had been so violent that the patient had been crying out loud. The bouts of diarrhoea and vomiting also became significantly less frequent and less severe. I departed in the middle of the night, leaving my brother with the patient.

NV, 27 Oct. 1893

THE PETERSBURG GAZETTE

The first signs of P[yotr] I[lyich] Tchaikovsky's dangerous illness were revealed on [Thursday] afternoon,[6] but its character as a usual stomach disorder aroused no alarm in the patient.

---

[6] The article reads 'Friday'—an obvious mistake, easily verified by reports in the other St Petersburg papers.

By six o'clock that evening, however, along with an increase in the diarrhoea and acute pains, vomiting began. Dr [Lev] Bertenson,[7] who was called in immediately, diagnosed the illness as cholera and, summoning the assistance of three expert colleagues, undertook an energetic attempt to defend the patient from the terrible epidemic.

PG, 25 Oct. 1893

NIKOLAY FIGNER

[In the evening] they sent for Dr Bertenson, with whom P[yotr] I[lyich] was great friends. Dr Bertenson wasted no time in getting there and diagnosing the most vicious form of Asiatic cholera; he claimed that he had no prior occasion to confront this particular form of cholera.

NBG, 26 Oct. 1893

SERGEY BERTENSON

Son of Lev Bertenson, later an actor and theatre critic.

To my father fell the sad duty of being the physician who directed the treatment of Pyotr Tchaikovsky. . . . I recall quite clearly [Sergey was then 8 years old—A.P.] the feeling of alarm that ran through our family when my father's brother, also a physician, whose help Pyotr Ilyich would always seek for his minor ailments, sent for my father with the news that Tchaikovsky had cholera. My uncle quite rightly could not assume sole responsibility for the outcome of the illness and had insisted that another physician be called in. After considerable persuasion the patient agreed to a consultation, but only on the condition that the second doctor be my father, in whose authority both he and his family had every confidence. Tchaikovsky was on friendly terms with my parents, sometimes visiting our home, and his name was surrounded within our family by a halo of adoration. My father, of course, left at once to go to the patient, shortly summoning his two assistants, doctors Alexander Zander and Nikolay Mamonov.

Sergei Bertenson, *Vokrug iskusstva*
(Hollywood, 1957), 20

[7] The report does not give Bertenson's first name. Three Bertensons were practising at that moment in St Petersburg: the brothers Lev and Vasily and their uncle Iosif, a distinguished physician, director of the clinic of the Duchess of Edinburgh (née Grand Duchess Mariya Aleksandrovna) in St Petersburg. Vasily Bertenson's initial visit, before that of his brother, did not become known to the public until about a week later, when Modest produced his account. For more on the Bertensons see *PBC* 11–18, 25–30.

NIKOLAY MAMONOV

Physician, assistant to Lev Bertenson.

Pyotr Ilyich Tchaikovsky was susceptible to stomach ailments in general, and last summer he felt ill with cholerine. I should tell you that P[yotr] I[lyich] regarded the cholera epidemic with great scepticism. . . .

On Wednesday morning he was already complaining of a loss of appetite and general indisposition, but did not pay any attention to this. . . . On Thursday, from nine in the morning, he began experiencing a severe upset of the stomach, which grew still worse after he drank two glasses of water. On this day it became clear to us what terrible illness had struck P[yotr] I[lyich]. By that evening the choleraic spasms appeared, along with retention of urine—which worried us most of all. His relatives began rubbing his body, and this somewhat eased the patient's condition.

Thursday night passed fairly calmly for P[yotr] I[lyich], and the spasms ceased.

NBG, 26 Oct. 1893

MODEST TCHAIKOVSKY

Lev Bertenson arrived with his brother at eleven o'clock and after examining the patient and his excretions determined that it was cholera. They immediately sent for a medical attendant. Including the doctors, there were eight of us with the patient: the [two] Counts Litke,[8] our nephew Davydov, Nazar Litrov, the medical attendant, and myself. At midnight Pyotr Ilyich began crying aloud and complaining of spasms. We began directing all our efforts to massaging him. The patient was fully conscious. The spasms appeared in various parts of his body at the same time, and the patient asked us to massage now this part of his body, now that. His head and extremities began to turn very blue and became completely cold. Not long before the appearance of the first spasms, Pyotr Ilyich asked me: 'It's not cholera, is it?' However, I concealed the truth from him. But when he overheard the doctor giving instructions about precautionary measures against infection, he exclaimed: 'So it is cholera!' The more important details of this phase of the illness are difficult to relate.

ZC 650

---

[8] The original has 'three counts Litke', which is obviously a mistake, since with three Litke's the total number would have been nine people present at Tchaikovsky's bedside, whereas Modest reported that there were only eight.

[NIKOLAY TCHAIKOVSKY]

Exceptional diligence was required of the physicians to stabilize the patient, who had no doubts about his condition for a minute. He never lost consciousness.

NBG, 26 Oct. 1893

22 October

LEV BERTENSON

Towards dawn on Friday, during my absence, there was a further deterioration in Pyotr Ilyich's condition: the spasms returned and the action of the heart fell so rapidly that my brother had to give Pyotr Ilyich an injection of musk and camphor. Early on Friday morning my brother was replaced by my assistant, Dr Mamonov, and I myself arrived at eleven o'clock. The patient's condition was such that I was convinced that the attacks that had threatened the patient's life during the night had passed.

'How do you feel?' I asked Pyotr Ilyich.

'Vastly improved,' he replied. 'Thank you: you have snatched me from the jaws of death.'

NV, 27 Oct. 1893

NIKOLAY FIGNER

It goes without saying that every measure was immediately taken, with two more physicians being called in, so that the patient had uninterrupted medical assistance. Indeed, thanks to the exhaustive efforts of the doctors treating him, they managed to eradicate the cholera. During this entire time the patient did not lose consciousness for a minute; on the contrary, he himself would indicate where exactly he was having spasms, and when the critical period passed he even joked with those around him. By Friday evening the choleric attacks had ceased and there was a hope that our friend's recovery was very near. Unfortunately, the prediction of Dr Bertenson, for whom the outcome of the illness was already clear by Saturday evening, proved correct. The cholera disappeared, but it was replaced by an affliction of the kidneys, which in turn led to poisoning of the blood.

NBG, 26 Oct. 1893

MODEST TCHAIKOVSKY

Right up to five in the morning it was one uninterrupted struggle with his spasms and numbness which, the longer these lasted, the less they yielded to our energetic rubbing and artificial warming of his body. There were several moments when it seemed that death had come, but an injection of musk and a tannin enema revived the patient.

By five o'clock the illness began to abate, and the patient became relatively calm, complaining only of depressed spirits. Up to this point the most frightening thing had been the moments when he had complained of the pain around his heart and of being unable to breathe; but now this ceased. Three quarters of an hour passed in complete rest.[9] The vomiting and bowel movements lost their alarming appearance, though they recurred fairly frequently. The spasms reappeared whenever he tried to move. He grew thirsty, but said that drinking seemed more pleasant in his imagination than in reality. Scarcely would we give him a teaspoon of something to drink than he would turn away from it in revulsion, but a few minutes later he would ask for the same thing again.

But generally what disturbed him most was that the outward signs of his illness caused such anxiety in those around him. In the midst of the most serious attacks he, as it were, apologized for the trouble he was causing, fearful that some details would arouse disgust and retaining his awareness sufficiently to be able to joke sometimes. Thus he turned to his favourite nephew, saying: 'I'm afraid you'll lose all your respect for me after all this nasty business.' He was continually urging everyone to go to bed and thanked us for the slightest service. Early in the morning, as soon as the patient no longer needed nursing, Vasily Bertenson sent me to notify the police orally of what had happened.[10]

On Friday, 22 October, at nine o'clock in the morning, Vasily Bertenson, who had not left my brother for a moment, was replaced by Dr Nikolay Mamonov. At that time there had been relative calm for about an hour. Vasily Bertenson recounted the case history to Dr Mamonov and left without waiting for my brother to wake up.[11] At this time the lividity had

---

[9] This phrase is missing in Modest's account published in *ZC*.

[10] As a result of it Tchaikovsky was included in daily bulletins listing cholera patients who fell ill in St Petersburg in the period from 12 a.m. on 22 October to 12 noon on 23 October. See *Viedomosti Sankt Peterburgskogo gradonachal'stva i stolichnoi politsii*, 24 Oct. 1893; *PL*, 24 Oct. 1893.

[11] Unpublished correspondence shows that Vasily Bertenson in fact left the the city on Saturday, travelling to the Smolensk region to visit another patient, GDMC, f. B[10], no. 466. For more on Lev Bertenson's assistants Nikolay Mamonov and Alexander Zander, who participated in Tchaikovsky's treatment, see *PBC* 18–20.

passed, though there were black spots on his face, but these soon disappeared. There came the first period of relief. We all breathed more easily,
but the attacks, though significantly less frequent, still continued, accompanied by spasms. In any event, he felt so much better that he considered himself saved. Thus when Lev Bertenson arrived at about eleven
o'clock he said: 'Thank you. You have snatched me from the jaws of death.
I feel immeasurably better than during the first night.' He repeated
these words more than once that day and the next. The attacks and the
accompanying spasms finally ceased around midday. At three that afternoon Dr Alexander Zander replaced Dr Mamonov. The illness appeared
to have yielded to the treatment, but by this time doctors feared the
second phase of cholera—inflammation of the kidneys and the typhoid
stage, though at that point there were still no signs of either illness. His
only discomfort was an insatiable thirst. This condition continued until
evening, but by night it had improved to such an extent that Dr Mamonov,
who came to replace Dr Zander, insisted that we all go to bed since he
foresaw no threatening symptoms that night.

ZC 650–1

EDUARD NÁPRAVNÍK

Pyotr Ilyich Tchaikovsky, who is visiting St Petersburg, has been taken
dangerously ill.

RIII, f. 21, op. 1, ed. kh. 227, ll. 57–8

THE PETERSBURG GAZETTE

How could Tchaikovsky, having just arrived in Petersburg a few days
earlier and living in excellent hygienic conditions, have contracted cholera?

According to the doctors who treated him, he ingested the epidemic
bacteria in some water and through an unfortunate choice of medicine,
taken on his own initiative without consulting a doctor, created within his
organism favourable conditions for their rapid and excessive reproduction.

According to Dr Bertenson, the first of the doctors summoned by Pyotr
Ilyich, if [Tchaikovsky] had taken castor oil when he first experienced
pain and convulsions in his stomach, and not Hunyadi-János [mineral]
water, as he did, it might have been possible to save him—although, as
this experienced doctor says, this was a case of true Asiatic cholera of rare
intensity.

In addition, too much time passed before medical help was sought.

In the morning, feeling ill, [Tchaikovsky] sent for a purgative water and treated himself with that all Thursday and part of Friday,[12] not suspecting that Hunyadi water merely caused him to secrete mucus, without expelling the solid . . . matter in which the fatal bacilli were nested. By the time Dr Bertenson was summoned the patient had already suffered a number of vomitive and diarrhoea evacuations, and the combined efforts of six people were necessary to restore sensation to the patient in the grip of infection, by rubbing various parts of his body. During the critical period of the illness the patient experienced seventy-five attacks of vomiting and diarrhoea. . . .

But [Tchaikovsky] was of such a strong and resolute nature that the strength of his resistance to the illness amazed the doctors and gave hope for his rescue.

PG, 26 Oct. 1893

It is here appropriate to point out a few aspects of primary importance bearing on the matter of Tchaikovsky's cholera. The material collected in this and the next chapter may indeed result in a confused impression as regards the course of his illness. Close scrutiny reveals a plethora of minor contradictions owing largely to the fact that most of the testimonies were provided by people without special knowledge—relatives, visitors, and newspaper reporters. Tchaikovsky's physicians, on the other hand, discussed it in terms of, and in accordance with, medical views of their own time, which in several respects differed from those of the present day.

One major problem to be recognized is the lack of certainty with regard to whether the composer did in fact survive the most dangerous stage of collapse (also known as the algid and asphyxial stage of cholera), and died from subsequent complications, as it was claimed by most of the lay informants, including the newspaper publications, while the few pronouncements by the medical practitioners on this particular issue remained ambiguous or evasive. The difficulty rests in the imprecise character of the medical jargon popular at the time, so that one term could refer to different phenomena and vice versa, as well as in a degree of wishful thinking, even on the part of the doctors, who hoped against hope that the famous patient might ultimately recover.

As is well known from legal practice, the reports by various witnesses about the same event rarely coincide. Different individuals tend to pay

---

[12] This is an error: the night before, Thursday, Lev Bertenson diagnosed cholera and started his own treatment.

10. Tchaikovsky in Kharkov, 14 March 1893

attention to different circumstances and details, and their impressions are easily confused or contaminated. One obvious example in the case at hand would be the contradictory statements by those present at the bed-side about the deterioration or improvement of Tchaikovsky's condition. Various people were present in the apartment at different times, and the doctors themselves were continually changing their minds about the patient's prospects. The resulting blend of fear and cautious hope which seems reflected in both the press and public opinion, is, therefore, not at all surprising.

Furthermore, with the exception of Modest's narrative, all other eye-witness accounts were in fact oral interviews given to journalists by the composer's physicians, relatives, and friends. It would be unfair as well as unreasonable to expect any of them, shaken as they must have been both by the tragic loss and by the mere fact of being interviewed, to be able to reconstruct the course of the fatal illness with accuracy or precision, and this includes even the doctors themselves, who were unlikely to be con-sulting their medical records during the interviews. It is important to recognize that what is often referred to as the account of Tchaikovsky's main physician is nothing but a transcript of an extempore oral interview given by Lev Bertenson the day after the composer's death to the re-porter of the *New Times* and published on 27 October. Moreover, the text of the interview has been arranged by the reporter topically, in three distinct sections (separated by ellipses at the end of the first and second paragraphs) which deal, respectively, with the origin of Tchaikovsky's illness, the progress of the disease, and his final hours. Such an arrange-ment implies little concern on the part of the journalist for accuracy of chronological sequence. At any rate, Dr Mamonov's interview, published on the previous day in the *News and Stock Exchange Gazette*, had already provided the correct order of events.

The other piece connected to Bertenson, which appeared in the *Peters-burg Gazette* on 26 October, was clearly composed of bits of information patched together from various sources of uneven reliability. The article attributed to a 'Dr Bertenson, the first doctor to be summoned by Tchaikovsky', various 'opinions', among them the claim that the com-poser did not begin to receive medical treatment on Thursday evening, but only on the following day, Friday, 22 October. Some biographers unabashedly called this another 'interview' and declared that it was given not by Lev Bertenson but by his brother Vasily, which in their judge-ment not only implies that neither of them had attended the composer on Thursday evening, but also serves as flagrant evidence of the supposed cover-up. That argument makes little sense. Unpublished correspondence shows that Vasily Bertenson in fact left St Petersburg on 23 October, to visit another patient in the Smolensk region. Any careful reading of the *Petersburg Gazette* article, meanwhile, leaves no doubt that it is the 'famous and honourable' physician, Lev Bertenson, and not his brother or uncle, who must be identified with the 'Dr Bertenson' it cited. The so-called 'interview' clearly states that the 'Bertenson' in question was present at Tchaikovsky's bedside at both the beginning and the end of his illness, and this could only be Lev and none other. That he is referred to as 'the first doctor to be summoned by Tchaikovsky' merely indicates the careless procedure employed by the reporter and successfully imitated by his modern followers. It goes without saying that Lev Bertenson uttered none of what the journalist attributed to him. In fact, close scrutiny of the text allows us to attribute most of 'Dr Bertenson's interview' to the exaggerated impressions of Tchaikovsky's illness of Nikolay Figner, who had been actively meeting all the time with the press despite the very fragmentary information that he possessed.

It was this very article in the *Petersburg Gazette*, reprinted in various other papers, that prompted Lev Bertenson to issue a refutation published the following day in the *New Times*, which read: 'Certain papers have in connection with the illness of P[yotr] I[lyich] Tchaikovsky ascribed to me opinions and comments in such distorted form that I am compelled to deny them, especially as I have seen no members of the press except a reporter from the *New Times*, and therefore cannot have spoken with any of them.' Thus one has to recognize that there was only one interview given by Lev Bertenson and none by his brother Vasily.

If medical records ever existed, they would certainly have been perused by Modest as he composed the lengthy account that was published in the *New Times* and the *News and Stock Exchange Gazette* on 1 November. It is unfortunate that Lev Bertenson's medical archive remains unlocated, though we may yet hope that it will someday come to light. It was alleged that a letter from Lev Bertenson to Modest, giving a detailed description of the development of cholera was seen in Tchaikovsky's archives by some scholars in the 1930s, but my own exhaustive search in the course of my several visits to Klin disclosed no sign of such a document. But even if it existed, it was in all likelihood not an instruction of how successfully to cover up a supposed suicide, but rather the opposite: a digest of medical records compiled by Bertenson and his associates and sent to Modest at the latter's request so that he might check his narrative against the documented facts.

Its very purpose makes Modest's account, from the point of the arrival of the doctors on the evening of Thursday, 21 October, the most reliable and comprehensive in terms of medical data, of the various testimonies we possess. If Modest's texts suffers from a flaw, it is a somewhat self-serving attitude on the part of its author, who was attempting to minimize his own burden of responsibility for the delay in summoning medical help. This explains Modest's persistent tone of apology and even the omission of some pertinent details in the earlier part of the narrative—such as the fact that he spent most of Thursday at the theatre, where dress rehearsals of his play *Prejudices* were under way, and that someone even had to be sent to find him there, according to another memoirist, with word that his brother's life was in serious danger.

When and under what circumstances Tchaikovsky became infected with cholera cannot, despite much speculation, be established, just as the world will never know when and where Nietzsche contracted syphilis. The incubation period for cholera can be anything from one to three days (nowadays some specialists describe the incubation period as even shorter—from twelve to twenty-eight hours). Be that as it may, the composer could not have contracted the disease earlier than Monday, 18 October, or later than the evening of Wednesday, 20 October.

From a medical standpoint, therefore, little credence can be given to any of the stories which began circulating at the time regarding a 'fateful' glass of unboiled water allegedly drunk by Tchaikovsky either at Leiner's restaurant on the eve of the onset of his illness (which Yury Davydov in retrospect pretended to have witnessed) or during the course of that night, or the next day around lunch-time. This last scenario is dramatically emphasized by Modest, which has led supporters of the suicide theory to ridicule this as a clumsy attempt at cover-up, arguing that the episode is irrelevant since, according to Modest himself, his brother was by this time already experiencing the first alarming symptoms. That it is irrelevant is undoubtedly true, yet to attack Modest on this point remains misguided: he was by no means a medical authority and must not be treated as such. In addition, Modest was clearly suffering pangs of guilt for failing to intervene sooner and so save his brother's life, which might well have been the case had he summoned a doctor at once and had a correct diagnosis been made several hours earlier that it was. His belief or, better yet, his wishful thinking that the infection occurred as late as Modest suggests may have helped him to alleviate his remorse somewhat.

Yet, in the final analysis, the entire question of how or when Tchaikovsky became infected is irrelevant. During the last century the water system in St Petersburg was notoriously outdated—as it remains to the present day. In the weeks after Tchaikovsky fell ill the cholera bacillus known as *vibrio cholerae* was reportedly found even in the water supply of the Winter Palace, the residence of the Tsar. Moreover, the sanitary commission discovered, in the course of a special investigation, that certain restaurants were mixing boiled water with unboiled tap-water in order to cool it before serving it to patrons, unaware that the cholera bacillus multiplies very rapidly when the water is warm, though it can also survive in colder temperatures.

Although the bacillus is transmitted most easily in water, it can also survive on foodstuffs, especially on fruit and vegetables which have been washed in infected water. It can live in butter for up to a month. Milk also provides a hospitable environment. These facts are important because the disease can only strike if the bacillus enters the human digestive tract. In effect, it can only be caught by putting an infected foodstuff or other substance into the mouth. It is transmitted easily enough by touching the mouth with infected hands. This opens up a further range of possibilities. The bacillus survives for up to 15 days on faeces and a week in ordinary earth dust. Infected clothes and linen, especially the bed-linen of victims, are important sources of transmission, should they be touched by others who then later unsuspectingly put hand to mouth. Person-to-person transmission usually occurs indirectly through infection of food or clothing or bathroom and toilet facilities.[13]

All of this relates to the common misperception (accepted by the promoters of the suicide version) that cholera only struck the lower classes, with their lack of sanitary conditions, and that Tchaikovsky's case was therefore somehow exceptional and is not to be taken at face value. In fact, it was nothing of the sort: during the week of Tchaikovsky's illness two out of thirty-two deaths from cholera occurred in private apartments—that is, the victims were persons of means. A few years earlier the composer Alexander Borodin contracted cholera, but recovered. And Tchaikovsky's own mother, after all, died of the same illness in 1854.

During the nineteenth century it was customary in describing the symptoms of Asiatic cholera to divide its course into successive stages with characteristics that might differ according to the views of a particular physician or a school of thought, and also because cholera symptoms do not always present themselves in so distinct a form as to be capable of separate recognition.

The Russian physicians traditionally saw the beginning of cholera in the onset of the so-called choleraic diarrhoea, as a rule of mild and painless character, which closely resembles a simple dietary indisposition and tends to pass disregarded. At first, there is no vomiting, and the diarrhoea attacks last from two to three days if the patient is to recover, or for only a few hours in cases where the illness passes to the more serious stage. This next stage, which is often called 'cholerine', brings watery vomiting

---

[13] Richard J. Evans, *Death in Hamburg: Society and Politics in the Cholera Years 1839–1910* (Oxford, 1987), 227. It would seem that the wide range of alternatives does not exclude the possibility that Tchaikovsky might have contracted cholera from one of his anonymous sexual encounters in St Petersburg, as Dr Thomas Stuttaford suggested, *The Times*, 4 Nov. 1993.

with large numbers of bacilli and is accompanied by severe stomach pain, while the diarrhoea turns more violent; the matter discharged, commonly termed 'rice-water evacuations', has a whey-like appearance and contains flakes of mucus. This stage of copious evacuations lasts in severe cases again for only a few hours, after which the patient's body becomes largely dehydrated and the algid stage follows. In the West, cholera specialists did not recognize this 'cholerine' as a separate stage of the illness, but considered it a part of the algid stage or stage of collapse.

The term 'convulsive' could at the time be applied either to the entire algid stage of cholera, or only to its earlier juncture when cramps of the legs, feet, and muscles of the abdomen come on, occasioning great agony, and when the signs of collapse make their appearance. This happens side by side with the suppression of urine and extreme dehydration. The body temperature may fall to 75° F. The surface of the body assumes a blue or purple hue, the skin is dry and wrinkled, indicating the intense draining away of the fluids of the body. The features are pinched and the eyes deeply sunken, the pulse at the wrist is imperceptible, and the voice is reduced to a hoarse whisper. The patient is restless but realizes his condition, for his mind is usually clear. Death may occur at any point during this period, the duration of which varies from a few hours to five days. If the patient survives the algid stage, the stage of reaction develops.

It is the ambivalent character of this next stage that is largely responsible for the confusion in the contemporary reports, since the very arrival at that point could mean that the patient is given the chance of recovery. At this stage the patient's condition appears to improve: blood pressure may rise to normal, colour return to the skin, the stool become less frequent, and the temperature restored to about normal. Furthermore, at this stage of reaction the patient ceases to be infectious, which fact may have caused lay persons to believe that it signified that the cholera proper had come to an end. This explains the misguided opinion found both in some newspapers and in private testimonies that since, according to a momentary belief, the composer appeared to have survived the algid stage of cholera, the disease itself was vanquished and that Tchaikovsky died from some consequent complication. In reality, at that point the outcome of the illness still remains wholly uncertain. The patient may in fact lapse back into the algid stage, or develop symptoms resembling typhus: high fever, severe headache, drowsiness (hence the use of the term 'typhoid' applied either to the entire stage of reaction, or to its closure), which in turn may or may not prove fateful. If during the algid stage there occurs irreversible changes in the kidneys and the suppression of urine persists, no effort can help to prevent uraemia and, even despite the possibility of temporary relief, the patient dies.

All these notions acquire significance when tested against the extant documentary evidence about Tchaikovsky's illness. Their scrutiny demonstrates beyond doubt that the disease ran in conformity with the general pattern, and the few specific minor developments that seem to deviate are easily explained by considering the peculiarities of the composer's organism, and in particular his long history of stomach disorders.

We learn that he started to experience the symptoms related to cholera's early stage, that is, diarrhoea and the vague feeling of being unwell, after a bad night, in the morning of the first day, 21 October. For some time, however, none of this upset his business routine, and it was only after eleven o'clock, when he was forced to abort the planned visit to the family of Eduard Nápravník, that Tchaikovsky may have realized, even though he refused to recognize it, that this time the trouble with his stomach seemed to have been worse than usual. Still, he felt strong enough to spend the early afternoon writing letters, of which one addressed to the manager of the Odessa Opera Theatre appears to have survived. In it the composer laid down plans for his stay in Odessa the following January and asked him to find him suitable accommodation.

The subsequent business lunch with Fyodor Mülbach concerned, as it becomes clear from the earlier correspondence, the terms of the loan Tchaikovsky intended to borrow from him so that he could help his brother Modest in paying the apartment's rent. In the course of that meal, while complaining of indisposition, the composer informed them that instead of castor oil he had earlier drunk a glass of the mineral water Hunyadi-János. Through this he might in fact have stimulated the growth of the cholera bacillus by neutralizing the stomach acids with the alkaline water, though of course not one of those present could have been aware of this. Modest, on the other hand, emphasized an irrelevant episode, that at the same time Tchaikovsky 'poured a glass' of 'unboiled water' and 'took a sip from it'. 'Of all illnesses cholera was the one he least feared.'

Although the composer's condition continued to deteriorate, he twice refused an offer to send for a doctor and, apparently, neither he himself nor anyone else felt particularly worried, having been accustomed, as they all were, to his habitual stomach problems. During Modest's absence (he had to attend the rehearsals of his play at the theatre), Tchaikovsky's condition must have dramatically worsened, as it seems, with the onset of nausea and vomiting, so that by the time Alexander Glazunov saw him at about five in the afternoon, Tchaikovsky undoubtedly felt very ill. Glazunov reports that on that occasion the composer mentioned the possibility of having contracted cholera, but this could well be the memoirist's afterthought since he was writing three decades after the event, in 1923.

Modest's conduct upon his coming back from the theatre at about the same time suggests that he felt worried enough to overrule his brother's protests and send for the trusted physician Vasily Bertenson who, as it later turned out, was not at home, but not concerned enough to stay or to proceed with emergency measures. He left again for the theatre at about six. It appears that the next two hours precipitated the patient's transition to cholera's algid stage. It was unfortunate that in the mean time Modest's manservant Nazar failed to engage a physician other than Vasily Bertenson, but the very need of those attempts speaks for the growth of the composer's sufferings. So far it seems that the thought of cholera was not seriously entertained: even Vasily Bertenson, who arrived finally at 8.15 p.m. (if one trusts Alina Bryullova, before Modest's own return from the theatre), hesitated to come up with a diagnosis, but chose to summon his elder—and more famous—brother Lev for consultation. When the latter arrived after 10 p.m., he definitively diagnosed cholera's algid stage: the patient began to experience violent convulsions, cramps, and numbness in the limbs.

Nowadays the infection of cholera is cured by the full replacement of the body fluids through intravenous injection of sodium chloride (salt) solution, combined with sodium bicarbonate or sodium lactate to counteract acidosis, and by the use of antibiotics that can shorten the duration of the diarrhoea and decrease the requirement for fluid replacement. None of this of course was available at the end of the nineteenth century when the treatment of cholera remained largely the treatment of its symptoms.

The main concern for physicians was to remove the poisonous agent of the disease from the body through the use of laxatives, to render it harmless by introducing medication, stimulating the patient's vital signs (camphor, musk, and other stimulants), to return to the body the warmth it had lost, and to regulate the altered circulation by prescribing a hot bath in the 'cold' or algid stage of cholera.

'Employing all the scientific measures prescribed for such situation', as Lev Bertenson put it in his interview, he chose not to prescribe the bath treatment on Thursday night, nor did he on Friday. Bertenson would later note that the death of Tchaikovsky's mother under similar circumstances had instilled in the composer and in his relatives 'a superstitious fear of the bath'. It appears to have been precisely the emotional resistance of Tchaikovsky's brothers, coupled with the fears of Tchaikovsky himself, that proved decisive in Lev Bertenson's long delay in ordering the hot bath.

Early on Friday morning, 22 October, Vasily Bertenson sent Modest to tell the police what had happened, in accordance with official regulations concerning cholera epidemics. At nine o'clock Vasily Bertenson was replaced by Dr Nikolay Mamonov, his brother' medical assistant; the latter was replaced in turn later that afternoon by Dr Alexander Zander. Everyone thought that the disease was gradually yielding to the treatment. Towards the morning, Saturday, 23 October, the crisis seemed to have been over and Tchaikovsky was thought to have survived the most dangerous 'algid' or 'convulsive' stage of cholera.

5

Hope

23 October–24 October

---

23 October

THE PETERSBURG GAZETTE

By Saturday morning all choleraic attacks had indeed disappeared and [Tchaikovsky] had been rescued from cholera proper. He had recovered to the point that after the disinfection process it became possible to allow his friends into the patient's room.

They came and shook his hand, and he, smiling, responded with a feeble handshake. . . .

The physicians made the visitors wash their hands in a solution of mercuric chloride as they left, but primarily as a formality, for they were quite confident that the infection, already driven out of the patient, had been completely eliminated.

PG, 26 Oct. 1893

LEV BERTENSON

The convulsive stage of cholera could be considered over. Unfortunately, the second stage—the reaction—had not begun. I should mention that in cholera cases as serious as that which Pyotr Ilyich had, the kidneys usually cease to function. This is a result of their rapid deterioration. From the onset of Tchaikovsky's illness complete failure of the kidneys had been apparent. This is very dangerous, for it entails poisoning of the blood by the constituents of the urine. On Friday, however, there were no marked signs of such poisoning. All measures were taken to revive the action of the kidneys, but nothing was effective. Still, one measure—the

11. Tchaikovsky in London, June 1893; the composer's last known portrait

bath—I did not take until Saturday, and the reason is this. The mother
of . . . Pyotr Ilyich had died of cholera—and had died at the very moment when she was placed in the bath. Pyotr Ilyich was aware of this
fact, and it had instilled in him and in all his relatives a superstitious fear
of the bath. On Saturday the signs of uraemic poisoning became evident,
and at the same time the patient had a new and very significant increase
in diarrhoea, which now indicated the paralytic condition of the intestines. This diarrhoea had a very dispiriting effect on Tchaikovsky, and he
turned to me with the words:

'Let me go, don't torment yourself. It's all the same to me if I don't
recover.'

NV, 27 Oct. 1893

MODEST TCHAIKOVSKY

On the morning of Saturday the twenty-third there was no improvement
in the patient's morale. He seemed in a more depressed state than the
previous evening. His faith in recovery had vanished. 'Leave me!' he told
the doctors. 'There's nothing you can do, I won't get better.' Some irri-
tability began to show in his treatment of those around him. The previous evening he had still been joking with the doctors and arguing with
them over his drink, but this day he merely followed their orders submis-
sively. The doctors began directing all their efforts to restoring the function of his kidneys, but all in vain. We all placed great hopes on the hot
bath, which Lev Bertenson prepared to give him that evening. I should
mention that our mother died of cholera in 1854, and that death took her
at the moment she was placed in the bath. My elder brother Nikolay[1] and
I involuntarily regarded this necessary measure with superstitious fear.
Our fear increased when we learned that, asked by the doctor whether he
wished to have the bath, Pyotr Ilyich replied: 'I'm very glad to wash,
only I shall probably die like my mother when you put me in the bath.'
We had to forget the bath that evening because his diarrhoea again
worsened, becoming uncontrollable, and the patient grew weak. Lev
Bertenson left after two o'clock in the morning, dissatisfied by the state
of affairs. Nevertheless the night passed relatively well. After two enemas
the diarrhoea decreased significantly, but the kidneys were still not
functioning.

ZC 652

---

[1] This is the first mention of Nikolay's presence at the patient's bedside, which indicates that
he arrived no later than 23 October and would have known about the events of the previous
days from his relatives.

RUSSIAN LIFE

From early morning on 23 October the sad news began to circulate through the city that our famous composer P[yotr] I[lyich] Tchaikovsky has fallen ill with cholera and lies near death.

RZ, 26 Oct. 1893

GRAND DUCHESS ALEXANDRA IOSIFOVNA

President of the RMS.
Telegram to Nikolay Stoyanovsky, vice-president of the RMS.

I have just learned with horror and grief about Tchaikovsky's grave illness; please let me know the condition of his health as well as his address. My children and I value him greatly. God help him! Alexandra.

PL, 27 Oct. 1893

VLADIMIR TUR

Secretary of the RMS.
Official report to Nikolay Stoyanovsky.

I have the honour to inform Your Excellency that Pyotr Ilyich Tchaikovsky fell ill with cholera on Thursday and is now in an extremely dangerous condition. Crisis is to be expected.

GDMC, A[12], no. 37[3]; *PBC* 104

AUGUST GERKE

Lawyer and member of the Directorate of the RMS. The following is from Gerke's notes intended for an official report about Tchaikovsky's condition at the request of the Grand Duchess Alexandra Iosifovna.

In the evening of 21 October Pyotr Ilyich Tchaikovsky fell ill in St Petersburg (Malaya Morskaya Street, 13) with a bad case of cholera when the epidemic in St Petersburg had already been declining. I learnt of this on 23 October at 5 p.m. . . . I visited the sufferer—in the evening of 23 October and saw there Davydov and Litke and later left for a quartet concert with Stoyanovsky.

GDMC, A[12], no. 36[7]; *PBC* 104

GRAND DUKE KONSTANTIN KONSTANTINOVICH

I was told that P[yotr] I[lyich] Tchaikovsky has a true Asiatic cholera that began on Thursday and that he is now in a very dangerous condition. I am very worried about Pyotr Ilyich.

GARF, f. 660, op. 1, d. 40, l. 134

STEPAN PETROV

Russian writer known under the pen-name 'Skitalets'.

As a first-year university student, not terribly musical by nature, I chanced to find myself within a circle of ardent music lovers who placed opera above everything else in the world. . . .

One of these passionate music lovers came running to me one morning with the news that Tchaikovsky had fallen ill with cholera. The news seemed preposterous—Tchaikovsky and cholera, heaven and earth, the sun and dust—but we hurried over to the 'city' (we lived on the island) to verify it at first hand. Telephones were as yet very scarce at that time, and there were no evening papers at all, so that it was difficult to find anything out until the appearance of the morning papers.

Tchaikovsky was then living on the corner of Gorokhovaya and Malaya Morskaya. . . . He was staying, if I am not mistaken, with his playwright brother Modest Ilyich, and did not have his own apartment in Petersburg. His private life in general was surrounded by a sort of fog, a haze of mystery. . . .

Near Tchaikovsky's building we saw a small crowd of students and young ladies. Yes, he had contracted cholera, but hope was not yet lost—even now Bertenson was expected, he would come and save him. No one gathered there knew Tchaikovsky, having seen him only at premières and in concerts, but we all felt that someone very near and dear to us lay suffering in the apartment above. The same feeling reigned throughout the city, and how everyone cursed the members of the city council for allowing water—the most essential object of consumption—to become the breeding ground for so dangerous a disease!

RU, 27 Oct. 1913

VASILY YASTREBTSEV

That evening I happened to find myself at the first quartet concert, which was celebrating, incidentally, the jubilee of Leopold Auer. During the interval I met Rimsky-Korsakov, who, when I asked him whether it was true that Tchaikovsky was so dangerously ill, informed me that today he himself had visited Pyotr Ilyich at home . . . and had learned that the rumours are correct; that last Wednesday (20 October) Tchaikovsky had been at the Chamber Music Society, and afterwards went to Leiner's, where, having eaten some macaroni, he drank a glass of unboiled water; that the same night he had developed all the symptoms of Asiatic cholera, with convulsions and spasms; that at present there is a turning-point, but the doctors (Bertenson and the others) fear that the cholera will reach the kidneys—and if so, everything will be over.[2] However, according to the doctors, there is little prospect that typhus will develop, and if so, he could survive, with God's help—but who really knows? This wasting illness might well have a ruinous effect on his inner state. 'You know,' continued Rimsky-Korsakov, 'Borodin suffered this foul disease, cholera, some two years before his death; and then when he recovered he was all but unrecognizable: he had almost completely lost his creative gift. What will happen in this case?'

Iastrebtsev, *Rimskii-Korsakov*, i. 125

ALEXANDER GRECHANINOV

In 1892 and 1893 cholera was raging in Russia. A few hours after my conversation with R[imsky]-Korsakov, I met a friend on the street who told me that he had just learned that Tchaikovsky had been taken ill with cholera. I was thunderstruck by the news. I did not want to believe it, and I went at once to verify the rumour at the home of Tchaikovsky's brother Modest on Malaya Morskaya, where Tchaikovsky always stayed. Sadly, the rumour turned out to be true. No one, not even close friends and relatives, was being allowed into the Tchaikovsky apartment for fear of infection. It was said that after the concert Tchaikovsky had supper in a restaurant and on returning home had immediately begun to feel ill.

Grechaninov, *Moia muzykal'naia zhizn'*, 41

VLADIMIR POGOZHEV

Three or four days after my meeting with Pyotr Ilyich I received word of his illness. I did not attach particular significance to this, as Tchaikovsky

---

[2] During that visit Rimsky-Korsakov could not have seen Tchaikovsky, since he definitely states in his memoirs that the last time he saw the composer was at the première of the *Pathétique* Symphony. Rimsky-Korsakov is mistaken in stating that Tchaikovsky went to the Chamber Music Society on Wednesday (as we know that this evening he was in the Alexandrinsky Theatre) and that after cholera typhus can develop (confusion with the so-called typhoid stage of cholera).

had experienced stomach ailments before and they had always passed
with no serious consequences. But his condition continued to worsen. Hope
for recovery flashed briefly for a moment, but in vain.

VC (1980), 197

24 October

GRAND DUKE KONSTANTIN KONSTANTINOVICH

Telegram to Modest Tchaikovsky.

The Grand Duchess and I are very much concerned about Pyotr Ilyich.
We would sincerely appreciate any known information regarding his state
of health. Please accept my apologies for this awkward request. Konstantin.

PBC 76

MODEST TCHAIKOVSKY

Telegram at 12.45 p.m. to Vasily Bertenson in Smolensk, Hotel
Germaniya, where he stayed while visiting his patient.

First period passed, full retention of urine, condition is grave.

GDMC, B^9, no. 206

MODEST TCHAIKOVSKY

By the morning of Sunday the twenty-fourth, the situation was not yet
hopeless, but the anxiety of the physicians about the inactivity of the
kidneys grew. Pyotr Ilyich felt quite bad. To all enquiries about his condition he several times replied: 'Rotten!' To Lev Bertenson he said: 'How
much kindness and patience you're wasting in vain! I can't be cured!' He
slept more, but it was an uneasy, heavy sleep: he was slightly delirious
and continually repeated the name of Nadezhda von Meck, reproaching
her angrily. Then he would quieten down as if listening to something—
now frowning intently, now seeming to smile. After he had slept his consciousness seemed more sluggish than on the other days. Thus he did not
immediately recognize his servant Sofronov, who arrived that morning
from Klin, but all the same he was happy to see him. Up until one o'clock

in the afternoon the situation appeared to those around him to remain unchanged. There was not a drop of urine, so we did not examine it even once. Lev Bertenson arrived at one o'clock and at once judged it essential to resort to what seemed to us the extreme measure for stimulating the activity of the kidneys—the bath. At two o'clock the bath was ready.

ZC 652–3

AUGUST GERKE

Letter to Modest Tchaikovsky.

And how is our poor dear patient doing? Are all dangers of cholera over by now and is there any improvement in his health? Yesterday at the quartet concert everyone whom I would start talking to about Pyotr Ilyich responded with grief and compassion. Would you scribble to me on any piece of paper, whether you need any help to keep vigil at the patient's bedside? I would willingly become his sick nurse. It could be a good idea to issue *Bulletins* with the doorman and to ask Dr Bertenson or Mamonov to take care of that. I am now going to the church and I will pray most heartily for Pyotr Ilyich.

GDMC, B^{10}, no. 1147; *PBC* 106–7

MODEST TCHAIKOVSKY

Letter to August Gerke.

The condition is almost the same. Faeces are thickened. Expecting urine, but in vain.

GDMC, A^{12}, no. 36^7; *PBC* 107

THE PETERSBURG GAZETTE

The sad news of P[yotr] I[lyich] Tchaikovsky's illness spread very quickly through the city and his numerous friends and admirers rushed to the house where he is living. Most, despite the protests of the doorman, mounted the stairs to the apartment and rang the door, disturbing the sufferer.

As a result the physicians decided to write bulletins on the progress of the illness, instructing the doorman to show them to all those seeking information but to allow no one access to the apartment bell.

PG, 26 Oct. 1893

BULLETIN

2.30 p.m.
The dangerous fits continue and are not responding to treatment; complete retention of the urine, together with drowsiness and a marked general weakness; the diarrhoea is not as strong as before, but still continues.

NV, 25 Oct. 1893

THE PETERSBURG GAZETTE

At three o'clock Pyotr Ilyich was placed in a hot bath.

PG, 25 Oct. 1893

[NIKOLAY TCHAIKOVSKY]

When, around three o'clock on Sunday afternoon, the doctors decided to place the patient in a hot bath, P[yotr] I[lyich] begged them not to do this, saying that his mother had died in a hot bath. After the bath he said in a faint voice: 'I feel weak!' He did not say another word after that, though apparently he did not lose consciousness.

NBG, 26 Oct. 1893

LEV BERTENSON

I suggested to Pyotr Ilyich that we should give him the bath. He readily consented. When he had been placed in it, I asked:
    'Do you find the bath unpleasant?'
    'On the contrary, it's pleasant,' he replied, but after a while, complaining of weakness, he began to ask to be lifted out.
    The immediate effect of the bath was beneficial: a warm sweat appeared, and with it a hope that the uraemic poisoning might diminish and functioning of the kidneys be restored.

NV, 27 Oct. 1893

MODEST TCHAIKOVSKY

Pyotr Ilyich was in a half-conscious state while [the bath] was prepared in the same room. He had to be roused. He seemed not to grasp quite

12. Lev Bertenson, Tchaikovsky's physician

clearly at first what they wanted to do with him, but then he consented to the bath, and when he was lowered into it, he was fully aware of what was happening. When the doctor asked him whether he found the hot water unpleasant, he replied: 'On the contrary, it's pleasant,' but very soon began asking to be lifted out, saying that he felt weak. And indeed, from the moment he was taken out of the bath his drowsiness and his sleep took on a certain peculiar character. The bath did not have the anticipated effect, though it produced a strong sweat; at the same time, according to the doctors, it reduced for a while the signs of blood poisoning from the urine. The perspiring continued, but at the same time the pulse, which up till then had been comparatively regular and strong, again weakened. It was again necessary to resort to an injection of musk to restore his failing strength. This was successful: despite the perspiration the pulse rose and the patient grew calm. Until eight o'clock it seemed to us that his condition was improving.

ZC 653

NIKOLAY MAMONOV

Saturday passed tolerably, but the absence of urine continued to worry us. On Sunday morning very clear signs of poisoning from the urine appeared and a bath was administered, which produced a strong sweat. After this the patient seemed to be better.

NBG, 26 Oct. 1893

AUGUST GERKE

4.30 p.m.
I arrived at 4.30 p.m. and after reading Dr Bertenson's bulletin (of 2.30 p.m.) . . . I went upstairs where I saw Nikolay Tchaikovsky and his cousin. . . . Downstairs there were Kamenskaya [singer], Varlamov [actor], Glazunov. . . . The bath took place, failure of strength caused injections of camphor and musk.

GDMC, A^{12}, no. 36^7; *PBC* 109

MEMBER OF TCHAIKOVSKY'S HOUSEHOLD

It was already too late by the time Pyotr Ilyich was placed in the hot bath, and after it he lost the last of his strength.

SV, 26 Oct. 1893

ALEXANDER ZANDER

Physician, assistant to Lev Bertenson. The following are the notes
of Boris Asafyev taken after conversation with Zander.

After taking the bath that had been forced upon him Tchaikovsky grew
completely quiet, drawing into himself and scarcely speaking. He no longer
showed any interest in those around him. You've had your way, he seemed
to say. You insisted on the bath, in which my mother died—now I'm in
your hands, though as far as I know, I'm sentenced to death. But what
of it? I'm ready. That is what was in his look.

RGALI, f. 2658, op. 1, no. 45, l. 30

MODEST TCHAIKOVSKY

Soon after Dr Mamonov had left, at about a quarter past eight, his replacement, Dr Zander, again noticed a sudden weakening of the pulse
and became sufficiently alarmed to consider it necessary to inform Lev
Bertenson immediately. According to the doctors, the patient was by this
time in a comatose state, so that when I went into his room the doctor
advised me not to leave him for a minute. His head was cold, his breathing laboured and accompanied by moans, yet still the question 'Do you
want a drink?' would bring him momentarily to consciousness. He would
answer 'Yes' or 'Of course', then would say 'That's enough', 'I don't want
any', or 'I don't need it'. Shortly after ten o'clock Dr Zander diagnosed
the onset of oedema of the lungs, and Lev Bertenson quickly arrived.

ZC 653

AUGUST GERKE

8.30 p.m.
Still the same bulletin. I was with [young cellist Dmitry] Bzul; saw Modest. Weakness continues, another fit, fall of strength, bath, a new injection. They wait for Lev Bertenson.

GDMC, A^{12}, no. 36^{7}; *PBC* 110

LEV BERTENSON

By evening hope [of improvement] was gone. Drowsiness set in and there
was a sudden weakening of the action of the heart, so severe that my

assistant Dr Zander, who had remained with Pyotr Ilyich, gave the patient an injection of musk and sent for me. I found Pyotr Ilyich in a comatose state and with a sharply weakened heartbeat, from which he could only manage to be brought out for the very shortest time. Thus, for example, when he was offered a drink, he accepted it with full consciousness, saying: 'That's enough', 'more', and so on. By half past ten that evening all hopes for a possible favourable turn in the course of the illness completely disappeared. The drowsiness became ever deeper, and the pulse remained undetectable, despite repeated and frequent injection of stimulants.

NV, 27 Oct. 1893

BULLETIN

10.30 p.m.
Urinary function has not been restored and signs of blood-poisoning from the constituents of the urine are extremely pronounced. Since three o'clock this afternoon there has been a rapidly growing decline in the action of the heart and fading consciousness. Since ten o'clock this evening the pulse has been almost imperceptible and there is oedema of the lungs.

NV, 25 Oct. 1893; *PG*, 25 Oct. 1893

EDUARD NÁPRAVNÍK

The state of P[yotr] I[lyich] Tchaikovsky's health is hopeless!!

RIII, f. 21, op. 1, ed. kh. 227, ll. 57–8

KONSTANTIN DE LAZARI

On 24 October, rather late in the evening I found myself at the Merchants Club. Rarely is anything other than money discussed there. Everyone is preoccupied, thinking about his losses or gains. If a group of people gathers, it probably has to do with some important occurrence. So it was on this particular evening. I saw several men standing together in animated conversation.

'What a pity! Such a talent! It will be a great misfortune if he dies!'

'Who are they talking about?' I asked.

'Do you mean you don't know? Pyotr Ilyich Tchaikovsky is near death, he may even be already dead.'

This news struck me like thunder. It was too late to go to Tchaikovsky's so I returned home utterly devastated by the news.

RO, 18 July 1900

MODEST TCHAIKOVSKY

At the request of [brother] Nikolay, a priest was sent for from St Isaac's Cathedral. Only by increased injections for stimulating the action of the heart could the condition of the dying man be maintained. All hope of improvement vanished. The father who came with the Holy Sacraments found it impossible to administer them to Pyotr Ilyich because of his unconscious state, and simply read loudly and clearly the prayers of the dying, not a single word of which seemed to reach his consciousness. Soon after this the fingers of the dying man moved strangely, as though he had an itch in various parts of his body.

The doctors continued tirelessly employing all possible measures to prolong the action of the heart, as if still hoping for a miraculous recovery. During this time the following people were by the dying man's bedside: the three doctors, the two Litke brothers, Buchshoevden, Nikolay Figner, [Dmitry] Bzul, Vladimir Davydov, my brother's servant [Alexey] Sofronov, [Nazar] Litrov and his wife, the medical attendant, my brother Nikolay, and myself. Lev [Bertenson] decided that there were too many people for the small room. The window was opened, and Figner and Bzul departed. Bertenson, judging all hope lost, left in extreme exhaustion, leaving Nikolay Mamonov to witness the final moments.

ZC 654

NIKOLAY MAMONOV

At eight o'clock uraemia set in. . . . Pyotr Ilyich was fully conscious, though of course very dispirited. He was often half-asleep, but one had only to ask him, 'Do you want a drink,' or something else, and he would acknowledge the speaker at once and express his wish. . . .

Beginning at ten o'clock, and for the next two hours, the oxygen mask had to be changed every five minutes, and during Tchaikovsky's illness fourteen cubic feet of oxygen were taken from the pharmacy.

At twelve o'clock the patient fell into his death agony.

It was not very agonizing, but it lasted a very long time—from twelve midnight until three in the morning [25 October].

NBG, 26 Oct. 1893

THE PETERSBURG GAZETTE

Since Saturday [the doctors] had been worried about a new danger sign —the continued retention of urine. They began to fear lest the blood, absorbing the bacilli, become infected by the retained urine, and concentrated their efforts on stimulating the discharge of the latter. But no diuretics were effective, the blood became infected, and with the success of the infection all hope vanished for a rescue of the dying man, not yet old and still in the full flower of his rare creative genius!

Dr Bertenson, an old and intimate friend of [Tchaikovsky], displayed an incredible feat of self-possession in concealing his despair from the still half-conscious patient and his relatives. For the rest of the morning and afternoon [on Sunday] he tore himself away only briefly to visit other dangerously ill patients, and from five o'clock until half past one in the morning he was never absent from Tchaikovsky's bedside, leaving him only when it became clear that there was nothing more he could do there.

Anyone who saw the respected doctor in that moment will never forget the indescribable grief in his face and in his voice as he uttered the terrible words 'He's dying . . .'.

Also present during [Tchaikovsky's] final hours was another close friend, N[ikolay] Figner, who was particularly struck by the strength of [Tchaikovsky's] resistance to the dreadful illness. Almost to the very last, he would turn and even slightly raise himself on the bed without any assistance, and during his attacks of vomiting he spewed the discharge with such force that it flew half-way across the room.

His voice failed a few hours before death and at the same time his hearing became dull, but if one spoke slowly into his ear he would indicate with a gesture and his eyes that he understood. Just before the end Tchaikovsky opened his eyes, which had remained closed for some time, glanced over at his nephew whom he so loved, then shifted his gaze to his brother Modest and, with a barely audible sigh, died.

PG, 26 Oct. 1893

NIKOLAY FIGNER

The final hours of P[yotr] I[lyich]'s life were truly terrible. I cannot recall without a shudder the painful death agony to which I was witness. The dying man remained conscious until almost the very last. It is impossible to convey the torments experienced by those around him, in particular [Tchaikovsky's] brother Modest and Lev Bertenson, who did not leave the bed of the dying man until the fatal moment.

NBG, 26 Oct. 1893

By the morning of Saturday, 23 October, sad news, that Tchaikovsky had been taken 'dangerously ill' began to spread through the city. Anxiety and concern about Tchaikovsky's condition touched not only the composer's friends and admirers, but also the general public and even the Imperial family. The flow of visitors began to invade the apartment, but also there is no evidence that anyone was admitted to the patient's bedside except the medical personnel, relatives, and a few close friends. It appears that information about his present condition was communicated to new arrivals in Modest's apartment antechamber.

It remains debatable whether Tchaikovsky did actually survive the algid stage of cholera. On the one hand, the sources claim that on Friday, 22 October, he experienced a period of considerable relief which seems to have lasted until the next morning. This was eagerly interpreted by the relatives, friends, and sympathizers as proof that the most dangerous moment of the crisis had passed, and that if the complications of the typhoid stage could be avoided, the patient might acquire the chance to recover. On the other hand, at least one physician, Lev Bertenson, must have entertained serious doubts as regards his patient's transition to the stage of reaction. The published text of his interview seems almost intentionally confused on this very point: he claims that the convulsive stage of the disease passed but, as it follows from the rest of his argument, the next stage—that of reaction—never arrived. This incongruity may of course be blamed on the sloppiness of the reporter, but it could also have betrayed Bertenson's subconscious desire to obscure the issue and to present his colleagues and himself in the best possible light. After all, it would not have been easy explicitly to concede that all their skill and knowledge proved of no avail and that they had failed to help their famous patient at the very crucial stage; to imply that he died from accidental complications after he seemed to have already embarked upon the route of convalescence would have gratified both theirs and public sentiments by sheer force of dramatization. In fact, under the 'convulsive' stage that, as he put it, 'could be considered over' Bertenson might have meant in his interview not the entire algid stage, but merely its initial development which, true enough, came to an end by the evening of Friday,

23 October, when regular spasms appeared to have ceased. This would have also made better sense of Modest's telegram to the absent Vasily Bertenson which he sent later on Sunday, 24 October, around midday stating 'the first period passed', but that the composer's condition remained grave. As already stated, the algid stage may last up to five days. It cannot be denied that Tchaikovsky's physicians fought it energetically, but the consequent relief, which they were prepared to construe as the sign that the stage of reaction was at hand, proved illusory: it appeared rather a temporary remission, and by Saturday evening the patient's kidneys must have collapsed and uraemic poisoning became apparent.

It was at this time that, according to his interview, Lev Bertenson set his mind, despite the superstition of Tchaikovsky's family, on a hot bath: the medicine of the period considered the body's immersion in hot water as a potentially effective means of restoring blood circulation and thus of stimulating the kidneys (a view which is no longer held). This plan, however, soon had to be abandoned since diarrhoea suddenly worsened and became uncontrollable, indicating the paralytic condition of the intestines.

Somehow, the fact that the idea of the bath was abandoned on Saturday was omitted from the published text of Bertenson's interview, creating an impression that the bath had been resorted to on Saturday rather than on Sunday and that Tchaikovsky died early on Sunday morning rather than Monday. Unnoticed by the press at the time, that slip became a big issue almost a hundred years later, when speculating biographers tried to find traces of conspiracy and cover-up among Tchaikovsky's doctors and relatives. While there could be the outside chance that Bertenson might have wanted to avoid the troubling question of the belated bath, it seems likelier that the day in question was simply lost in the process of the interview and omitted by the reporter in his haste to write it up.

Close reading of this text, published in the *New Times* on 27 October, suggests that it was clearly divided into three sections. Ellipses at the end of the first and second sections indicate that the three parts very probably represent Bertenson's separate responses to three questions posed by the reporter. In these questions, which were edited out of the printed version of the interview, the reporter would appear to have asked Bertenson to describe how Tchaikovsky became ill, the course of the illness, and Tchaikovsky's last day. It may never have been the reporter's intention to get a full day-by-day account, and it may well have been the reporter, not Bertenson, who jumped ahead to the events of Sunday, interrupting the physician before he could explain that despite his desire to administer the hot bath on Saturday, it was postponed until Sunday because of the patient's condition.

The renewed diarrhoea had a very depressive effect on the already weak Tchaikovsky at the end of the Saturday. Lev Bertenson left after two o'clock in the morning, dissatisfied with the state of affairs.

That night passed relatively well, but starting with Sunday morning, 24 October, the composer showed signs of further deterioration. By the time Lev Bertenson arrived at one o'clock in the afternoon, he found his patient in a state close to semi-coma. Seriously alarmed by the inactivity of Tchaikovsky's kidneys, he decided finally to administer the hot bath. The subsequent immersion, around two o'clock (some newspapers insist that it happened at three o'clock), of the patient's body in hot water achieved little. It seemed that Tchaikovsky was losing his last strength which compelled the doctors to attempt a new injection of musk, and this apparently worked: despite the perspiration, the pulse improved and the sufferer calmed down. This last remission, much shorter than the one before, lasted for only five hours. After eight o'clock in the evening, in the words of Modest, 'all hope of improvement vanished'.

On the advice of August Gerke and in response to the stream of people enquiring about Tchaikovsky's health, doctors issued bulletins on the progress of the illness on Sunday, which were sent first down to the door-man, who later posted it on the front door of the apartment building. Two bulletins were written by Bertenson himself, the last one by his assistant.

The alleged discrepancies between Modest's account and the medical bulletins are in fact illusory. The first bulletin was posted up at 2.30 p.m., that is, half an hour after the bath. It tells us that 'the dangerous symptoms are still present, and are not responding to treatment'. Modest speaks of this very moment: 'The bath did not have the anticipated result, though it produced a strong sweat; at the same time, according to the doctors, it reduced for a while the signs of blood-poisoning from the urine. The perspiring continued, but at the same time the pulse, which up till then had been comparatively strong, again weakened.' It is clear that the same situation is described in both texts: no improvement in the patient's condition. Only after injections (two hours later) did the signs of a temporary and brief recovery appear, which naturally could not have been reflected in the first bulletin. The second bulletin was posted up at 10.30 p.m., after this temporary remission had already ended—at 8.15 p.m. the pulse had weakened sharply, sending the patient into a coma. So despite the fact that 'up to 8.00 p.m. his condition seemed to us to improve', the general picture was one of irreversible worsening. Hence the language of the second bulletin is understandable: 'Since 3.00 p.m. (and up until 10.30 p.m.) there has been increasing weakness.'

Lev Bertenson's last visit to the apartment took place after ten o'clock in the evening. One can imagine the physician's sense of frustration and despair: his patient was in coma and clearly dying, his pulse remained undetectable, the overall condition further complicated by oedema of the lungs. Bertenson judged that there was nothing more to be done, and chose to leave, according to Modest, in a state of 'extreme exhaustion'.

This survey of the period's medical opinions and documentary data still necessarily falls short of determining with full confidence the exact details of Tchaikovsky's last illness. None of the surviving records meets the modern standards of scientific accuracy. On the balance of evidence, however, it seems very likely that the composer, despite protestations of the less informed sources, failed to survive the algid stage of cholera, which was diagnosed too late for any effective treatment, and died from uraemic blood-poisoning, caused by the eventual paralysis of the kidneys.

6

Death

25 October

―――――

25 October

BULLETIN

1.30 a.m.
The patient's condition has so worsened that a sanitary inspector and police officials have arrived at the house.

PZ, 26 Oct. 1893; *PG*, 26. Oct. 1893

[NIKOLAY TCHAIKOVSKY]

Not ten minutes before his death he opened his eyes: his gaze rested on his nephew and his brother. Infinitive love and anguished farewell could be read in that look. A few minutes later P[yotr] I[yich] fell asleep forever.

NBG, 26 Oct. 1893

SERGEY BERTENSON

Until the very moment of the composer's untimely end a mood of such depression reigned in our home as if the dying man were in our midst. To this day I cannot forget the look on my father's face when he returned home and said, 'It's all over', and broke into sobs.

Bertenson, *Vokrug iskusstva*, 20

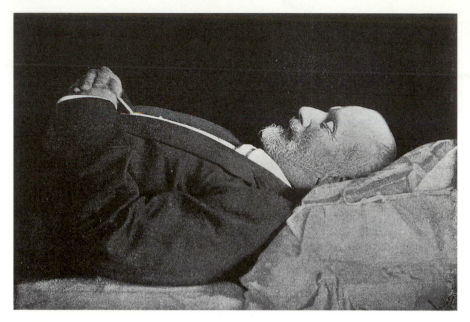

13. Tchaikovsky on his death-bed, 25 October 1893

MODEST TCHAIKOVSKY

His breathing grew more shallow, though he could still be brought to consciousness, it seemed, by asking him whether he wanted to drink: he no longer responded with words, but only with affirmative or negative sounds. Suddenly his eyes, which up until then had been half-closed and glazed, opened wide. An indescribable expression of full consciousness appeared. He rested his gaze in turn on the three people who were standing near him, then lifted it towards the sky. For a few moments something in his eyes lit up and then faded with his final breath. It was a little after three in the morning.

ZC 654

Letter to Ivan Klimenko on 9 November 1893.

He passed away like a saint. The expression of his eyes at the minute before he died was so loving and courageous; it appeared that even at this moment he was not thinking about himself but was rather asking our forgiveness for causing us such terrible grief.

I. A. Klimenko, *Moi vospominaniia o
P. I. Chaikovskom* (Riazan, 1908), 75

EDUARD NÁPRAVNÍK

Shortly after three o'clock this morning our finest modern Russian composer, Pyotr Ilyich Tchaikovsky, passed away from Asiatic cholera after a four-day illness.

RIII, f. 21, op. 1, ed. kh. 227, ll. 57–8

ALEXANDER GRECHANINOV

The doctors struggled desperately to save this life so dear to Russia. Several times a day, terribly worried, I went over to [Malaya] Morskaya Street. There were always large crowds of people standing in front of the bulletins posted on the wall. Despair changed to hope and then gave way again to despair. Finally, on 25 October Tchaikovsky passed away. The entire musical world was stunned by this news. Neither before nor since have I witnessed such unanimity of profound grief as seized everyone then.

Grechaninov, *Moia muzykal'naia zhizn'*, 42

THE NEW TIMES

The renowned composer Pyotr Ilyich Tchaikovsky fell ill from cholera on Thursday. [Yesterday] at 3 p.m. the decline in cardiac activity rapidly increased, his consciousness dimmed. . . . Between the third and fourth hour after midnight P[yotr] I[lyich] died.

NV, 25 Oct. 1893

Tchaikovsky passed away in the apartment of his brother Modest Tchaikovsky, the playwright, with whom he habitually stayed when he visited Petersburg. The deceased lies on an ottoman as if alive, and appears, as it were, to have fallen asleep. The photographer of the Imperial Theatre [Nikolay Gundviser] took pictures of the deceased.

NV, 26 Oct. 1893

In the morning a death mask was taken of the deceased [by sculptor Sławomir Celiński]. The face retained its customary expression and bore an imprint of complete tranquillity.

NV, 27 Oct. 1893[1]

---

[1] For some reason this report on the events of 25 October was not published in the *New Times* next day, as was the usual practice of St Petersburg newspapers, but two days later. Cf. *NBG*, 26 Oct. 1893; *SV*, 26 Oct. 1893; *BV*, 27 Oct. 1893.

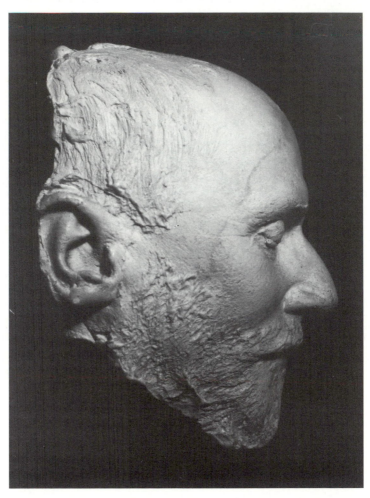

14. Tchaikovsky's death mask, taken on 25 October by Sławomir
Celiński

GRAND DUKE KONSTANTIN KONSTANTINOVICH

With Dmitry I went. . . .[2] I have just received a telegram from Modest Tchaikovsky: Pyotr Ilyich died at three o'clock this morning. My heart bleeds. I loved him and respected him as a musician. We were good and genuine friends, and I shall miss him. . . .

For a long time I could not recover after having received the grievous news about Tchaikovsky's death. Another person in the treasury of Russian art is no more. I corresponded with him and I possess not a few of his letters.[3]

Yesterday morning I was not really myself. I lamented the untimely death of Tchaikovsky. Everyone was struck by it. I tried to write a poem on Tchaikovsky's death, but nothing worked out. The Tsar and the Tsarina are very upset by the death of Tchaikovsky.[4]

GARF, f. 660, op. 1, d. 40, l. 137

IVAN VSEVOLOZHSKY

The director of the Imperial Theatres.
Letter to Count Illarion Vorontsov-Dashkov, the Minister of the Imperial court.

This night at 3 a.m. Pyotr Ilyich Tchaikovsky died. I know that his family is under financial strain. Perhaps the Sovereign will be willing to bury him at his Majesty's expense.

RGB, 58/II, kart. 140, no. 25

ILLARION VORONTSOV-DASHKOV

Letter to Alexander III.

Your Majesty, could not it be allowed to conduct Tchaikovsky's funeral at Your Majesty's expense?

---

[2] The original diary entry has 24 October. As usual, the Grand Duke wrote his diary entry on the morning of the next day and this entry is made on the morning of 25 October in the Grand Duke's residence in Strelna, near St Petersburg. Right at the moment of writing 'With Dmitry I went', describing events of 24 October, the Grand Duke must have received the telegram about Tchaikovsky's death. Dmitry is the younger brother of Konstantin Konstantinovich.

[3] This paragraph is written in different ink, probably at the Tsar's residence of Gatchina.

[4] This paragraph is the diary entry of 25 October, written by the Grand Duke on the morning of 26 October in Gatchina.

If your order to do so will follow it seems to me that it would be fitting to entrust the organization of the funeral to this Ministry's official.

RGB, 58/II, kart. 140, no. 25

ALEXANDER III

The note to the upper part of the letter of Vorontsov-Dashkov.

Of course, it can be done. What a pity and such a disappointment!

RGB, 58/II, kart. 140, no. 25

ALEXANDER KUGEL

Journalist and man of letters, correspondent of the Moscow news-paper *News of the Day*, writing under the pen-name 'Qvidam'.

Tchaikovsky has died! I cannot convey to you all the force of the impression caused by this death. How can one express the sense of emptiness and fear facing the majesty of death that turns the majesty of life into nothing. Side by side with Lev Tolstoy, Pyotr Tchaikovsky: two names in which Russian Genius found its expression, and one half is now no more! It is snatched by cholera. Fate played a nasty joke by mixing cholera with symphony. Incidentally, I was told that the new symphony which Tchaikovsky conducted last Saturday ended not with the usual *Allegro*, but with a melancholic *Adagio lamentoso* as if some kind of presentiment oppressed the author's soul. . . .

In the morning I visited the apartment of the deceased. He lived in the apartment of his brother on Malaya Morskaya, in the house where the restaurant *Vienna* is located. The plump and well-meaning doorman looked entirely distressed:

'Such a modest gentlemen. He would go to Leiner's for a dinner . . . and such a crowd now . . . And he was not even a general. . . .'

Downstairs I met a music critic of one newspaper. He started to speak to me and cried. 'My God', his dry lips kept repeating, and his eyes, red from tears, stared into space without expression.

Upstairs everything was ready for the requiem. On the catafalque, covered with a quiet—one would say, lyrical—expression on his face, lay the deceased, transparent, wax-like, without any traces of suffering, or—to put it better, with the traces of suffering reconciled. He was dressed in a frock-coat and covered with a transparent shroud. . . . Two students carried a wreath—a temporary one; there will be another, made of silver.

Two ladies in black stood in the corner and cried. Nearby, with a tense expression on their faces stood singers, musicians, critics—the whole assembly of people who were nourished by the great muse of the deceased. No later than on Thursday Chernov [a baritone with the Maryinsky Theatre] was singing during the concert at Duma Hall Tchaikovsky's song 'Amid the din of the ball'—and now. . . . A medical attendant applies to the lips and nostrils of the deceased a handkerchief with disinfecting liquid. What is the ball? What is life? Everything ends with one hopeless chord.

ND, 26 Oct. 1893

THE NEWS AND STOCK EXCHANGE GAZETTE

From early morning a great number of students, colleagues, and admirers of the deceased composer arrived at the apartment of M[odest] Tchaikovsky. Even though reports of P[yotr] I[lyich]'s death had already appeared in . . . the newspapers, many people refused to believe that the announced death was an actual fact. Among the visitors were many prominent individuals. In view of all the people who came to ask about the final moments of the deceased's life, the street door did not close from morning on wards.

Today, 25 October, at 12.30 p.m. in the chapel of the Imperial School of Jurisprudence, a requiem service was held for the former student of the School, Pyotr Ilyich Tchaikovsky, attended by the School's Director, Lieutenant General Alexander Panteleyev, the entire teaching staff, and all the students. Tomorrow at twelve noon the School of Jurisprudence will conduct a solemn requiem over the coffin of the deceased and lay a wreath.

At half past one, people began gathering for the requiem. So great was the crowd wishing to attend this requiem that even the fairly large apartment occupied by the composer's brother could not accommodate everyone. Among those present were: the director of the Imperial Theatre, Privy Councillor Ivan Vsevolozhsky; the St Petersburg deputy-governor, Privy Councillor [and Tchaikovsky's former classmate from School of Jurisprudence] Ivan Turchaninov; the director of the Imperial School of Jurisprudence, Lieutenant-General Panteleyev; several representatives of the musical world, including [Eduard] Nápravník, [Herman] Laroche, [Anatoly] Lyadov, [Nikolay] Rimsky-Korsakov, Dlusky, [Josef] Palechek, [Nikolay] Solovyov, and others; [choral director] Alexander Arkhangelsky; the singers [Mariya] Dolina, [Mariya] Kamenskaya, [Nikolay] Figner, [Arkady] Chernov, [Leonid] Yakovlev, and others.

NBG, 26 Oct. 1893

EDUARD NÁPRAVNÍK

Attended the first requiem at two in the afternoon. The male chorus of
the Russian Opera sang at all the requiems. All expenses for the burial are
being borne by the Ministry of the Imperial Court.

RIII, f. 21, op. 1, ed. kh. 227, ll. 57–8

THE PETERSBURG GAZETTE

At two o'clock the doors were opened to the room where the deceased lay.
It is a small corner room with five full-length windows looking out over
the intersection of Malaya Morskaya and Gorokhovaya. The furniture
has been removed from it. P[yotr] I[lyich] Tchaikovsky's body rests on
a low catafalque draped in white satin. The deceased is dressed in a black
suit and covered up to the neck by a transparent shroud; his face, completely exposed, no longer reflects the suffering of the painful illness: it is
of a parchment-like yellow, but tranquil, impassive—the face of an exhausted man sleeping peacefully, and only the presence near the head of
someone continually touching the lips and the nostrils of the deceased
with a bit of light-coloured material soaked in carbolic solution reminds
one of the terrible illness that struck down the deceased. . . .

In view of the fact that Pyotr Ilyich died not from cholera (the cholera
had been arrested on Friday) but from an infection of the blood and that
there can therefore be no question of contagion, his coffin remained open
for a time.

PG, 26 Oct. 1893

STANISLAV GABEL

Professor at the St Petersburg Conservatoire.

When I hurried over to his apartment, I found him dead; a small cloth
lay upon his cold lips. Near his corpse I found my predecessor as Conservatoire inspector, [Vasily] Samus, and [Eduard] Nápravník.

BV, 24 Oct. 1913

I was one of the first professors to learn about his death. People reported
that he had been poisoned, that it was most likely a stomach illness.

SR 4 (1913), 7

THE NEW TIMES

Now and then [during the requiem] someone will pass through with a hissing atomizer [of antiseptic, for disinfecting the air in the apartment].

NV, 27 Oct. 1893

THE NEWS AND STOCK EXCHANGE GAZETTE

The brother of the deceased, Modest Tchaikovsky, is so struck by grief that he is unable to be present at the requiem; he remains in another room in the company of a few devoted persons; no one except Nikolay Figner goes in to see him.

NBG, 26 Oct. 1893

THE PETERSBURG LEAFLET

The chorus of the Russian Opera under the direction of Fyodor Bekker sang at the requiem. The harmonious singing of the opera chorus brought heartfelt tears to the eyes of the many mourners. . . . The voices of the chorus members trembled with the emotion that gripped all present; several mourners sobbed as the doleful tunes were sung. . . . None wanted to believe that there upon a black catafalque in the small low room lay the lifeless body of the great composer, whose features, even after the terrible illness that carried him to the grave, still bore the same imprint of exceptional geniality and kindness which until so recently had endeared Tchaikovsky to everyone who met him.

[A second] requiem that evening again attracted a crowd of people wishing to pay their last respects to the composer, whose body still lies on the catafalque.

PL, 26 Oct. 1893

THE NEW TIMES

At seven o'clock in the evening a second requiem service was held, at which were present Leopold Auer [violinist], [Tchaikovsky's classmate from the School of Jurisprudence] Ivan Turchaninov, Nikolay Figner, Pavel Vasilevsky, Alexander Verzhbilovich [a cellist], Vasily Krylov, Nikolay Potekhin, and others. The male chorus of the Imperial Russian Opera sang.

The coffin has been covered with wreaths from the staff and direc-
torate of the Imperial Theatres, 'To the unforgettable P[yotr] I[lyich]
Tchaikovsky from the orphaned Medea and Nikolay Figner', 'To the
unforgettable P[yotr] I[lyich] Tchaikovsky from N[ikolay] R[imsky]-
K[orsakov], A[natoly] L[yadov], and A[lexander] G[lazunov]', from
Count P. A. Bennigsen, from Mrs Nadezhda von Meck, and others.

NV, 26 Oct. 1893

NIKOLAY RIMSKY-KORSAKOV

How odd that although death was the result of cholera, there was free
access to the requiems. I remember that Verzhbilovich, totally drunk
after some sort of binge, kissed the corpse on the face and head.

Rimskii-Korsakov, *Polnoe sobranie sochinenii*, i. 193

THE NEWS AND STOCK EXCHANGE GAZETTE

At 9 p.m. Pyotr Ilyich's body was placed in a metal coffin in the presence
of his relatives and a few close friends, Alexander Nasvetevich, Nikolay
Figner, and others, during which special prayers were offered. . . . The
coffin was soldered . . . in the presence of the police.

NV, 26 Oct. 1893

THE NEW TIMES

The body of the deceased was placed in the coffin, with all precautionary
measures being taken: the body was wrapped in a sheet soaked in a solution of mercuric chloride, the inner coffin, made of metal, was soldered,
and the outer, made of oak, was screwed shut.

NV, 27 Oct. 1893

THE SON OF THE FATHERLAND

Yesterday following the requiem the body was placed in the coffin. It is
a simple coffin of varnished oak with a carved wooden cross on its lid, and
a metal coffin inside.

The coffin was sealed and soldered with lead and the entire apartment
disinfected.

SO, 26 Oct. 1893

EDUARD NÁPRAVNÍK

I am unable to express how grievously this unexpected death has struck me. The divine flame that shone so brightly, warming us all, has been extinguished. . . .

I mourn the deceased not only as one of Russia's greatest sons, but also as my best friend and a marvellous person, whose image shall never be erased from my memory. The sole consolation for all of us whom he has left behind will be his songs—full of beauty, strength, and inspiration.

NBG, 26 Oct. 1893

GRAND DUCHESS ALEXANDRA IOSIFOVNA

Telegram to Modest Tchaikovsky.

With all my heart I share your family's grief over the unforgettable Tchaikovsky. His fame is the pride of the conservatoire that trained him. He is dead, but his fame will live forever in his works and inspire new forces to the selfless service of our precious Russian art.

BV, 26 Oct. 1893

SOFIYA TOLSTAYA

Letter to Lev Tolstoy.

We learned today of a sad event: the composer Tchaikovsky has died of cholera in Petersburg.

L. N. Tolstoy, *Polnoe sobranie sochinenii*
(90 vols.; Moscow, 1929–64), lxxxiv. 201

ANTON CHEKHOV

Telegram to Modest Tchaikovsky.

The news staggered me. It is a terrible loss. I felt deep respect and affection for Pyotr Ilyich, and was greatly indebted to him. I sympathize with all my heart.

A. P. Chekhov, *Polnoe sobranie sochinenii*
(12 vols.; Moscow, 1974), v. 240

AUGUST GERKE

Letter to Modest Tchaikovsky.

After last evening's bulletin I was already fearful, but still I hoped in the mercy of the Lord! Clearly it was God's wish to summon our dear Pyotr Ilyich unto Himself. It is terrible: Pyotr Ilyich Tchaikovsky is no more! I can scarcely believe it, how hard it will be to get used to this! . . . I hasten to embrace you heartily and clasp you to my breast. I wish you and those close to our dear departed one the strength and fortitude to endure this blow and your loss!

GDMC, B[10], no. 1148; *PBC*, 115–16

LEV BERTENSON

My very dear Modest, I should like to embrace you warmly and tell you how deeply shocked I am by our horrible common misfortune, but I am unable to do so because I can hardly walk and cannot go out.

The dreadful disease that took the life of your unforgettable brother has linked me with him, with you, and with all those to whom he was dear.

I cannot recover from this terrible tragedy that I have had to witness, and I am going through now! I can tell you only one thing, that I feel what you feel.

GDMC, B[10], no. 493

YURY YURYEV

I wanted to see Pyotr Ilyich's relatives right away. But there was nothing for it but to wait for the first requiem. Once it was announced I set off for the Tchaikovsky home well before it was to begin, assuming that I would be one of the first. But on approaching [Malaya Morskaya] Street I saw that it was already completely blocked by the crowd. . . . Mounted policemen were everywhere. Leaving the cab on the corner of Nevsky [Prospect], I somehow made my way through the crowd to the entrance, but getting up the stairs was an enormous feat. The entire staircase was literally choked with people straight up to the fifth floor, where the Tchaikovskys lived. I barely managed to squeeze through. . . . The door to the apartment was wide open—and it was the same picture there as on the stairs: it was utterly impossible to penetrate into the apartment.

Iur'ev, *Zapiski*, ii. 84

VASILY YASTREBTSEV

I stopped by for a moment at the Rimsky-Korsakovs' to find out something about Tchaikovsky's sudden tragic end, but neither Nikolay [Rimsky-Korsakov] nor [his wife] Nadezhda was at home: they were at the requiem, and so, asking Andrey [Rimsky-Korsakov's son] to convey my most sincere and warm gratitude to [Rimsky-Korsakov] for his kindness and the scores, I disappeared.

Iastrebtsev, Rimskii-Korsakov, ii. 126

WALTER NOUVEL

Who could have thought that night [when the Sixth Symphony was performed, on 16 October] that this would be the funeral song of the composer himself?

A few days later Diaghileff came to me in a great state of agitation. Tchaikovsky was seriously ill—cholera, most likely. There had been a serious epidemic the previous year, but now it was abating, only mild cases remained, and deaths were few and far between. We had great hopes for his recovery. Diaghileff was living near the composer, and went several times a day to find out the latest news, which he communicated to me. On the eve of October 25th, he told me that his state was desperate, and the following morning I received a note from him, announcing the death of the great composer.

From the earliest hour Diaghileff was in the house of death, and he it was who brought the first wreath. At one o'clock I went thither to pray with my brother. The news had not yet been publicly announced, and there were few people there save relations and close friends. All were weeping.

Haskell, Diaghileff, 48

SERGEY DIAGHILEV

The following is taken from a letter to his stepmother and memoirs written in 1928.

I was the first to lay the wreath. The sad news was not yet published, and there were present only a few people, those who were either related to the deceased or his close friends. Everyone wept.

IRLI, f. 102, ed. kh. 97, l. 425

Suddenly [on 25 October] I saw a sentence inserted at the foot of [*New Times*] announcement: 'Piotr Ilyitch Tchaikovsky died yesterday.' I could not believe my eyes.... In despair I rushed out of the house, and although I realized Tchaikovsky had died of cholera I made straight for Malaya Morskaya, where he lived. The doors were wide open and there was no one to be seen. The place was upside down. In the entrance hall the score of the Sixth Symphony lay open on a table, and I noticed on a sofa the camel-hair skull-cap which Tchaikovsky wore all the time. I heard voices from another room, and on entering I saw Piotr Ilyitch in a black morning coat stretched on a sofa. Rimsky-Korsakov and the singer Nicolai Figner were arranging a table to put him on. We lifted the body of Tchaikovsky, myself holding the feet, and laid it on the table. The three of us were alone in the flat, for after Tchaikovsky's death the whole household had fled. Piotr Ilyitch looked little different from when he was alive, and as young as ever. I went off to buy flowers. For the whole of that first day my wreath was the only one lying at his feet.

A lot of people assembled to hear the prayers for the dead, among them Vsevolojsky, Director of Imperial Theatres, and Napravnik. Everyone kept his mouth covered with a handkerchief and spat constantly into it, which was what we were advised to do to avoid catching cholera.

Buckle, *Diaghilev*, 23

LEOPOLD AUER

The death of Pierre Tchaikovsky ... struck musical circles in Russia like a bolt from the sky, and its reverberation was felt throughout the world of music. In the full flower of his strength and at the apogee of his glory, he was carried off after a few days' illness, a victim of the cholera which was ravaging the city at the time and against whose onslaughts the medical science of the day was helpless.

Auer, *My Long Life in Music*, 284

ALEXANDER ARENSON

Musician, author of one of the first biographical essays about Tchaikovsky.

Everyone at the [Moscow] Conservatoire already knew about Pyotr Ilyich's illness on the evening of Saturday, 23 October. This news struck like lightning both the public and the musicians at the symphony concert that evening. Next day, 24 October, reassuring information appeared in the newspapers as if 'the danger was over'. On Monday morning, a young friend of the deceased, Mr Poplavsky, convinced us definitively, on the basis of telegrams received the previous night, that Pyotr Ilyich was recovering, and we quietly continued to play the quartet. Suddenly our Inspector, Alexandra Hubert, rushed into the classroom and informed us, with tears in her eyes, that Pyotr Ilyich had died.

A. Arenson, *P. I. Chaikovskii: biograficheskii ocherk*
(Riga, 1898), 20

MIKHAIL BUKINIK

Cellist and music critic.

I shall never forget the day when the news resounded through our Moscow Conservatoire: 'Tchaikovsky is dead!' It was Monday, 25 October . . . 1893. On those days we usually had our quartet class, which was conducted by Ivan Hřímalý, a pupil of the famous [Ferdinand] Laub.

The ensemble class was required for all violinists and cellists of the senior classes. We usually played quartets, but in order to keep students waiting their turn occupied, we would also play sextets and octets.

This particular time we were learning Tchaikovsky's *Florentine* string sextet [*Souvenir de Florence*], which had just recently been published. We took turns playing—some one movement, the others the next movement.

The first movement was played by the cellists Modest Altschuler and Vl[adimir] Dubinsky. I was to play the next movement. When one group of students was playing, the other was obliged to sit and listen to the professor's remarks. But usually those who were not playing grew bored and would constantly seek some reason for going out into the corridor, whether to smoke, or to flirt with the female students, or simply to gossip.

Modest Altschuler, having finished his part, left the classroom. But not five minutes later he suddenly burst back in with a shout: 'Ivan Voitsekhovich! Tchaikovsky's dead!' His cry produced the same effect as if he had announced, 'The Conservatoire's collapsed!' or 'War's been declared!'

The professor clutched at his head and, letting out a cry of 'Ah!', instantly ran out of the classroom. The students were struck dumb. Our instruments fell from our hands.

Of course, we all went into the corridor, and there general commotion already reigned. Confused professors, agitated students, the young ladies already sobbing. There was a feeling as if each of us had lost something dear to himself personally. We wanted to express this feeling in some way. But how? The director of the Conservatoire, Vasily Safonov, knew how to express our feelings. He immediately invited the clergy to conduct a requiem service on the conservatoire premises. An announcement of the time of the requiem was posted. We all milled about, saddened and confused.

Gradually the Conservatoire began filling up with people we had never seen before. Classes ended spontaneously. Everyone poured out of the classrooms. Students, professors and teachers, servants, and the outsiders who had appeared filled every free corner and corridor of the building, and everyone was possessed by a single common dread, a common grief: 'Tchaikovsky is dead!'

The clergy arrived. Preparations began. They put on their robes. When everything was ready, Safonov, grave and with a religious air, passed into the hall, accompanied by the professors and students. We prepared for the service. It grew quiet and solemn. The church tapers were distributed. There were many of them. No one remained without one, old or young. Even those who were not Orthodox took them.

As the 'With the Saints give rest' was sung, we all fell to our knees. The sound of the people dropping to their knees, together with the mournful light of the candles in the broad daylight, the audible weeping, and the obedience to fate expressed by the bowed human figures—all this had such an effect upon me that I could scarcely keep from sobbing hysterically.

When the service ended and everyone rose, pale with tearful eyes, I felt lonely and somehow empty.

Soon we learned that the professors had gathered and had decided to send a deputation to Petersburg for the funeral. The students did the same. They left that same day.

NZ 28 (1952), 239–40

IGOR STRAVINSKY

Tchaikovsky's death . . . affected me deeply. Incidentally, the fame of the composer was so great that after he was known to have cholera the government issued bulletins about the progress of his illness. Not everyone was aware of him, though. When I went to school and awesomely announced to my classmates that Tchaikovsky was dead, one of them wanted to know which grade he was in.

Stravinsky and Craft, *Expositions and Developments*, 87

VASILY BERTENSON

Telegram to Modest Tchaikovsky from Moscow.

There are no words to express my grief, may the Lord give you the strength
to endure such a terrible loss.

GDMC, B[10], no. 466

The material presented in this chapter is valuable in two respects. On the
one hand, it reflects Tchaikovsky's extraordinary status as a national
treasure and the sense of profound shock that the general public experienced with the news of his sudden death. It was no accident that in one
testimony Tchaikovsky is placed side by side with Lev Tolstoy as the
supreme manifestation of Russian genius: one must realize that by this
time Tolstoy was elevated to the status of sage and considered by thousands the most celebrated writer in the world. Apparently the composer's
death caused distress in the highest spheres of the government. The
members of the Imperial family sent telegrams of condolence, and the
decision was taken to finance Tchaikovsky's funeral from the Imperial
treasury, which was tantamount to the contemporary notion of state
burial. If the personal reaction on the part of Alexander III may seem
somewhat mute, one must recall that at this time the Emperor was already terminally ill and died less than a year later. The diary of the Grand
Duke Konstantin Konstantinovich testifies to the fact that both Alexander III and the Empress Mariya Fyodorovna were upset, which is confirmed by the words written in the Emperor's own hand on the petition
to cover the funeral expenses: 'What a pity and such a disappointment!'
meaning, of course, both the untimeliness of the death and the irreparable loss suffered by Russian culture.

For the purpose of this study, however, the material in this chapter
provides sufficient evidence to prove beyond doubt that Tchaikovsky's
immediate environment, including his physicians, took every precautionary measure required by the government's regulations against further
possible spread of the disease—the fact that was questioned, and even
denied, by the supporters of the suicide theory who chose to distort or
ignore the relevant contemporary documentation.

The discovery of *vibrio cholerae* by Robert Koch ten years earlier
fundamentally transformed medical views on both the etiology and

epidemiology of cholera. If up till then emphasis was placed on the need to enact the strictest possible quarantine in order to prevent any contact between those infected and the outside world, by now it was established that cholera was spread basically through the ingestion of contaminated water and not through mere contact with the sick person.

Thus it was recognized that the most elementary hygienic precautions were sufficient to ensure that, in the words of the authoritative encyclopaedia of the period, 'one can almost certainly avoid contracting cholera'.[5] Likewise, it was now known that the body of someone who had died from cholera did not, in fact, represent a further threat of contagion.

The years immediately preceding Tchaikovsky's illness witnessed in Russia a number of scientific publications which expounded on the relatively non-contagious character of cholera and the limited threat of infection provided that the elementary rules of hygiene were observed. Thus, in 1892 the noted Swiss hygienist, who lived at this time in Russia, Fyodor [Fridrich] Erisman, stated in an article specifically addressed to medical personnel that 'as such the cholera patient does not represent a danger to those around him'.[6] A similar view was echoed in the same year by another expert, Mikhail Galanin, who wrote: 'If proper measures of precaution are taken, contact with the patient entails no special danger; in fact there is a greater chance of getting infected when one neither sees a patient nor suspects any danger and, consequently, remains unconcerned about it.'[7] Nikolay Gamaleya, who was to become an internationally renowned microbiologist, argued along the same lines in a dissertation on that very subject successfully defended in 1892, and so did another prominent doctor, Grigory Zakharin, in the course of lectures he delivered the following year at Moscow University.[8] Incidentally, the latter emphasized the crucial significance of the timely diagnosis which, as we know, in Tchaikovsky's case failed to take place. The composer's doctors, especially, the Bertenson brothers, were highly learned medical practitioners, well informed of the developments in their science. In fact, in 1905, twelve years after his death, Vasily Bertenson published an article in which he used the example of Tchaikovsky's illness to illustrate the thesis that treatment of cholera represents no possible danger to the patient's physicians.[9]

---

[5] *Entsiklopedicheskii slovar F. A. Brokgauza and I. A. Efrona* [F. A. Brockhouse and I. A. Yefron, *Encyclopaedical Dictionary*], 41 vols. (St Petersburg, 1890–1907), s. v. 'kholera'.

[6] *PBC* 22.

[7] Ibid. 23.

[8] Ibid. 23–4.

[9] V. B. Bertenson, *O kholere* (St Petersburg, 1905), 3.

That very year, 1893, finally saw those scientific conclusions on the nature of cholera find their way into official documents. In March 1893 the government's statement entitled *Regulations Concerning the Executive Sanitary Commissions* appeared in an updated version, which contained significant changes in comparison with its predecessors. One major example is the pointed removal of an earlier injunction against crowded funerals and funeral banquets. Elsewhere I demonstrated at length how all prescribed rules were implemented to the letter after the composer's death by the police and the members of the sanitary commission.[10]

Most of the testimonies on those matters are contemporary to the events they described. One notable exception is Sergey Diaghilev. His letters to his stepmother, written shortly afterwards, are in concordance with the testimonies of other witnesses, notably his friend Walter Nouvel, who accompanied him on this occasion. In contrast, Diaghilev's later memoir, written in the 1920s, is heavily fictionalized and should serve as a warning to those modern biographers who rely excessively on this type of recollection. Numerous newspapers ran daily reports on what was happening there, of which this chapter offers a representative selection.

At the same time, it must be recognized that popular and lay opinion remained, despite the newest scientific developments, largely confused as to the workings of cholera. This is manifest, for instance, in the somewhat muddled reporting of the *Petersburg Gazette*, where we read, on the one hand, that, since Tchaikovsky had died not from actual cholera (meaning its algid stage) but from its after-effects (meaning the supposed typhoid stage and uraemia), his dead body was not contagious and his coffin could safely remain open; but that, on the other, the face of the corpse was periodically dabbed with carbolic solution—presumably, to prevent the spread of infection. This last measure was in fact a matter of routine and over-caution owing to the Russian custom of kissing the forehead of the deceased. But in the end, the public acted in accordance with their own view of the epidemic, their own fears or lack of them. It is this that explains the episode, blown out of proportion by the supporters of the suicide theory, of the cellist Alexander Verzhbilovich kissing Tchaikovsky's body on the face and head. Nikolay Rimsky-Korsakov, who reported the incident, found it 'odd', simply expressing his medical ignorance. As was shown, Tchaikovsky's body was thoroughly sanitized. Moreover, we are told by the same witness that when Verzhbilovich performed his act of homage he was 'totally drunk after some sort of binge'—and so could hardly have been aware of what he was doing in any event.

---

[10] Poznansky, 'Tchaikovsky's Suicide', 210–11.

Incidently, the attempt by some of Tchaikovsky's biographers to interpret the serene expression on the composer's death mask as a proof that he died not from cholera, but from poison, makes no sense. As we know, Tchaikovsky survived the convulsive stage of the disease and died close to a state of coma, so there is no reason why his face should have borne any expression other than that of peace. Some of Tchaikovsky's death-bed photographs, as well as his death mask, seen at a certain angle, actually reveal signs of emaciation, as a result of the protracted agony.

Of particular significance is the fact that none of the newspaper articles covering Tchaikovsky's death and its aftermath betray even the slightest hint at improper conduct on the part of the police or the civil authorities. It seems inconceivable that so many journalists could have failed to perceive the alleged flagrant violation of standard measures or, perceiving it, connived with officials to ignore it. (Incidentally, one may note the outcry over the lack of precautions with regard to the city's water supply and restaurant practices, which began a public campaign ultimately resulting in the exposure of serious sanitary deficiencies.) On the other hand, one should perhaps not expect any special accuracy as regards details. Since in this period the newspapers were notoriously amateurish, it could even have happened that the events of two consecutive days were conflated into a single sequence with little concern for precise chronology.

Therefore, the only viable approach to this material requires that a valid reconstruction proceed on the basis of the broadest possible consensus found among the extant reports, disregarding the exceptions. When applied to our evidence, this approach enables us to establish beyond doubt that the coffin containing Tchaikovsky's body was properly sealed, in full accordance with all government regulations, following the second requiem held at Modest's apartment, around nine o'clock in the evening on Monday, 25 October, the day of his death.

One must disregard the dating of this episode as Wednesday, 27 October, found in the *Moscow Register*, which is a flagrant contradiction to St Petersburg's newspapers. Moreover, it was the same correspondent who informed his readers that the late composer was survived by a wife and children.

Of the individual responses to Tchaikovsky's death one should single out the letter and the telegram sent to Modest by Lev and Vasily Bertenson, respectively. Both were private communications never intended to be published and therefore unrelated to any further imaginary cover-up. The deeply sympathetic tone of the two documents, in particular, Lev Bertenson's reference to the 'dreadful disease' seems entirely genuine and would have been certainly inconceivable in the case of their complicity in any foul play. The same is true of the lawyer August Gerke who at one point was even identified as the deliverer of poison to provide the composer with the means of suicide. Gerke's tribute, found in the Tchaikovsky archives, with its reference to 'God wished to summon our dear Pyotr Ilyich unto Himself', strikes one as exceptionally moving.

7

Tribute

26 October–27 October

---

26 October

THE NEW TIMES

Along the staircase leading to Modest Tchaikovsky's apartment two counter-currents of people flow unceasingly. The apartment door stands constantly open. A thousand people have passed through it today. The corner room, in which the coffin lies, makes a distinctive impression: its whole tropical décor [the correspondent has in mind the palms and other tropical plants in the room—A.P.], the drawn white curtains at the windows, and the garlands hung about the walls, breathe an air of still and silent sorrow. Throughout the day the crowd scarcely diminishes, but despite its presence the room is quiet.

The mood of the visitors is reverential. Everyone speaks in a whisper, as if afraid to disturb the eternal slumber of the late brilliant composer. . . . The room is half in shadow, as two lamps burn in the corners and thick wax candles flicker dimly around the coffin. The adjoining rooms are also filled with people, and there too everything, from a mirror turned to face the wall to a piano with its keyboard locked, reminds one of the sad event. The ottoman on which the deceased passed away stands in the same spot, but nobody sits upon it. . . . On the coffin lies a black velvet pillow with the Order of St Vladimir, Fourth Class, and a mass of wreaths which cover virtually half the coffin.

NV, 27 Oct. 1893

THE WORLD

A solid wall of people presses into the narrow corridor and the three small rooms. Beneath the low ceiling the chanting by the priests of the 'With the Saints give rest' sounds dully, its sorrowful melody mingling with the weeping of the ladies, and now and then loud irrepressible sobs are heard.

SV, 27 Oct. 1893

THE PETERSBURG LEAFLET

Today . . . three requiem services will be conducted over the coffin of the deceased: the first at twelve noon for students of the School of Jurisprudence, the second at one o'clock for the Russian Opera, and the third at two o'clock . . . yet another requiem is scheduled for one o'clock at the Conservatoire, with the participation of the student chorus.

PL, 26 Oct. 1893

THE WORLD

Relatives of the deceased went to the Holy Synod to petition to move the body of Pyotr Ilyich to St Isaac's Cathedral. The carrying out of the bier is planned for today, Tuesday, and the burial for Wednesday.

SV, 26 Oct. 1893

THE PETERSBURG LEAFLET

The requiem [at twelve noon—A.P.] was sung by the chorus of the Life Guards of the Semyonov regiment. . . .

At one o'clock this afternoon at the Petersburg Conservatoire a solemn requiem was held for Tchaikovsky, a former student of the Conservatoire, and its pride and glory. Present at the service were all the members of the Directorate of the Imperial Russian Musical Society, and the professors, teachers, and all the students of the Conservatoire. . . .

On account of Tchaikovsky's death all classes at the Conservatoire have been suspended for three days and all musical evenings for the current week have been cancelled. The next (second symphony concert, scheduled for Saturday, 30 October, has been postponed until 6 November. It will be dedicated to the memory of Tchaikovsky; Mr Nápravník will conduct the concert, and the programme will be made up exclusively of compositions by Tchaikovsky.

At two o'clock a requiem was performed over the coffin of the deceased with the participation of the Arkhangelsky and Sheremetyev choruses under the direction of Mr Arkhangelsky. This requiem was of particular musical interest, as it was composed by Mr Arkhangelsky himself and is almost unknown to the public. . . . The singing of Mr Arkhangelsky's chorus was remarkably balanced and harmonious; it impressed itself deeply upon the hearts of the mourners.

PL, 27 Oct. 1893

THE SON OF THE FATHERLAND

A deputation from the Moscow Conservatoire (the director of the Conservatoire, [Vasily] Safonov, and the most senior of its professors, [Nikolay] Kashkin) arrived from Moscow, and just before the evening requiem at six o'clock laid a large, elegant metal wreath of roses. Arriving with the same train was nearly an entire carriage filled with boxes of wreaths from the Moscow Imperial Theatre and many others.

SO, 27 Oct. 1893

THE NEWS AND STOCK EXCHANGE GAZETTE

Towards evening, the government council member Nikolay Stoyanovsky laid a sumptuous wreath of natural flowers in the name of the august president of the Imperial Russian Musical Society, Her Imperial Highness Grand Duchess Alexandra Iosifovna. A deputation from the St Petersburg Conservatoire—the deputation was made up of the director Ioganson and Professors Rimsky-Korsakov, Lyadov, and Samus—also laid a wreath of natural flowers. A similar wreath was laid by the Moscow Conservatoire deputation, Messrs Safonov and Kashkin. It is impossible to list all the wreaths.

NBG, 27 Oct. 1893

NIKOLAY KASHKIN

I was quite certain that we would see each other on Saturday, 23 October, because Pyotr Ilyich liked to be very exact in keeping to his intentions. It was with this same certainty that I arrived at the concert of the twenty-third, and only there did I learn that Vasily Safonov had received a telegram about Tchaikovsky's illness but the telegram had been reassuring in nature, saying that the terrible danger was over. This later turned out to be a grievous mistake—in fact the irreversible had already occurred when the reassuring telegram to Moscow had been sent.

We had no information about Tchaikovsky's illness, and the telegram we had received was quite incomprehensible, while circumstances, moreover, were such that it was impossible to make any immediate enquiries. In recent years Pyotr Ilyich had always stayed with his brother Modest when in Petersburg, but the latter had moved not long before, and none of us knew his new address. Vasily Safonov sent a telegram to the Petersburg Conservatoire, but as it was Sunday it lay there unanswered; in short, we knew nothing, and not until eight o'clock on Monday morning, 25 October, did Dimitry Gringmut [an editor-in-chief] of the *Moscow Register* inform me that my dear friend was no more. I left for Petersburg that day and there found the coffin already closed and sealed.

Kashkin, Vospominaniia, 183

THE NEW TIMES

Following the evening requiem one more service, both moving and characteristic, was conducted. Around half past seven a priest entered the apartment with a large pectoral cross and asked whether there were any sacerdotal robes about. 'Let us hold one more requiem and pray,' he said. 'People are still arriving, and perhaps they would like to pray.' The priest, whom, incidentally, no one there knew, was told what robes they had, but that there was nobody to sing, no choristers. 'It doesn't matter,' he replied firmly. 'I'll start the service. Perhaps somebody will turn up who can sing. There are students here. But if not, I'll sing myself. Such a great artist, all Russia knows him. It's a sin not to pray.' Someone present again pointed out some obstacle. 'Don't worry,' replied the priest. 'Everything will be fine.' A moment later near the coffin was heard: 'Blessed is the Lord our God . . .'. 'Amen,' sang a shy voice from the crowd. The ektenia began. The first voice was joined by the second, then a third, and finally everyone present started to sing. The singing was out of tune, choppy, and dissonant, yet everyone sang straight from the heart, as best he could. The requiem turned out to be unusual, distinctive, and touching. Many were weeping. As they sang the 'With the Saints give rest' and later the 'Eternal memory', all dropped to their knees. When the service ended, the priest removed his robes and, bowing to the coffin, quietly went out of the room without a word and left the apartment, never telling anyone his name.

NV, 27 Oct. 1893

THE PETERSBURG LEAFLET

People say that the cause of Tchaikovsky's cholera was that he used unboiled water from the Neva for drinking during the days preceding his illness, which he never used to drink.

PL, 26 Oct. 1893

THE NEWS AND STOCK EXCHANGE GAZETTE

It is said that Tchaikovsky was taken ill from having drunk unboiled water in a certain major restaurant.

NBG, 26 Oct. 1893

THE SON OF THE FATHERLAND

This is fairly plausible if we recall what abominable water Petersburgers are treated to. . . .

Yet we find it extremely strange that a good restaurant could have served unboiled water during an epidemic. There exists, as far as we can recollect, a binding decree that commercial establishments, eating houses, restaurants, etc., should have boiled water. . . .

But when such an incident occurs in a first-class restaurant and the victim of this negligence on the part of the bartender or the *maître d' hôtel* happens to be someone who is the pride of all Russia—this is a scandal and an outrage for which one can scarcely conceive a fit punishment.

Our restaurants are in general quite fine. They sometimes have procedures one cannot make out: is this commerce—or a crime?

SO, 26 Oct. 1893

GRAND DUKE KONSTANTIN KONSTANTINOVICH

The Empress [Mariya Fyodorovna, Alexander III's wife] sent me music and several songs on the poems of Rathaus. I played two of them. I left Gatchina with Nicky [the future Emperor Nicholas II] . . .

I could not attend the requiems for Tchaikovsky since at home they fear infection. I returned to Strelna by four o'clock.

GARF, f. 660, op. 1, d. 40, l. 138

15. The Grand Duke Konstantin Konstantinovich

TSESAREVICH NIKOLAY ALEKSANDROVICH

Heir to the throne; the future Nicholas II. The following is from his private diary.

A terrible misfortune happened yesterday—our wonderful composer Tchaikovsky died.

GARF, f. 601, op. 1, no. 231

LEV TOLSTOY

Letter to Sofiya Tolstaya, the writer's wife.[1]

I feel very sorry about Tchaikovsky, sorry, because it seemed to me that we had something in common. I visited him, and invited him to visit me, but apparently he was offended that I was not at *Eugene Onegin*. Sorry about him as a man with whom something was not quite clear, even more than as a musician. It was so quick, and so simple and natural, and un-natural, and [it strikes] so close to home.

Tolstoy, *Polnoe sobranie sochinenii*, lxxxiv. 200–1

27 October

THE NEWS AND STOCK EXCHANGE GAZETTE

All day long a solid wall of admirers of the deceased stands along the staircase, in the apartment, near the front entrance; all rooms are packed with people. It is impossible to move. Those arriving with wreaths are forced to wait a long time before managing to reach the apartment, where relatives of P[yotr] I[lyich] accept the wreaths. A few manage to squeeze through the crowd to lay their wreaths on the grave of the beloved artist. And the crowd keeps growing. Young people predominate—university students, female students, lyceum pupils, law students, gymnasium pupils, vocational school students, conservatoire students. The priest hardly managed to get up the stairs. During the requiem, held at two o'clock

---

[1] Probably as a result of a misunderstanding Orlova, followed by Holden, attributed to Tolstoy in this letter a text he never wrote (see Orlova, 'Tchaikovsky: The Last Chapter', 137; Holden, *Tchaikovsky*, 408).

16. The closed coffin, with wreaths

with the chorus of the Russian Opera, the crush reached extreme limits.

The walls of the room in which the coffin with the remains of P[yotr] I[lyich] is displayed are completely draped with wreaths: so many were collected that they had to be hung along the walls. The coffin cannot be seen behind the mass of wreaths. Already today the number of wreaths laid amounts to one hundred.

In view of the fact that the flood of mourners after the requiem reached incredible proportions, those in charge are asking the public to pass by the coffin without stopping—one enters by one door and exits by another. This helps to avert a jam and its inevitable consequences.

NBG, 28 Oct. 1893

THE NEW TIMES

At the evening requiem [at eight o'clock] there were so many people that not only the apartment but the entire staircase from top to bottom was literally overflowing. The building management ordered the front entrance to be locked. Two caretakers were placed near the street door. An enormous crowd of some hundred and fifty people formed on the pavement.

Despite the fact that it was all but impossible to get inside, the public persisted in demanding that the doors be opened, and there were even moments when some of the more impatient managed to force their way into the house. Only those who produced tickets entitling them to participate in tomorrow's funeral procession were allowed inside. The tickets were being distributed at the Directorate of the Imperial Theatres, and this afternoon a long winding queue of people was standing there, as at a railway booking office window. Eight thousand tickets were distributed. For the Kazan Cathedral six thousand tickets were distributed, while several tens of thousands of applications for tickets were submitted. When the requiem was over it took the mourners nearly half an hour to file out, and only after this were all those waiting in the street allowed inside. There was a terrible crush at the door. About a hundred people vigorously mounted the stairs, but on the fourth floor all were met with disappointment: at the doors of the fifth-floor apartment above, those in front were told that owing to the lateness of the hour no more visitors would be admitted.

NV, 28 Oct. 1893

EUGÈNE OUDIN

English singer (baritone) and pianist.
Letter to Herman Klein, music critic of the *Sunday Times* of London.

I did not find him in Petersburg on my way to Moscow, but there received word from him that he would attend without fail my début in the latter city. Instead a telegram arrived telling me of his sudden illness, that the danger was over and there was hope. This was last Saturday. Monday morning a telegram informed me of his death!

Last Thursday he was healthy and fine. He drank a glass of unfiltered water from the Neva, and cholera infected him! It's terrible! All the Russian musical societies are in mourning, and the concert at which I was to make my Petersburg début (next Saturday, the eleventh) has been postponed a week. It will consist entirely of works by the late maestro. I shall sing an aria from *Onegin* and several songs. A joint appearance will take place the following day.

Herman Klein, *Thirty Years of Musical Life in London*
(New York, 1903), 349–50

ANNA GALPERSON

Reporter for Moscow's *Modern News*.
Letter to Nikolay Shakhovsky, a St Petersburg journalist.

Tchaikovsky's death is indeed terrible, but the dreadful illness obviously did not turn society away from him. Or does it only seem thus from afar? According to the newspaper accounts, admirers crowded around his coffin, while the accounts themselves and all the obituaries are so unreservedly rhapsodic that involuntarily the loathing for the disease which carried him to his grave has been completely effaced.

RNB, f. 847, ed. kh. 107

THE WORLD

Today in St Petersburg they debated the telegram received from Mr Taneyev in which he asserts that Tchaikovsky wished to be buried in Klin or in Moscow. Meanwhile the brothers of the deceased were saying that Pyotr Ilyich in the same manner spoke to them about St Petersburg, and generally thought that one should be buried where one died.

SV, 27 Oct. 1893

THE PETERSBURG LEAFLET

The session of the capital city council [city Duma] was opened by the Mayor Vasily Ratkov-Rozhnov with the speech in which he spoke of the heavy loss suffered by Russia: our Composer of genius passed away at the peak of his powers from the epidemic that still snatches so many victims every day. . . .

St Petersburg city council has repeatedly seen the need to memorialize Russia's prominent sons: thus, to honour the memory of Glinka the city school was founded and one of the capital's streets was given his name. . . . Consequently, the Mayor suggested the establishing of a stipend drawn from city funds to be given the name of the late composer, and generally discussed how the city administration could immortalize the great composer's memory. . . .

[Some members of the city council] proceeded with the statement in which they suggested starting a fund-raising campaign first among its members in order to erect a monument at the grave of the deceased, as well as in Teatral'naya Street, where the Conservatoire is located and in which Tchaikovsky received his musical education, to be given in his name. . . .

Following the Mayor's speech, the city council member Sergey Khudekov declared that the name of the late composer is so great that one should not limit oneself to a monument on the grave only, but one should petition for permission to embark upon a national fund-raising campaign with the purpose of building a monument to Tchaikovsky on one of the capital's squares.

PL, 28 Oct. 1893

The material found in this chapter (for the most part, self-explanatory), is necessarily selective, but it suffices to demonstrate that the public response to Tchaikovsky's death rapidly acquired the scale of national mourning. The increasingly crowded requiems continued—four of them on 26 October, the day after the coffin was officially sealed (at noon, 1 p.m., 2 p.m., and 6 p.m.).

Although of the initiatives introduced by the St Petersburg's city council to immortalize Tchaikovsky's memory, only a few were immediately implemented (a Tchaikovsky stipend was founded, his bust was erected, and the memorial plaque placed on the building in which he died; also two city schools were given his name), it is worth noting that shortly afterwards a public fund-raising campaign was launched by special permission of Alexander III so that three years later the monument on the composer's grave was solemnly inaugurated (by the sculptor Pavel Kamensky). It was, however, not until the Soviet period in 1923 that Tchaikovsky's name was given to one of St Petersburg's streets (formerly Sergiyevskaya).

It was also in the days immediately following Tchaikovsky's death that public opinion started to enquire into the ultimate causes of what had happened: the first accusations had been directed so far, against the restaurant owners who allowed unboiled water to be served to their customers. This attack intensified, eventually leading to the creation of a special committee to investigate the city's water supply and the subsequent scandal.

Finally, one observes a curious passage in Lev Tolstoy's letter to his wife. There were attempts to read in it the insight of a genius into what 'really' happened, implying that the words 'natural, and unnatural' relate to the circumstances of the composer's death. Such an interpretation is quite out of the question, as it thus would deprive the following words, 'and so close to home', of any meaning. In fact, it is difficult to say with any certainty what Tolstoy meant when he wrote it, which no doubt reflects the emotional state of Tolstoy himself. In this period, Tolstoy had grown increasingly preoccupied by the subject of death. Surely this letter says as much, if not more, about the great writer than about the deceased composer.

8

Funeral

28 October–2 November

---

28 October

THE NEW TIMES

Today Tchaikovsky's funeral was held. A funeral is a sad ceremony, but when it is performed so majestically, so solemnly as it was today, this sadness is made somewhat less evident; this scene of universal respect for the deceased offers us the consolation that the life and labours of a man do not pass without leaving a trace.

The whole of the city's intelligentsia turned out to bury Tchaikovsky; everyone capable of feeling, appreciating, and perceiving musical impressions longed to pay their last respects to the great composer, to catch a glimpse of his coffin, to sigh bitterly over such an untimely loss. Dignitaries, students, artists of word and thought, and crowds of common people came *en masse* to accompany Tchaikovsky to his grave; everyone entreated God to grant peace to the soul of the extinguished 'leading light of Russian musical art', as was written on one wreath.

At nine o'clock in the morning the relatives and friends began gathering at the apartment of the deceased, while at the same time the deputations taking part in the procession gradually began to assemble as well. As for the public, as early as eight o'clock groups of people had been standing along Malaya Morskaya and near the theatre.

Yesterday evening a wreath from Their Imperial Highnesses Grand Duke Vladimir Aleksandrovich and Grand Duchess Mariya Pavlovna was laid upon the coffin. Grand Duchess Elizaveta Mavrikiyevna sent a wreath shortly after receiving the news of the composer's death. This morning a luxurious wreath of natural flowers from their Majesties was laid.

Many other new wreaths were laid both late yesterday evening and today; among them was a wreath sent by the actor with the French company [Lucien] Guitry, in the form of a lyre made of laurel leaves, with broken strings and the inscription: 'To a great artist from Guitry'. To the telegrams with expressions of condolence already received from various corners of Russia and abroad a new pile was added today.

The deputations were a long time lining up. The order of the procession was arranged by the Directorate of the Imperial Theatres. Numerous institutions had announced their desire to pay homage to the deceased by seeing him off, several of them appearing *in corpore*, therefore the entire procession had earlier been divided into eight parts and each section had its own monitors, people from the artistic and musical world. Altogether, there were nine deputations and institutions in all eight sections of the procession. This number alone indicates how much space must have been taken up by the procession. It stretched for more than a mile.

The streets were closed to traffic, and the deputations took up their formation silently and with decorum. A mood of reverence reigned in the crowd.

His Highness Prince Alexander Oldenburg arrived.

Toward ten o'clock the priests of the metropolitan see arrived at the apartment of the deceased, and Archimandrite [Nikander] performed the liturgy. Only the brothers and relatives of the deceased were present. Before the liturgy the wreaths were carried out. The Tsar's wreath and the wreaths of the relatives remained on the coffin. The other wreaths were all piled on special chariots. Two chariots and three landaus were heaped high with the wreaths, creating entire mountains of flowers.

At ten o'clock . . . two choruses—singers from the Life Guards of the Finland and Semyonov regiments—took their place in the middle of the street behind the deputations and began to sing the Sanctus. From the apartment, followed by the priests, the coffin was carried out by all three of the deceased's brothers, Prince Oldenburg, the singers Melnikov, Yakovlev, Figner, and others. The coffin was placed on a hearse, to which were harnessed six horses in black open-work horse-cloths bearing coats of arms. The hearse was light in colour, with white draperies and four lamps along the edges of the platform. At the four corners of the canopy were hung lyres with the initials P[yotr] T[chaikovsky] done in lilacs. Once the coffin was in place and covered with a gold pall and surrounded by another pile of wreaths, six students from the Imperial School of Jurisprudence stood along the sides of the hearse and held the tassels of the canopy.

The procession set out. Malaya Morskaya was packed with people; further along there were fewer people, yet several thousand marched in the procession itself. . . . The traditional doorman opened the procession; three

17. The funeral procession on Malaya Morskaya Street, 28 October 1893

students from the School of Jurisprudence carried a black velvet pillow with the Order of St Vladimir Fourth Class. . . .

Behind the deputations came the choruses, the clergy in their white cassocks, the archimandrite, the sad hearse—and behind that, the relatives, friends, and wave after wave of mourners, among whom one could see five moving mountains of wreaths.

The procession turned from Malaya Morskaya Street onto Bolshaya Morskaya and, heading towards Maryinsky Theatre Square, passed by the theatre, skirted the Conservatoire building, still under construction, and went up Ofitserskaya to come out again onto Bolshaya Morskaya, turning finally towards Nevsky [Prospect] and the Kazan Cathedral.

Crowds of people were in the scaffolding of the Conservatoire building, several taking photographs from above.

The Maryinsky Theatre stood in mourning, the columns of its pediment draped in black cloth and decorated with crossed palms. Wreaths hung between the windows. Above the pediment was hung a lyre shrouded in transparent black crepe. The lamps all round were lit.

In front of the theatre stood a solid wall of deputations with wreaths. Represented were the Imperial Russian Opera, the opera chorus, the ballet company, the orchestra of the Alexandrinsky Theatre; from Moscow, the opera company (with a silver wreath), the orchestra of the Bolshoy

Theatre, the opera chorus, the Malyi Theatre, the ballet company; and from the private theatres, the Kharkov Opera, the Russian Choral Society, and the St Petersburg Amateur Musical and Dramatic Circle, on whose stage Tchaikovsky's *Eugene Onegin* had first appeared in April of 1883. . . .

Slowly, the hearse drove past the theatre and came to a halt. One by one the deputations laid their wreaths.

It was nearly twelve o'clock when the procession reached the [Kazan] Cathedral and the coffin was carried through the west doors; senior students from the School of Jurisprudence stood near the cathedral. The deputations tried to enter from Nevsky [Prospect], but the cathedral was already nearly full. The coffin was placed in the centre on a high catafalque, then surrounded by candles and covered with the pall and the wreaths. The six senior law students stood on watch near the body. The Right Reverend Nikander, the bishop of Narva, began the liturgy. . . . Present in the church were Grand Duke Konstantin Konstantinovich, Prince Alexander Oldenburg, Government Council member N[ikolay] Stoyanovsky, the Minister of the Imperial Court Adjutant General [Illarion] Vorontsov-Dashkov, many high-ranking individuals, all the luminaries of the musical, dramatic, and artistic world, men of letters, and, finally, all the deputations and the Imperial Musical Chorus. . . .

The church service lasted a long time, until almost two o' clock. There is no need to comment on the singing—anyone who has heard the chorus of the Russian Opera can imagine it. They sang Glinka's Cherubic, and Tchaikovsky's 'We sing to thee' and 'Our Father', as well his 'Gladsome Light of the Holy Glory' in place of the communion anthem. Profoundly moving, the funeral melodies rose, expressing fully both aching grief and submission to the will of the Lord, and as the 'With Saints give rest' was sung the thought of the worshippers seemed also to be borne over into 'life eternal', and quietly, quietly, after the high notes, the final 'eternal memory' died away. Many people were moved to tears by the singing.

At the conclusion of the service, the procession formed again for the journey to the Alexander Nevsky Monastery.

Opposite the west doors, on the square, stood the music chorus of the Life Guards of the Finland regiment, and to the sounds of the hymn 'Glorious is the Lord', with the singing of the Sanctus, friends and artists bore the coffin from the church and placed it on the catafalque. The bishop and priests prayed by the hearse.

The procession started out towards the monastery. Everything was the same: the deputations and the two choruses, from the Kazan Cathedral and the Finland regiment, marched in the same order—only there were still more priests. The whole way there was heard alternately the singing of the Sanctus or the doleful strains of a funeral march. The procession passed between two rows of spectators, and Grand Duke Konstantin Konstantinovich and Prince Oldenburg walked some time behind the coffin as far as the monastery.

At the gates of the cloister the sorrowful procession was met by a bishop accompanied by the abbot-general of the monastery, the Archimandrite Isaya, the monks, and the monastery choir. Here another liturgy was performed, and another requiem sung. . . . The coffin was taken down and borne through the holy gates to the old cemetery, the musical chorus following behind, playing. . . .

At the Alexander Nevsky Monastery, where admittance was also by ticket, the public had began to gather at the grave as early as twelve noon. The space surrounding the grave was restricted to certain members of the deputations, representatives of the Conservatoire, and newspaper and journal reporters. The grave is situated near the wall of the cemetery, in the same corner where the composers Borodin . . . Mussorgsky, and a little further off, Serov lie. The grave, faced inside with brick, was lined to the very bottom with gold brocade. Following the burial, the coffin was covered over as well with a vault of brick. At an angle near the wall, encompassing a fairly large area around the grave, wooden trellises for wreaths had been constructed from planks and nails. All the surrounding monuments and their fences were crowded with people. . . . Everywhere, on all sides, and deep into the heart of the cemetery, the entire space was filled with mourners. Several students had contrived to find seats along the top of the cemetery's stone wall. A photographer's camera also looked across the wall towards the façade of the monastery, waiting for an opportune moment. The police and organizers managed to keep the space around the grave free of people.

At 3.45 the first, distant sounds of the chorus and then of the orchestra were heard. Everyone grew animated, but it was another twenty minutes before the strains of the hymn rang out at the monastery gates, signalling that the procession had arrived at the gates. At precisely four o'clock the students of the School of Jurisprudence hastily approached the grave with the cushion on which they had borne the Order of the deceased at the head of the procession. Behind them appeared the chorus and soon the clergy arrived in their white cassocks, with Bishop Nikander at their head. At five minutes past four the heavy coffin was borne through the narrow passage and along the planked footpath. A tight circle of people close to the deceased immediately grouped around it. Bishop Nikander performed the final liturgy. The chorus near the coffin responded its amen, and as the ektenia was spoken the second chorus, located in the cemetery behind, among the crowds outside the barrier, sang 'Lord have mercy' in distant echo. The first chorus performed the 'Eternal Memory'. The bishop blessed the remains, and they were lowered into the grave and sprinkled with earth. The ecclesiastical ceremony ended and the priests withdrew. The orators mounted the platform near the grave, surging to and fro in a solid wave, clambering upon their fences. . . .

The director of the Conservatoire, Mr Safonov, gave a quiet and barely audible, yet heartfelt, speech, in which he spoke of the deceased as artist and composer.

Also beautiful was the speech by Mr Gerard, as a fellow student, colleague, and friend of the deceased. Modest and well liked even in childhood, Pyotr Tchaikovsky was able in later life as well to inspire the warmest affection and love in everyone who knew him and met him in daily life and in society. Mr Gerard's speech rang with the warm but sorrowful note of a friend saying his final farewell:

Everyone in Russia who is capable of thought, and especially of feeling, is deeply shaken. Tchaikovsky's music—for the most part a music of quiet sadness, of profound sorrow—has always found an echo in Russian hearts. This is understandable: Russian hearts hold so much room, so many reasons for quiet sadness and profound sorrow. But within the great Russian family there is a numerically tiny but cordially and strongly united family of Tchaikovsky's comrades from the School of Jurisprudence. This family has suffered an even greater loss: it is now burying a beloved comrade. We who grew up with him, shared the joys and anxieties of his childhood, knew what a human being he was. I do not believe that any perceptive expert in the human heart would be able to define his character so well as his comrades at boarding school could; and we all loved him because there was among us no one more charming, more cordial, more kind and sympathetic than Pyotr Tchaikovsky. These were the distinctive features of his character that attracted everyone who became close to him; these are also the distinctive features that shine brightly in his creative works. Farewell, our dear one! The earth will be light on you, I do not doubt. It is always light for one who leaves of himself an eternal and dear memory; and for Tchaikovsky his eternal memory is in his works, and in the love of those who knew him. Farewell!

August Gerke gave a remarkably warm speech which greatly impressed everyone present by its sincerity.

A good many heartfelt verses were spoken over the open grave.

When all the speeches and verses were over, the singer of the Imperial Theatres, Nikolay Figner, could only say, with tears in his eyes and a trembling voice: 'Farewell, dear friend! May your memory live forever!' Everyone devoutly made the sign of the cross, and the cold clods of damp earth began to thump against the lid of the coffin.

The funeral ended around five o'clock. Following the speeches the crowd slowly began to disperse. The area near the platform was slow to empty and many people remained a long time near the grave, under whose vault were hidden forever the remains of the brilliant composer.

All expenses, by order of the Emperor, have been undertaken by His Imperial Majesty.

NV, 29 Oct. 1893

ALEXANDER GRECHANINOV

The funeral was grandiose, a crowd of deputations coming from every corner of Russia, a sea of flowers and wreaths. I carried a silver wreath, bought with money I collected among my friends. The length of the funeral procession can be judged by the fact that when the head of the procession was at the Nikolayev Station, its end was still at the Kazan Cathedral, in which the burial service for Tchaikovsky was read. And at the Alexander Nevsky Monastery, where he was buried, no more than half the mourners were able to get inside.

Grechaninov, *Moia muzykal'naia zhizn'*, 42

SERGEY DIAGHILEV

An immense crowd flocked to Tchaikovsky's funeral; and although it was broad daylight, the street lamps were lit all the way along the processional route. The coffin was borne past the Maryinsky Theatre to the Cathedral of Kazan. We expected the Emperor to attend, but only the Grand Duke Konstantin Konstantinovich came. . . . I followed the hearse with Rimsky-Korsakov, who said to me, 'Here's a man gone in good time. Look at Gounod—he so outlived his fame that no one noticed his death.' Gounod had died earlier that year.

Buckle, *Diaghilev*, 23

EDUARD NÁPRAVNÍK

A solemn, grandiose, and magnificent funeral. . . . I attended the liturgy, the service in the Kazan Cathedral, and the burial at the Nevsky Monastery.

RIII, f. 21, op. 1, ed. kh. 227, ll. 57–8

18. Kazan Cathedral in St Petersburg, where Tchaikovsky's last requiem was held on 28 October 1893

VLADIMIR NÁPRAVNÍK

During Pyotr Ilyich's illness I was not permitted to visit him, and I saw only his closed coffin, which was moved to the Kazan Cathedral the day before the funeral. I personally cannot recall such a moving, crowded, and sorrowful funeral as this one.

VC (1980), 223

GRAND DUKE KONSTANTIN KONSTANTINOVICH

Yesterday was one month after I received Tchaikovsky's last letter, and now he is already buried. I intentionally went to the city so that I could attend a funeral mass in the Kazan Cathedral. The Sovereign financed the funeral that was organized by the Directorate of the Imperial Theatres, which managed it with great solemnity. In the Cathedral the Right Reverend Nikander, Bishop of Narva officiated, and the chorus of the Russian Imperial Opera sang. Six students of the School of Jurisprudence, the alma mater of the deceased, stood at each side of the coffin.

The church was full, only those who had tickets were admitted. For a long while I had not witnessed so solemn a liturgy. They sang the Credo and the Te Deum from the liturgy composed by the deceased. I wanted to cry and thought that the dead one could not help hearing his own music that accompanied him to the world beyond. I could not see his face, the coffin was sealed. It was painful, and sad, and solemn, and good in the Kazan Cathedral. From there the casket was moved to the Alexander Nevsky Monastery, where he was buried at the cemetery. I had a terrible headache.

GARF, f. 660, d. 40, l. 138

NEWS OF THE DAY

Both capital newspapers merged into one friendly family. Each newspaper devoted half of the issue to Tchaikovsky, and not a single false note appeared in this entire newspaper requiem. It was rare to encounter such a moving consensus. And I assure you, one needs to be of truly great worth in order to cause such consensus. One has to be a Tchaikovsky!

ND, 28 Oct. 1893

TCHAIKOVSKY'S BURIAL CERTIFICATE

This is given by the parish of St Panteleymon's Church, the community of the Holy Trinity St Alexander Nevsky Monastery to commit to the earth the body of the court counsellor (retired), the composer Pyotr Ilyich Tchaikovsky who died of cholera on 25 October, 53 years of age, and whose funeral mass was officiated on 28 October this year, with His Majesty's permission in the Kazan Cathedral by Right Reverend Nikander, the Bishop of Narva.

St Petersburg, 28 October, 1893.
Seal of St Petersburg's Panteleymon Church; signed by
Archpriest: Vasily Peretersky; Deacon: Vladimir Voznesensky; Sexton: Alexey Bystrovsky.

RGIA, f. 815, op. 13, no. 405, l. 297

29 October

HERMAN LAROCHE

Several weeks before his death he spoke to me about subjects for a new opera, which had by turns attracted him. Among other things, this past summer he had read a French translation of George Eliot's *Scenes of Clerical Life*, whose novels, beginning with *The Mill on the Floss*, he had come to enjoy immensely in the last years of his life. Among the stories comprising this little volume there is one, 'Mr Gilfil's Love-Story', which takes place in the eighteenth century and which particularly enthralled him by the pathos of its subject-matter. He found it to be a subject on which he 'could very easily write an opera'. Not long before this, however, he had been thinking (whether seriously or just 'offhand', I cannot say) about *Karmozina* after the famous drama by Alfred de Musset, which had made a profound impression on him when he was still quite young. Oddly enough, about *The Captain's Daughter* [after Pushkin], news of which appeared so often in the papers, he spoke to me least of all; but on the other hand he mentioned *Romeo and Juliet* repeatedly and at various times in his life, and it seems to me that of all these subjects it was the Shakespeare one that attracted him most strongly. Besides operas he was full of plans for various instrumental works: thus, about two years ago, he intended to write a concerto for two pianos and orchestra, but when he had finished a sextet for strings, evidently feeling that it had turned out well, and fascinated by the unusual group of instruments, he announced that he 'now would like to write another sextet'. In this instance his words had been half in jest, but in general, musical ideas and images, intentions, and undertakings occupied him perpetually: he did not compose, like many (and at times even talented) Russians, 'in snatches', but quite literally lived in a word of sounds, adrift in a boundless element, and even though in the last ten or twelve years he had become far less prolific, far more cautious, and more demanding of himself, this inner singing continued as strong as ever, and even, I feel, with progressively increasing strength. People close to him, with whom he could be himself, are well aware of how he would often fall suddenly silent during a conversation or fail to respond to questions, and they knew enough not to pester him by asking him 'why have you grown quiet?' or 'what's the matter?'—knowing that, quite likely, instead of the mundane topic then being discussed, some extended chord in sixths for divided cellos had appeared before him, or some melody for cor anglais.

The hair on his head had long since turned white, but this was the only sign of old age in that vigorous, hearty, and blooming body. To say that he 'remained young at heart' would be not only banal, but also incorrect. Youth of the heart is set in opposition to a sickly and enfeebled body. At his home in Klin Pyotr Ilyich used to walk a dozen miles every day, undaunted by either rain or snow, just as he was undaunted last year by the rolling during his stormy and dangerous journey from Europe to America; arriving in Petersburg or Moscow for a few days, like a true country dweller who could not grow tired of the spectacles of the city, he would never miss an evening at the theatre, knowing that in his backwoods he was unlikely ever to see the latest French comedy, or dramatic adaptation of [Gogol's] *Dead Souls*, or [Rubinstein's opera] *Die Makkabäer*, or [Massenet's] *Esclarmonde*. It was in his final years that he learned to conduct, beginning in the mid-1880s; in the summer of 1884, staying with his brother in the country, he took it into his head to devote a quarter of an hour every morning to English, and partly with the help of one of his friends, but mostly by teaching himself, he made remarkable progress in a short time. Not only his creative imagination, but also his memory and receptivity, his talent for enjoying nature or art, his mental and physical energy—all remained untouched in him right up until his final illness. As far as his creative imagination is concerned, I find that it was constantly growing: true, he had a harder time writing, trusted himself less, and nervously destroyed entire compositions which he had completed only suddenly to take a dislike to them, but his music became richer, clearer, and more individual.

No, I refuse to think that he had said everything he had to say, that he had 'accomplished everything earthly within the earthly span'! On the contrary, I believe that he carried to his grave an entire world of captivating visions, and that had he lived but another fifteen years we might have discovered new and unexpected facets of his genius. There was in him that happy balance between 'the search for new paths' and an instinctive attachment to the classical tradition, the very balance which gives an artist the strength for the boldest of innovations, for solid and true achievements. He was passionately fond of Mozart, not merely in theory but in practice, and successfully advanced his cause—but in Tchaikovsky's own compositions there was never any turning backward, nothing archaic or in opposition to the age, and it is remarkable that in the final years of his life it was the extreme left among our musicians, the musical youth—those one might expect to find influenced by the criticism which once responded with such hostility to his early attempts—who in fact flocked around him and formed the circle of the most enthusiastic admirers of his works, and his most devoted personal friends.

He worked tirelessly and daily when at home: his trips to the capitals, which necessarily disrupted his routine, were always a burden to him, and he used to return joyously and eagerly to his little wooden house surrounded by its large garden, where he was accustomed to experience the sweet torments of creation. Never going a day without working, from his youth on he made it a rule to write during fixed hours. With his usual mild irony he would tell interviewers that he worked 'just like a hack'. This intensive life within the world of harmony was not free of a certain strain: musical images haunted him everywhere, and would even, as he said many times, appear to him in his sleep, fantastically interweaving with images and events from everyday life. To the superficial observer this artist's immersion in his work was scarcely noticeable. Tchaikovsky was a true virtuoso in his use of time, and outside his fixed hours—in the morning and the afternoon—he would write only in the most exceptional cases. The rest of the time he gave the deceptive yet refreshing and soothing impression of a man who, finished with his daily labour, has no need to make up for lost time, and who is free and able to devote himself to a favourite entertainment, playing piano duets with a friend who has arrived on a visit, or a game of vint for small stakes if several arrive, or after an early supper, country-style, listening to somebody reading aloud from his beloved Gogol, Lev Tolstoy, Turgenev, Ostrovsky, and Flaubert.

In speaking of his musical genius, I used the word 'balance'. I can think of no other word that more aptly characterizes him not only as a musician, but in general. In Burckhardt's book *Die Kultur der Renaissance in Italien* [*The Civilization of the Renaissance in Italy*] there is a chapter entitled 'Die Entdeckung des Menschen' — 'The Discovery of Man'. I have always felt that this same discovery has been made by all of us who have had the good fortune to be at all close to Tchaikovsky. He was, if I may say so, the consummate example of a great artist. Complete harmony reigned within him: there were no contradictions between activity and vocation, between task and strength, between mind and character, between manner of life and inner desires. Fond of depicting in his symphonic poems the worldly sorrow, and torments of a restless soul, he himself, even in his youth, struck me, on the contrary, as the reconciled and enlightened Faust of the second part [of Goethe's epic], contemplating life and a people with love, but without agitation. It is said that such harmonious natures were more often met in classical antiquity than they are today. But it is also said that the ancient world had little of the element of goodness or warmth of feeling. In that respect I cannot venture to write that Pyotr Ilyich had a classical nature.

We willingly forgive men of genius a certain egoism, a certain dryness of the heart. They are concerned with themselves, and for the sake of this concern it has become the custom—perhaps even to an exaggerated and biased extent—to consider it legitimate that they should not remember their neighbours. There is nothing more widespread than the biographical fiction, which holds that a great genius is without fail also a beautiful person and the kindest of souls. This fiction has as its source the same undemandingness. Pyotr Ilyich's future biographer will have no need of this, no need to go searching for facts for the sake of some conventional and sugary idealization.

Pyotr Ilyich was exceptionally kind. He possessed both the sort of kindness which strikes the eye, and the sort which no one ever suspects. He was kind in every way and in all directions. Those who viewed him from afar could judge only by his financial generosity, which constituted but the most superficial and material aspect of his kindness. With his lively temperament, which was by no means devoid of a capacity for fits of irritation or anger, he was somehow predisposed to every kind action, loving to look for, and able to find, the good in both the composition of a musician and the soul of a person. Without taking pains or making any effort, he managed by his presence alone to soften extremes, to reconcile enemies, to bring warmth, light, and joy. His loss for art is a heavy one, and perhaps greater than we, his contemporaries, can conceive; but even this loss pales before that which we have borne in the person of this amazing embodiment of the radiant aspects of mankind.

TG, 29 Oct. 1893

GRAND DUKE KONSTANTIN KONSTANTINOVICH

In the train I was composing a poem in Tchaikovsky's memory, but nothing came out of it.

GARF, f. 660, d. 40, l. 138

ALEXEY SUVORIN

Editor-in-chief of the *New Times (Novoe vremia)*. The following is an excerpt from his diary.

Tchaikovsky buried yesterday. Dreadfully sorry for him. He was treated by the Bertensons, two brothers, and they did not give him a bath. To my mind these Bertensons are not at all deserving of their Jewish-made reputation.

RGALI, f. 459, op. 2, ed. kh. 140, l. 104,
Suvorin, *Dnevnik*, 73 (incorrectly)

30 October

ANTON RUBINSTEIN

Letter to his sister Sofiya.

What did you say of Tchaikovsky's death? Could even that be God's will? What a loss for music in Russia! And it happened at the peak of life—he was only 50!—and all this caused by a glass of water! Everything indeed is nonsense—life, creativity, and all the rest.

A. G. Rubinshtein, Literaturnoe nasledie (3 vols.;
Moscow, 1986), iii. 140

1 November

GRAND DUKE KONSTANTIN KONSTANTINOVICH

I added one stanza to the poem in memory of Tchaikovsky, but it seems that it does not proceed any further.[1]

GARF, f. 660, d. 40, l. 138

MUSIC AND LIFE

In the last days of October 1893 the Vyatka Society [Vyatka was a town in the north-eastern part of Russia, and Tchaikovsky was born in its province] received a telegram announcing the sudden death of P[yotr] I[lyich] Tchaikovsky. The Vyatka Society, having a circle of local music lovers at its centre, decided to honour the memory of Pyotr Ilyich with a solemn requiem at the cathedral. A deputation with a respectful request for permission and assistance was sent to Vyatka's then Bishop Sergey. . . .

The deputation, it is true, was small, being only two individuals, but individuals fairly prominent in the Society and the musical circle. . . . Both men were well known to the bishop. They presented themselves. They received his blessing. They sat down. Briefly they stated their request. 'And who is Pyotr Ilyich Tchaikovsky?' asked the bishop, knitting

---

[1] The Grand Duke ultimately failed to produce a poem devoted to Tchaikovsky's memory. There exists one earlier poem of his, dedicated to Tchaikovsky and written in 1889.

his distinctively long and thick brows. He was a composer, explained the respectful visitors.

'A com-pos-er? A musician! You should be ashamed to come here with such a request!!' began the bishop and was off. . . . Bishop Sergey was a scholar—a *magister theologiae*—but for all his scholarly merit he was very quick-tempered and irascible.

'A musician means a buffoon. Your Tchaikovsky is a buffoon! The Church does not pray for buffoons.'

The bishop rejected their arguments. The people of Vyatka, however, were undeterred and a solemn liturgy and requiem service were conducted at a local convent, such that it was long before the nuns were to forget it. The Mother Superior was all but anathematized. Even Tchaikovsky's music was, at the bishop's order, committed to the flames. The bishop thundered against the name of Tchaikovsky in sermons and exhortations. But then it was reported in the newspapers that the memory of Pyotr Tchaikovsky had been granted the highest consideration. The Sovereign himself had taken part in the funeral of the famous—'as it turned out'—composer. And about Tchaikovsky there was never another peep.

'Aha!' rejoiced the Society, 'so much for your "buffoon"!'

MZ 1 (1910), 9–10

2 November

THE NEWS AND STOCK EXCHANGE GAZETTE

'Give us the precious remains of Tchaikovsky'—this was the entreaty made by Muscovites after the death of the unforgettable composer. He is ours, ours by right, ours because such was the will of the deceased, expressed by him not long before his death in a conversation with the well-known musicians Taneyev and Brandukov, who have declared that the late P[yotr] I[lyich] wished to be buried at Klin, where he worked on his compositions, which henceforth constitute the pride of the whole of Russia and the property of the entire world, where he created for himself this 'monument not of human making'.

In the mean time the family of Pyotr Tchaikovsky decided otherwise, and Tchaikovsky's remains rest peacefully in the cemetery of the Alexander Nevsky Monastery, which has sheltered more than one figure of Russian music in the shadow of its graves.

We were curious to learn from the late composer's brother, Modest Tchaikovsky, whether it was indeed the wish of P[yotr] I[lyich] to be buried in Moscow or at Klin, and also the reasons for the decision made by the family, which would appear, at first glance, to have gone against the will of the deceased.

'You see,' said Modest, 'my brother was able to admire and delight in every corner of nature which, in one way or another, whether by the beauty of its landscape or the serene quiet of its surroundings, caught his attention. A dreamer by nature, with a somewhat romantic soul, he would be drawn to such a spot, and, overcome with the emotions evoked by his beloved Mother Nature, he often exclaimed in such cases: "Here's a fine place to be buried!" Probably, indeed certainly, Klin, as a place where more than once P[yotr] I[lyich] was visited by the inspiration which dictated to him the musical ideas he embodied in so many works of art, was dear to my brother and he, admiring at some point the countryside around Moscow, expressed a desire to be laid to rest there, to find there eternal peace. Moscow truly loved the deceased and wished to see his remains buried there. I was informed that the Muscovites wanted to bury my brother in the Danilov Monastery Cemetery, but precisely this cemetery had always, and even not long before Pyotr Ilyich's death, made a painful, melancholy impression upon him with its gloomy air, and he used to shudder at the thought of being buried there.'

'And Petersburg? Why, here my late brother's best years were spent; here he received his education, first at the School of Jurisprudence, then at the Conservatoire; here his operas and symphonies enjoyed their first successes, here he had so many artistic attachments!'

'But this was not the only reason Pyotr Ilyich held Petersburg dear.'

'Here in Petersburg our parents died and were buried, and as late as last year our sister also was laid to rest in the Alexandrovskoe Cemetery.'[2]

'It is clear that Tchaikovsky could not have been buried anywhere else, and that wherever his remains might lie, the gaze of all educated Russians will be directed in prayer and reverence to that place which has been destined to be the final resting-place of the untimely deceased composer.'

NBG, 2 Nov. 1893

FREDERIC LAMOND

Thanks to Tchaikovsky's efforts during his stay in Moscow at the beginning of that month, the RMS decided to invite the young Scottish pianist to play in Russia, but it happened to be three

---

[2] A mistake on the part of the reporter or Modest: their sister Alexandra (or Sasha) died in 1891, not 1892.

years later, in October 1896. He successfully performed Tchaikovsky's First Piano concerto and attended the Requiem Mass on
25 October for Tchaikovsky.

At nine in the morning there was a Requiem Mass for the soul of Peter
Ilitsch Tchaikovsky. I drove in a sleigh to one of the chief churches of
Moscow and found all the professors of Conservatoire gathered in a small
side-chapel. I stood between Scriabin and Taneiev. When the officiating
priest began to read the Mass for the dead I was aware of an unnatural
paleness on the part of Scriabin. Taneiev wept and sobbed: knelt down
and kissed the icy flags of the chapel: something tense, even gloomy lay
on the whole gathering. As the priest of the Orthodox Greek Church, his
deep, impressive bass half intoning, half speaking, raised his voice to a
threatening, booming cry, it was as if the wings of angels of Death were
rushing over the gathering in the semi-darkness of the ice-cold chapel.

Frederic Lamond, *Memoirs* (Edinburgh, 1949), 97

The accounts of Tchaikovsky's funeral require little comment. Perhaps
most striking is the degree to which the populace took part in the sombre
ceremony, turning it into an event of national significance comparable
only to the funeral of Fyodor Dostoevsky in 1881. The display of love and
admiration for the deceased on the part of the masses was indeed remarkable. One also notes the attendance of so many dignitaries, as well as the
fact that the expenses were covered by the Emperor. On the day of the
funeral Alexander III himself was at his suburban residence at Gatchina,
celebrating the anniversary of his marriage, and for that matter alone
could not attend the other ceremony. He was suffering from kidney disease and died a year later. Furthermore, during the last years of his life
Alexander III was hunted by terrorists, who killed his father, and each
public appearance entailed security problems. The Emperor was fond of
both the man and his music and, according to oral tradition, is said to
have exclaimed upon learning of his death: 'We have many counts and
barons, but only one Tchaikovsky.' The wreaths sent by the Emperor and
Empress, as well as those from other members of the Imperial family,
were prominently displayed in the funeral cortège. Two of the Grand
Dukes were actually present, one of them even serving as a pallbearer. To
interpret this pomp and ceremony as an attempt at a cover-up of some
kind, or to suggest that the Church or its priests knew or even suspected
that they were conducting a service for a suicide would, particularly given
the scale of the ecclesiastical participation in the funeral, make a joke of

their Christian beliefs. (The reluctance of the provincial priest in Vyatka to perform a requiem at the request of the local music society was the result of his crude ignorance and no more.) Alternatively, for a practising Christian to deceive the Church authorities on so serious a matter as the manner of death would have constituted a mortal sin, something all but inconceivable in the case of at least one of the chief perpetrators of the alleged fraud, namely, Modest, who was a passionate believer. The existence of the burial certificate issued by the appropriate Church authorities of the Alexander Nevsky Monastery shows clearly that nothing wrong was happening behind the scenes.

One of the most prominent speakers at the civil ceremony at the graveside was Vladimir Gerard, a former classmate of the composer's from the School of Jurisprudence and now an established lawyer. Gerard evoked the world of his friend's early years, before he decided upon a career in music. His was a noble eulogy; one contemporary journalist found it 'beautiful'.

Finally, we read with appreciation the moving tribute to his late friend written by Herman Laroche, one of the foremost music critics of the time. We learn of several of Tchaikovsky's plans for future creative projects, among them the rather unusual idea of an opera based on a story from George Eliot's *Scenes of Clerical Life*. More important, Laroche offers his own insights into Tchaikovsky's personality, and his picture of the man is radically different from conventional modern-day portraits of a self-abusive neurotic perpetually on the verge of hysteria and collapse. Laroche's Tchaikovsky is a harmonious Renaissance man, 'contemplating life and people with love, but without agitation'. It may be argued that Laroche was biased in his perception, but then, so have been the composer's later biographers. In fairness, we must recognize that his perspective is, at the very least, no less legitimate than theirs, and that, in contrast to those who came later, he had known Tchaikovsky intimately for many years, starting from their early youth together—a fact which endows his testimony with a weight that cannot be dismissed.

9

Aftermath

3 November–5 December

———

I

3 November

LEV TOLSTOY

Letter to the critic and essayist Nikolay Strakhov.

Today I read [Modest] Tchaikovsky's description of the illness and death of his celebrated brother.[1] Here is a reading helpful to us: sufferings, cruel physical sufferings, fear: can it be death? Doubts, hopes, an inner conviction that it is death, and still, all the while, unceasing suffering and exhaustion, a dulling of the senses and almost a reconciliation and oblivion, and, just before the end, a kind of inner vision, an elucidation of everything—'So that's it'—and . . . the end. Here is for us a necessary, a good reading. Not that we should think only of this and not live, but rather we must live and work, yet constantly with one eye seeing and remembering this source of everything steadfast, true, and good.

Tolstoy, *Polnoe sobranie sochinenii*, lxvi. 419

ALINA BRYULLOVA

As always with such a virtually unexpected death, no one can believe it, and so everyone starts inventing various fictions and goes straight off in

———

[1] Modest Tchaikovsky's article, 'The Illness of Pyotr Ilyich Tchaikovsky', was published in the *News and Stock Exchange Gazette* and *New Times* on 1 Nov.

search of those responsible. And in this case all the Petersburg salons crashed down around Bertenson. The fact is that when the kidneys are affected a bath is indicated. Tchaikovsky was in general very superstitious, and his mother had also died of cholera when she was placed in the bath. That event had left an indelible trace upon Tchaikovsky's heart. . . . Bertenson, a close acquaintance who knew Tchaikovsky's psychology well, hesitated a long while before resorting to this treatment, fearing that the ever smouldering memory associated with the bath might have such an effect on him, might so weaken the vigorous elements of the organism in its struggle with the illness, that any beneficial effects of the bath would be nullified. Whether he was right or not is impossible for the layman to judge, and is conjectural in any event. On Sunday, when Pyotr Ilyich was already unconscious, they did resort to the bath, but to no avail.

VC (1980), 119

ALEXEY SUVORIN

The following is an excerpt from his editorial comments in the *New Times*.

I returned to Petersburg when we had grown fewer by one great man, one resounding and splendid talent. While in Berlin, I learned of Tchaikovsky's death at the Hotel Bristol the moment when I came back from seeing an acquaintance. The hotel's doorman, who knew that I am Russian, met me with the words: 'Do you know that Tchaikovsky is dead?' These words surprised me: 'How do you know Tchaikovsky?' 'For pity's sake,' he answered, 'I have been in Leipzig, and there I heard his symphony. This is astounding music!' This should make clear to you that the name of our composer was becoming truly popular abroad as well. And to have died of cholera! . . . It is a dreadful shame. . . .

Not only am I indignant at this death, I am also displeased with Mr Bertenson, who treated Tchaikovsky. I know that it is easy to blame any doctor and that they are often blamed unjustly and even senselessly. . . . I am displeased with Mr Bertenson, not because he did not cure Tchaikovsky, but because he left the patient, handing him over to his brother and his 'assistant'. . . . Mr Bertenson did not do everything necessary, and there seems to me to be grounds for asking him: why did he not hold a consultation? Because he trusted his own authority or because he believed in the patient's recovery? Whether he trusted in the one or the other, he was, in any event, mistaken, and the words of the dying man, who obtained some relief at first, 'you have snatched me from the jaws of death', ring now with cruel and just irony for Mr Bertenson. And this irony is not eliminated by the letter of Mr M[odest] Tchaikovsky, who records *en toutes lettres* the names and patronymics of the two Bertenson brothers and testifies to their unremitting concern for the patient. Everything, he says, was done, but death is inexorable. No, everything was not done. . . . Bertenson stresses the fact that Tchaikovsky's mother had died of cholera when she was placed in the bath and that this is why he delayed so long in proposing this remedy to him. Mr Bertenson evidently sees in this act of his a particular delicacy towards this patient. But what we have here is simply an utter failure to understand the patient and a lack of genuine delicacy on the part of the doctor. Who can prove that Tchaikovsky would have been opposed to a consultation if it had been held without having asked him? Who can say positively that the doctors gathered for a consultation would not have persuaded him against this prejudice about the bath and would perhaps have inspired him with moral energy as well? And can Mr Bertenson not affirm that Tchaikovsky believed in him as in God and that this faith was never once shaken in him? And if this was so, then Mr Bertenson did not do everything that he ought to have done, having in his charge a patient dear to all Russia. . . .

My lines may strike Mr Bertenson as cruel, especially as they are altogether useless to him who has died, but I write them for the living in general and for physicians in particular, who can draw from this event a certain lesson for themselves.

NV, 3 Nov. 1893

SERGEY BERTENSON

I remember as though it were yesterday a visit to our home one evening by a very pleasant gentleman, hitherto unknown to me, with greying hair and whiskers and a soft, soothing way of speaking and a quiet voice. The man was weeping, and he and my father talked together for a long time about something. He turned out to be Modest Ilyich Tchaikovsky, with whom we children later became great friends. He had come to express sympathy to my father on behalf of the entire Tchaikovsky family concerning the recent appearance in the newspaper the *New Times* of an article by Alexey Suvorin, in which he accused my father of insufficiently competent and attentive treatment of the deceased composer. This article was picked up by certain other journalists of the sensation-hungry minor press and a full-fledged defamation of my father began. Modest put an end to this by printing in all the Petersburg papers an open letter on behalf of the Tchaikovsky family expressing profound gratitude to my father and his assistants for the exceptional care shown to the deceased.

Bertenson, *Vokrug iskusstva*, 21

5 November

LEV BERTENSON

Letter to Modest Tchaikovsky.

I am very sorry that you limited yourself to leaving your card today and deprived me of the pleasure of shaking your hand.

This persecution by Suvorin and his blackguardly colleagues who hide behind his back has, of course, had its effect: my nerves are so shattered that for two days now I have been unable to visit my patients in the city and was even forced to spend today in bed.

I have taken great comfort in the kind and precious expressions of sympathy on the part of many fine and noble people: they have all been unanimous in their indignation at Suvorin, expressing their kindly feelings to me personally and in letters. At the same time, they all urge me with one accord not to honour Suvorin and his associates with a response.

I have firmly resolved to keep silent, answering this villainous persecution with contempt.

I am very grateful to you for your desire to defend me, but I shall give you no instructions. I dare say your own feelings will tell you what you should do. If indeed it is worth undertaking anything.

GDMC, B[10], no. 494

THE NEW TIMES

In the city there is much talk about the unsatisfactory cholera treatment of the late Pyotr Tchaikovsky. In conversations concerning this the opinion is heard that, to justify himself before Russian society and physicians, Dr Bertenson ought to present to one of the Russian scientific societies . . . a detailed report on his treatment of Tchaikovsky, so that by means of a scientific and, in addition, a public examination it might be possible to determine whether and how conscientiously scientific methods were applied in attempting to save the patient. Only the corporate spirit has kept many physicians from expressing censure of their colleague in print and in professional meetings. . . . The corporate spirit must not, however, hinder a clarification of the truth and determination of blame, if someone was to blame in this. By all indications, someone was, be it only in the respect that no consultation was called. Dr Bertenson should have called it in that he himself, in all probability, is little familiar with the treatment of Asiatic cholera. This treatment is familiar to clinical physicians and in particular to physicians of the large city hospitals, and since the symptoms of cholera were diagnosed in Tchaikovsky (though they were, apparently, diagnosed too late), Mr Bertenson was obliged immediately to call in doctors of one of the city hospitals. . . . From these doctors he would have learned that in the hospitals the majority of cholera cases, if treatment was begun before the period of spasms, had a happy outcome.

NV, 5 Nov. 1893

PETERSBURG GAZETTE

It was pointed out that Lev Bertenson, who treated the late Mr Tchaikovsky, had not really made every effort to seize the famous composer from the grip of death. Not without reason, it was said that 'Tchaikovsky's death from cholera' is indeed a shame.

That cholera is a powerful, perfidious, and multifaceted disease, there is no doubt; that cholera is not curable is already proved; that it could be undermined is shown by hundreds of facts. The question is, *who exactly ought to have treated* Tchaikovsky? At any rate, not Mr Lev Bertenson, nor his brother Vasily Bertenson.

When cholera was diagnosed, Tchaikovsky should immediately have been surrounded by junior and supernumerary house doctors from the Alexandrovsky hospital for manual labourers, who had experience of treating, in the course of two cholera outbreaks in Petersburg, several hundred cholera patients. Lev Bertenson could merely have shared with them his knowledge of Tchaikovsky's medical history, without undertaking the supervision of the cholera treatment, especially since, according to his own words, the case was without precedent for him.

If this case was without precedent for him, he should have referred to those who saw all sorts of cholera cases, and this means, we must repeat, largely, junior and supernumerary house doctors from the hospitals, the Alexandrovsky for manual labourers, the Obukhovsky, Barachny, etc. They receive the patients into their care; they supervise the course run by the dreadful disease; they know the specifics of each 'case', its tricks and turns, and all unexpected things. Would any of these people refuse to attend constantly at the bed of such a patient so dear to the entire world as Tchaikovsky? Would any of them, after accepting supervision of the treatment, leave the patient at one o'clock in the morning and return the next day at eleven, and even then by invitation?

Be that as it may, by no means everything that medicine can do was done as regards the late Tchaikovsky. Only a small part of the weaponry was taken from its arsenal, but even that was not fully employed. Medicine was taught a hard lesson by this loss. The failure to hold a consultation with doctors who had experience of cholera is an unforgivable error.

PG, 5 Nov. 1893

RAY

The details of Tchaikovsky's death are still rumoured in the city. The charismatic composer is indeed fortunate to receive so much sympathy from society. Everyone is sorry about him! But we have a custom: if an outstanding person dies, there arises an immediate need to find the guilty party. Just as it was among the ancient Hebrews, there is a thorough search for a scapegoat to be burdened with the sins of others. . . .

The accusation raised by Suvorin certainly remains his responsibility: he has all the cards in his hands. Personally, I do not belong to any musical circle and do not know any composer closely. I only heard that Tchaikovsky died from drinking unboiled water and from the attempt at self-cure with the help of Hunyadi mineral water. The deceased developed the most serious case of Asiatic cholera. Then the fashionable doctor Bertenson arrived, together with his brother, also a doctor (a third Bertenson in a row). No consultation took place.

As far as we remember, this is not the first time that Bertenson was at fault because of not calling for a consultation in a dangerous case. . . .

But why, just as happened at Tchaikovsky's bedside, did a consultation not take place? Why is there so much self-confidence, which may cost a human life?

Suvorin reproaches Bertenson for the belated use of the bath which could have saved Tchaikovsky. We are not doctors. How can we judge whether the bath would have saved him or not? But the bath had to be prescribed at that time, puting aside sentimental reminiscences and considerations to the effect that the patient's mother also died from cholera when she was placed in the bath, and therefore this measure might have upset the suffering Tchaikovsky.

While treating so precious a patient whose life was important to society,

Bertenson should not have been absent (once more for the sake of financial gain and in order not to lose other patients) for so long and should not have abandoned Tchaikovsky, who fighting a lethal illness, to the hands and care of his brother.

LU, 5 Nov. 1893

6 November

THE SON OF THE FATHERLAND

Immediately following the tragic death of P[yotr] I[lyich] Tchaikovsky, who according to rumour contracted cholera from drinking unboiled water in a restaurant, we reported the scandalous disorder in Petersburg eating establishments. Our words have now been confirmed by official sources. The sanitary commission conducted an investigation of 'boiled' restaurant water, which according to compulsory regulation every establishment of this sort must have, and arrived at the most troubling conclusions. The analysis showed that boiled water is everywhere diluted with unboiled water before being served to patrons. . . . Incidentally, the restaurant [Leiner's] that has been named in the stories about Tchaikovsky's illness is now suffering financial hardship.

SO, 6 Nov. 1893

7 November

THE NEWS AND STOCK EXCHANGE GAZETTE

Threatening accusations have rained down upon the fresh grave of Pyotr Tchaikovsky against Dr Lev Bertenson, who treated the patient but was unable to save him.

This practice is nothing new. Physicians in such cases are deprived of any opportunity of defence.

The practice, at the same time, is a clumsy one. It is called finding a scapegoat.

The mob disorders during last year's cholera epidemics occurred primarily because savage and ignorant people had been spreading rumours that the doctors were poisoning the cholera victims.

The savage and ignorant masses may yet be forgiven such views. But a man believing himself to be educated and humane should not search blindly for a scapegoat to feed his grief, however deep and sacred.

It is well known that medicine today knows no reliable, specific treatment for cholera and therefore recommends exclusively precautionary measures. Last year and this have seen only experiments in treating cholera, which have provoked heated debates among the physicians themselves.

The blame here may be placed on medicine, but certainly not on each individual physician who in his medical practice finds himself faced with a case of cholera.

Summon a hundred of the finest physicians to the bed of a cholera victim, and still the chances for recovery will depend on the strength of the infection and the degree to which the patient's organism is predisposed to this sort of illness.

Tchaikovsky's death is a terrible lesson.

When hundreds and thousands of peasants and petty bourgeois die of cholera, the thought of danger barely occurs to us.

But cholera, it turns out, can make dreadful leaps to the side, unexpectedly striking those who are well-to-do, and who live amid the finest material conditions.

The conclusion: continue to fight against cholera with all our strength, cleanse the breeding-grounds of infection, stamp out the root-cause of cholera's spread, that is, the hunger, cold, and ignorance of the masses.

NBG, 7 Nov. 1893

MODEST TCHAIKOVSKY

Letter to the Editor of the *New Times*.

On behalf of all those who were constantly with my late brother during the final days of his life, I ask you to put in print in the *New Times* that we consider any reproaches whatsoever directed against the treatment of Pyotr Ilyich's fatal illness to be absolutely unjust.

Despite the fact that we sense the bitterness of this loss more strongly than anyone, none of us feels for Lev Bertenson, his brother Vasily Bertenson, and assistants Nikolay Mamonov and Zander anything other than a sense of gratitude for their sincere and irreproachably thorough treatment of the deceased's illness.

NV, 7 Nov. 1893

8 November

THE NEW TIMES

Of what significance can such a statement [by Modest Tchaikovsky] be? In our opinion, almost none at all. It is of almost no significance, because in the present case a certain portion of the responsibility falls on Mr [Modest] Tchaikovsky, who delayed in summoning the doctor and did not see to it that a consultation was called, and also because the doctors whom Mr Tchaikovsky defends are obliged to answer not only to the relatives of the late composer but also to Russian society.

NV, 8 Nov. 1893

PETERSBURG GAZETTE

One more letter from Mr Modest Tchaikovsky. . . . Alexey Suvorin believes that Mr Bertenson's treatment was not entirely thorough. Modest Tchaikovsky finds that the treatment was 'entirely thorough'.

The same thing happened to Mr Bertenson as to the late Tchaikovsky: Tchaikovsky was treated by three specialists in pulmonary diseases.[2] Mr Bertenson is criticized as a physician by two men of letters. We wish Mr Bertenson only this: if this criticism upsets his nerves, God forbid that his nervous disorder should be treated by two midwives. Everyone is suited to his own place.

Opinions are divided. In order to find the truth, Mr Bertenson is left with the option of calling for a consultation with other physicians and allowing them to decide whether his treatment of the patient was 'entirely thorough' or 'entirely unthorough'. Without such a consultation in this case it will not do. One should have started with it. One is compelled to end with it. It is better late than never.

PG, 8 Nov. 1893

SERGEY BERTENSON

A few years later at a large dinner of the Literary Fund, Suvorin made a public apology to my father for his unjust accusation.

Bertenson, *Vokrug iskusstva*, 21

---

[2] The fact that Lev Bertenson was particularly known as a specialist in pulmonary diseases should not obscure his competence in the treatment of infectious illnesses, such as cholera, on which he had published several learned papers. For further information about Bertenson's brothers, as well as other doctors who treated Tchaikovsky, see *PBC*, 11–20.

3 December

VLAS DOROSHEVICH

Prominent journalist and writer.

The outbreak of cholera, which now, fortunately, begins to subside, continues to be the topic of the day. . . . Every epidemic possesses a character. Cholera is most treacherous. . . . Cholera is half Mephisto and half Iago. Its speciality is malice, combined with irony. It jumps from dark corners at people who at that moment do not expect it and may be resting from the tedious routine of fear, when they relax a little; when they stop being frightened. In July everyone would have taken a most trivial disorder for cholera and sent for a doctor. At the end of November one can take a true cholera for a trivial disorder. This explains why most patients were brought to the hospitals in a hopeless condition.

In the same treacherous manner out of the dark corners cholera destroyed Tchaikovsky. In July he would hardly have drunk unboiled water.[3]

PG, 3 Dec. 1893

II

6 November

ALEXANDER GRECHANINOV

At a special meeting of the Imperial Russian Musical Society it was decided that Tchaikovsky's final work, recently heard under the composer's direction, would be repeated at the next symphonic concert. It was to be directed by the conductor of the Maryinsky Theatre and the Russian Musical Society, Eduard Nápravník. I have no words to describe the impression produced by this symphony when it was performed anew under the masterly direction of Petersburg's talented and beloved conductor. Consumed with grief for his lost friend, Nápravník surpassed himself, conducting the symphony with such feeling, and such exaltation, that

---

[3] Ironically, Mr Doroshevich was not right. As we have seen, it was precisely in July that Tchaikovsky suffered a mild form of cholera because of careless drinking of unboiled water.

many in the audience were brought to tears, in particular during the performance of the final movement, full of profoundly doleful music. Under the direction of a true master the symphony appeared in a completely new light. Attention was also paid to the fact that the theme of the 'With Saints give rest' runs through the horn line in the elaboration of the first movement. Certainly this is a presentiment of death! And how lightly we had reacted to this swan-song, when we heard it from the composer two weeks before.

Tchaikovsky was but 53 when he went to his grave. He was loved during his lifetime as perhaps no living composer has ever been loved, and people had looked forward to many more new and brilliant compositions from him, and that is why all of Russia mourned him so sincerely and inconsolably.

To try to work out the grief I felt in my heart, I composed an elegy for orchestra, 'To the memory of Tchaikovsky', but I was not satisfied with it, and it was not released. Only several years later, when living in Moscow, did I take it up again, and it was performed at one of Belyaev's Russian Symphony Concerts, but it was not a success, and I never returned to it. I recall this with some sadness, as I so sincerely wished to compose something worthy of the memory of an artist, for whom I felt such profound respect and warm affection.

Grechaninov, *Moia muzykal'naia zhizn'*, 42

NIKOLAY RIMSKY-KORSAKOV

Shortly after the funeral the Sixth Symphony was again performed in a concert conducted by Nápravník. This time the public responded to it with enthusiasm, and from this moment on the symphony's fame continued to grow, gradually spreading throughout Russia and Europe. It was said that Nápravník made the Petersburg audience understand the symphony with his performance and that Tchaikovsky, not being a talented conductor, had not been able to do this, for which reason the public response had been rather restrained at its first performance under the direction of the composer. I believe this is untrue. The symphony went off splendidly with Nápravník, but it had also gone well with the composer. The public simply did not get to the heart of it that first time and did not pay sufficient attention to it, just as some years before it had not paid attention to Tchaikovsky's Fifth Symphony. I imagine that the composer's sudden death (which gave rise to all sorts of rumours), as well as stories of his presentiment of approaching death (to which mankind is so prone) and, further, the propensity to seek a connection between the gloomy mood of the symphony's final movement and such a presentiment—all these now focused the public's attention on this work, and the splendid composition soon became famous and even fashionable.

Rimskii-Korsakov, *Polnoe sobranie sochinenii*, i. 194

GRAND DUKE KONSTANTIN KONSTANTINOVICH

I attended a wonderful symphony concert dedicated to Tchaikovsky's memory and consisting exclusively of his works. The bust of the deceased, surrounded by palm trees, stood over the orchestra. They were performing the Sixth Symphony, the *Pathétique*. To hear it was inexpressible. Those sounds, as a last testament, farewell to life. Some excellent baritone, half-American, half-French, sang superbly in English from *Onegin* as well as several songs.[4] Auer played the violin concerto, and then, when he was called back on stage, he played the arrangement for violin and orchestra of the Andante from the string quartet [No. 1]. This was marvellous, and it seems that many were weeping.

GARF, f. 660, d. 40, l. 138–9

VLADIMIR NÁPRAVNÍK

On 6 November 1893 the Sixth Symphony was repeated in the hall of the Nobility under the direction of my father. I was at the first rehearsal. My father, full of emotion, addressed a few heartfelt words about Pyotr Ilyich to the orchestra. The symphony made a powerful impression and was a tremendous success.

VC (1980), 223

THE CITIZEN

The last movement of *Adagio lamentoso* by coincidence is of so deeply doleful a character that can be easily imagined in the music of death. Therefore it is not surprising that many of those who heard the symphony found that Tchaikovsky wrote a requiem for himself as if he anticipated the approach of his own death. As regards its musical aspects, it may also appear strange that, contrary to common practice, the late composer chose to end the symphony with a slow movement, not a fast

---

[4] Eugène Oudin, English singer, who had sung Eugene Onegin for the first time in England.

one. Be it as that may, in virtue of its exclusively subjective sentiment we listened to it with special attention, and it made on us the deepest possible impression.

GR, 8 Nov. 1893

11 November

SERGEY DIAGHILEV

The following is taken from a letter to his stepmother, after attending one of the requiems for Tchaikovsky in St Petersburg.

We are all shaken by Tchaikovsky's death. I wept throughout the entire requiem. It was particularly terrible after we had seen him conducting the orchestra, full of his powers.

IRLI, f. 102, ed. kh. 97, l. 427

NIKOLAY FENDEIZEN

Editor-in-chief of the *Russian Musical Gazette*.

Rarely is one a witness to such sincere universal grief as that with which the Russian cultural world met the death of one of its most attractive and cherished artists—Pyotr Ilyich Tchaikovsky, who passed away . . . at a time when his inspiration was not yet faded, when the artist might yet have given us more beautiful and powerful works. And it cannot be denied—with unprecedented unanimity, the society sought to express its worship, its affection for the departed composer-poet.

Still fresh in everyone's mind is the memory of universal sorrow, and of the solemn burial of the artist's body. This very solemnity, and the participation in it of even the Emperor himself, express the general mood of this event; the hundreds of wreaths testify to the consciousness of having lost a precious artist. Finally, there has been no lack of tributes in the press—a future biographer will find a wealth of material there, the most important being Mr Laroche's reminiscences about his late friend. . . . But hardly have there been *musical* 'obsequies' more powerful, sincere, and magnificent than Tchaikovsky's.

The remarkable circumstance here is that the Russian Opera, or rather, the Directorate of the Imperial Theatres—which, almost more than any

19. Tchaikovsky's funeral in the city streets, 28 October 1893

other institution, ought to have honoured Tchaikovsky's memory—
seemed to forget its duty, and the very day of the composer's burial a
second-rate French opera was performed in the evening at the Maryinsky
Theatre, while that morning the pediment of the theatre was still draped
in mourning. The Maryinsky Theatre took no part in the musical obsequies, if one does not count the singing of the opera chorus in the liturgy
at the Kazan Cathedral.

However, the Russian Musical Society, the Chamber Music Society, Mr
Bedyaev, the organizer of the 'Russian Symphonic Concerts', and other
Petersburg institutions have devoted an entire month and a half to the
memory of Tchaikovsky.

On Wednesday, 3 November 1893 two concerts—by the Chamber
Music Society and the Russian Quartet Society (in the hall of the
Conservatoire)—began a series of celebrations honouring the memory of
the musical artist. The magnificent, melancholy, and solemn *Andante
funebre e doloroso* from the E flat minor Quartet (No. 3, Op. 30) opened
the first of these concerts.

Tchaikovsky wrote his quartet while he was mourning the death of his
favourite violinist, Laub—and this same work served, as it were, as a

musical expression for the musician and artist of the marvellous, profound words 'eternal memory'. The Andante is full of sadness, full of sighs, so artistically expressed in one of its first phrases:

This Andante, despite it poetic and talented elaboration, produces such a melancholy, painful impression precisely because Tchaikovsky has splendidly conveyed the character of the Orthodox funeral song and recitative in the ecclesiastical spirit. Altogether this Andante was performed three times (two of these at the quartet concerts of the Imperial Russian Musical Society), and unfortunately not once was the E flat minor Quartet performed in its entirety, even though, of all Tchaikovsky's quartets, it is this one which is least familiar to the public.

Besides the Andante from the Third Quartet the Chamber Music Society also presented on the same evening the Second Quartet (Op. 22, in F major), with its marvellous, artful Scherzo (*Allegro giusto* in mixed 6/8 and 9/8 time), and the lovely sextet *Souvenir de Florence*, dedicated to the Society. The programme of the quartet evening at the Conservatoire was devoted to Tchaikovsky's first two quartets (Op. 11 and 22), as well as several of his songs. If we also add to this the remarkable and profoundly inspired trio (Op. 50) dedicated to the memory of Nikolay Rubinstein, which was performed at the second quartet concert of the Russian Musical Society, we have almost the entire series of chamber works written by Tchaikovsky. In them Tchaikovsky's genius is at times as vividly and poetically displayed as in his finest symphonic compositions. In this realm of music (chamber music, and in particular quartets) Tchaikovsky was a subtle, often witty (as for example in the Scherzo from the F major quartet), and, more often still, deeply poetic artist.

To hear this whole series of wonderful works was decidedly a pleasure.

The next concert dedicated to the memory of the well-loved composer was the second symphonic concert of the Imperial Russian Musical Society (on Saturday, 6 November), with the participation of Mr [Leopold]

Auer, the baritone Eugène Oudin, and Eduard Nápravník at the podium. The columns of the Hall of the Nobility behind the orchestra were decorated with tropical plants, from out of which rose a bust of the late composer by the sculptor Bach. The concert opened with a performance of Tchaikovsky's final work—his Sixth Symphony, the *Pathétique*. This time it made a powerful, and at moments profound, impression; with a second performance, and moreover one so excellent and, under Mr Nápravník's direction, so artistically polished, the Symphony in B minor benefited considerably.

After the symphony the beautiful Violin Concerto (D major, Op. 35) was performed by Leopold Auer (who also played the Andante from the First Quartet as an encore), and Eugène Oudin sang Onegin's arioso and two songs ('A Tear Trembles' and 'Serenade'). The final number on the programme was Tchaikovsky's first symphonic poem, or rather, his fantasy overture, *Romeo and Juliet*—that glorious youthful and profoundly poetic work by Tchaikovsky. This page—of tender, serene love—is one of the most perfect pages in Tchaikovsky's genius. Unfortunately the performance was too cool, not enthralling enough. On this evening Messrs Nápravník and Auer were honoured—the former with a laurel wreath, the latter with a lyre.

On Thursday, 11 November, the Society also devoted its second quartet concert to a celebration of the composer's memory, at which only the Op. 50 trio (in A minor), dedicated to 'the memory of a great artist', was new among Tchaikovsky's chamber works performed. The marvellously written piano part was played by Sergey Taneyev. The entire concert was repeated a second time on the afternoon of Sunday, 28 November, in the same hall of the Credit Society.

It should also be mentioned that the programmes of all these musical gatherings of the Imperial Russian Musical Society were decorated with a portrait of the late composer, as was the programme of the first Russian symphonic concert (on Saturday, 20 November, in the Hall of the Nobility), though here it looked more elegant.

This latter concert, with the participation of a famous opera singer, the pianist Felix Blumenfeld, and Nikolay Rimsky-Korsakov directing the orchestra, was one of the most interesting of the Petersburg concerts dedicated to Pyotr Tchaikovsky.

Tchaikovsky's Fourth Symphony (F minor, Op. 39), which opened the concert, belongs to his most successful and magnificent compositions. In my view, the finest movements are the first and the third, in particular the grandiose and powerful fanfare of brass instruments in the introductory *Andante sostenuto*, which makes such a strong and tremendous impression with its appearance at the end of the Finale. In addition, the main theme of the first movement is related to one of the 'Hades' motifs in the brilliant *Francesca* fantasy; the opus numbers (*Francesca* is Op. 32) demonstrate that Tchaikovsky was not yet free of the influence of his recent, truly inspired work. The Scherzo, a piece of exquisite filigree work, and which was repeated at the concert, is utterly charming. In general the entire symphony bears the traces of genuine creativity. *Francesca da Rimini*, performed after the symphony, is a brilliant work, in which Tchaikovsky's inspiration reached its highest limits. Together with *Romeo and Juliet*, *The Tempest*, and several passages from *Manfred*, this fantasy constitutes the late composer's finest and most wonderfully sumptuous monument. Both scenes, marvellous in their contrast—wild, frenzied Hades, in which even the moans are swept away in the horrific whirlwind, and the tender, marvellous, painfully passionate love of Francesca and Paolo—are amazingly fine and poetic.

Later Mme *** sang Joan's famous aria from the opera *The Maid of Orleans* and two songs, and the talented Mr Fel[ix] Blumenfeld played four piano pieces (including, for the first time, the lovely Impromptu in A flat major from the jubilee album for Anton Rubinstein and *Tendres Reproches* from Op. 72). The concert concluded with the *Slavonic March* (Op. 31), which belongs to Tchaikovsky's weakest works, despite its effective orchestration. In it Tchaikovsky took three Serbian folk melodies and added the weak, unsuccessful, and completely non-folk theme of [Alexey] Lvov's hymn 'God Save the Tsar'.

Two additional musical evenings were dedicated to the memory of Tchaikovsky. The first of these was 'An Evening of Church Singing', by the Arkhangelsky Chorus, organized in the hall of the Municipal Credit Society on 3 December, on the fortieth day after the composer's death, to benefit the Musical Artists' Fund (of which Tchaikovsky was a member). Besides a concerto by Bortnyansky and a second part which included a requiem by A. Arkhangelsky and a portion of his funeral mass, four passages were performed from Tchaikovsky's *Liturgy of St John Chrysostom*, which has rarely appeared in the programmes of our church concerts and seems never to have entered the repertoire of our church choirs (however, at the funeral mass at the Kazan Cathedral on 28 October the chorus of the Russian Opera also performed several passages from Tchaikovsky's liturgy).

Finally, on Sunday, 5 December, in the Hall of the Nobility Mr Raphof's school organized something in the way of a 'Franco-Russian funeral banquet'—an evening in memory of Tchaikovsky and Gounod, at which the students of the school performed songs, arias, and piano works by these composers, and even a few orchestral pieces.

But apart from all these musical evenings and concerts, there have been many other and frequent performances of works by the late Tchaikovsky in Petersburg lately, far too many to describe them all here; one private opera company even restaged one of Tchaikovsky's first works, his opera *The Oprichnik*.

But it is not only Petersburg that has solemnly celebrated Tchaikovsky's obsequies; Moscow, Kiev, Kharkov, Warsaw, Helsinki—almost every city where a circle of musicians is to be found—all have celebrated, perhaps not as richly but no less sincerely, the same musical obsequies. Finally even abroad, in the major musical capitals, everyone has hastened to pay his respects to the late artist.

And at these lavish obsequies, at this sorrowful celebration, strongest and saddest of all, like the artist's swan-song, sounds his final Andante from the *Pathétique* Symphony:

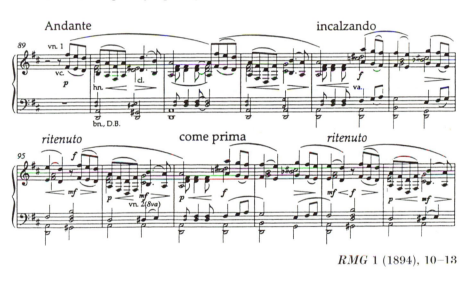

RMG 1 (1894), 10–13

The chapter starts with Lev Tolstoy's private reflections on Modest's account of Tchaikovsky's death—reflections which are reminiscent in their tone and import of the passages from his masterpiece *The Death of Ivan Ilyich* written seven years earlier, in 1887. This quotation stands in sombre contrast with the controversy that broke out in the press shortly after Tchaikovsky's funeral, which stemmed not from any suspicion of foul play or a subsequent cover-up by the family and physicians, but from a perception of incompetence on the part of the physicians. The conservative editor of the *New Times*, Alexey Suvorin, accused Lev Bertenson of malpractice and specifically of failure to call a medical consultation that might have saved his patient's life. The charge was unfair. After all, Lev Bertenson was himself a recognized expert, whose practice included 'the entire artistic world of the capital'. Ironically, he was unlucky with respect to musicians: it was he who some years earlier had attended Mussorgsky, enduring great embarrassment upon his death.

An issue made prominent by the newspapers in Tchaikovsky's case seems to have concerned Lev Bertenson's delay in prescribing for his patient the immersion in the bath, a treatment still believed—wrongly— by those of the period to produce a beneficial effect in cholera cases. It cannot be ruled out that Bertenson, who evidently suffered greatly from the futility of his efforts to save the composer, may himself have been plagued by a certain remorse in connection with the matter of the bath treatment: and that this may represent an alternative explanation for his inadvertent 'loss', mentioned earlier, of a day in the *New Times*, such that the reader might not realize that the bath was given to the patient not on Saturday, 23 October, but a day later, on Sunday,while the question of who was responsible for the delay might be side-stepped. Be that as it may, the sense of righteous indignation and indeed outrage at Suvorin's attack so visible in Lev Bertenson's private communication to Modest can hardly be reconciled with the theory that the two of them were actually guilty of far worse crimes, including perjury, fraud, or conspiracy.

Quite different questions raised by the St Petersburg press around the same time resulted in an official inquiry which made some very unsettling disclosures about the city's water supply. Particularly disturbing—and pertinent—was the finding that in all the restaurants and eating places of the city boiled water was routinely diluted with unboiled water before being served to patrons. As Tchaikovsky had taken a good many of his meals in restaurants, he could have contracted the *vibrio cholerae* at virtually any point over the course of the five days preceding the appearance of the first alarming symptoms.

The second part of the chapter reverts to the public perception of the Sixth Symphony. As mentioned earlier, the interpretation of the *Pathétique* as an alleged expression of Tchaikovsky's presentiment of his own death can be traced to the working of hindsight in the truly exceptional success of the second performance of that work on 6 November 1893 under the direction of Eduard Nápravník. Two reliable and expert witnesses— Nikolay Rimsky-Korsakov in this chapter and Nikolay Kashkin in the first chapter—both made it clear that such a connection was misguided. Yet the public, in the grip of its own emotions, refused to listen to the more sober voices, for the very reasons cited by Rimsky-Korsakov: the

suddenness of the death, the power of the music, the habit of superstition, and the desire for mystery so deeply imbedded in the human
psyche. All this could not fail to contribute to the emergence and circulation of the first of early fictions alleging Tchaikovsky's suicide, to which
Rimsky-Korsakov apparently alluded.

10

Hearsay

1890s

IVAN KLIMENKO

An architect and Tchaikovsky's friend from the early 1870s.

Soon after Pyotr Ilyich's death there appeared, and for a while perse-vered, a legend that he had died not from cholera, but because he had voluntarily poisoned himself. I personally started to believe in this leg-end without much difficulty after I became acquainted with the Sixth Symphony, the content of which seemed to provide enough reason to do so. Indeed, the general sombre mood that permeates all movements of the symphony, one may say, 'smells of death'. . . .

In the last movement of the symphony (*Adagio lamentoso*) the very first notes emanate utter hopelessness and irreparable anguish. Those heavy sighs which resound in the orchestra so powerfully describe the soul's suffering, the sombre mood rises to such an unbearable degree of tension that it becomes self-evident that only death the deliverer can stop all this torment. . . .

My interpretation of the Sixth Symphony's meaning was the very rea-son that the legend of Tchaikovsky's poisoning of himself seemed to me rather plausible, but I ceased to believe in it after I heard from Modest Tchaikovsky, Nikolay Kashkin, and the late Pyotr Jurgenson persistent assurances that in the last period of his life Pyotr Ilyich, while he was fully comfortable financially, was full of exceptional *joie de vivre*, high spirits, and an unstoppable creative urge and that, consequently, one could not speak at all of any predisposition on his part towards suicide.

I. A. Klimenko, *Piotr Il'ich Chaikovskii. Kratkii biograficheskii ocherk* (Moscow, 1909), 24–7

1900s

R. ALOYS MOOSER

Swiss musicologist and critic who worked in St Petersburg from 1896 to 1909. The following is a published summary of Mooser's account by his translator Mary Woodside.

It was during his [Mooser's] first winter in the capital that he heard the rumours of Tchaikovsky's homosexuality and some unspecified time later the related story of the composer's suicide, just three years before Mooser's arrival. His informant was Riccardo Drigo, composer and conductor of the Imperial ballet troupe, who had worked with Tchaikovsky on that composer's three ballets. Somewhat incredulous, Mooser verified the story with the composer Alexander Glazunov, whose upright moral character, veneration of the composer, and friendship with Tchaikovsky are stressed in his introduction as a 'witness'. . . .

Tchaikovsky is said to have seduced the son of his apartment custodian, precipitating a complaint to the police. The local commissariat, uncomfortable at dealing with such an accusation against a major public figure, passed the complaint upward through the chain of command until it reached the Tsar himself. His majesty, shocked, declared sentence at once: the man 'must disappear immediately.' This having been conveyed to the composer, the poor man, realizing his career was at an end, poisoned himself. . . .

Mooser finishes his account by inviting the reader to draw his own conclusion, indicating, I think, that he himself is not convinced that either tale is true.

Comment & Chronicle, *19th Century Music*, 13 (1990),
273–4

EKATERINA KAKHANOVA

Daughter of the senator Mikhail Kakhanov, the friend of Anatoly and Modest Tchaikovsky. The following is from her private diary of 1903.

For the entire day I kept reading [Modest's] biography of Pyotr Ilyich. I am pleased that the detailed description of the last year of his life removes every shadow [of credibility] as regards hints [current] in the public that he might have poisoned himself and that it was taken for cholera!

It is clear from his letters that the Sixth Symphony was written in such sad vein by chance in order to communicate the nostalgia he fell prey to during his solitary travels. It was called *Pathétique* also by chance and not by his own choice, but on the advice of Modest. [Tchaikovsky] was pleased with the realization that his talent had by no means been exhausted and the symphony succeeded, which from the spring of 1893 caused him to feel remarkably calm and cheerful. Meanwhile, his well-known phrase that this is his requiem only intensified the rumours within the public, and even Father, especially after he heard this symphony, tended to have his doubts and spoke about this in my presence to Anatoly. But knowing the love of both brothers for Pyotr Ilyich, even the possibility of such a suggestion, and now in particular, would have been painful to them, and given their commitment to the truth—in the case of Modest at times even excessive—[their knowledge of] could not have helped becoming transparent. . . .

RNB, f. 1000, op. 2, no. 588/1, 162–3

VASILY BERTENSON

Despite the fact that all thoughtful Russians, and not only Russians but also Europeans, stricken by such loss, read with intense interest all the details of Pyotr Ilyich's last days (in accounts written by his brother Modest and published in the *New Times* and the *News and Stock Exchange Gazette*), despite the presence at the patient's bedside of four physicians, there were people even then, as there are now, who declared confidently that Tchaikovsky did not die from cholera at all but perished from poison taken with the intention of committing suicide! . . .

Is it worth even speaking about such insinuations, particularly in the light of the nasty innuendoes about the reason that provoked the suicide?!

IV 128 (1912), 814

1920s

SERGEY DIAGHILEV

This memoir was written in 1928.

Various myths soon sprang up around the death of Tchaikovsky. Some said he caught cholera by drinking a glass of tap water at the Restaurant

Leiner. Certainly, we used to see Piotr Ilyitch eating there almost every day, but nobody at that time drank unbottled water, and it seemed inconceivable to us that Tchaikovsky should have done so.

Others invented the legend of Tchaikovsky's suicide, alleging that he poisoned himself for love of a certain member of his family [his nephew Vladimir Davidov], to whom he dedicated one of his principal works [the 'Pathétique']. These people claimed that if Tchaikovsky had really died of cholera his flat would have been put out of bounds; and that the cholera epidemic was over (he was, in fact, one of the last to die of it). I myself place little credence in these stories. I knew all of Tchaikovsky's circle, and was a close friend of the person who was alleged to have caused his death; and I think there is no evidence to support the theory of suicide.

Buckle, *Diaghilev*, 24

RICHARD SPECHT

German biographer of Brahms and other composers.

Perhaps [Brahms's] thoroughly sound nature became unconsciously aware of [Tchaikovsky's] homosexuality and was instinctively repelled by it, perhaps he merely disliked the all too mundane demeanour, the perfumed Cossack's savagery and gilt-edged melancholy, of the composer of the *Pathetic Symphony*, who was so elegant and yet so inwardly torn by the tragedy of his unhappy disposition, which at last drove him into voluntary death.

Richard Specht, *Johannes Brahms* (London, 1930), 289

1930s

NINA BERBEROVA

Tchaikovsky's biographer, distinguished Slavic scholar and memoirist. While working on the composer's biography in the 1930s, she met a few of Tchaikovsky's friends and relatives in Paris.

I asked [Vladimir Argutinsky-Dolgorukov, who belonged to Tchaikovsky's intimate circle in St Petersburg in the 1890s]: How was it that the descendants of Rimsky-Korsakov, who had survived the Revolution and emigrated to Paris, continue to spread the suicide story, as if there had

never been any cholera? [Argutinsky's] answer was clear. The Mlles
Purgold had decided in their youth that they would marry, one of them
Musorgsky, the other Tchaikovsky. Their plan had failed. One of them
had married Rimsky, and the other a certain Molas. Vindictive and en-
vious, known for their perverse initiatives and unpleasant natures, they
had launched that piece of tittle-tattle.

Nina Berberova, 'Looking Back at *Tchaikovsky*',
Yale Review, 80 (1992), 68

PRASKOVIYA TCHAIKOVSKY

> The wife of Anatoly Tchaikovsky, the composer's younger brother,
> emigrated to the West after 1917. This memoir was written at the
> end of the 1930s.

A number of biographies have appeared lately, containing the most extraordinary statements. Among these may be mentioned the legend that
he did not die of cholera, but that he poisoned himself. There is no truth
in this. The famous doctor, professor Bertenson, who attended him during his last illness, published daily bulletins. These still exist. Peter Ilyitch
was terrified of death and often said: 'I hope this vile sorceress will not
come near me for a long time.'

To me it seems that he had a dim presentiment of his approaching end.
It appears in the tragic music of his last Symphony, which he conducted
in person in the [Hall of the Nobility].

Music & Letters, 21 (1940), 109

ROSA NEWMARCH

> English writer on music; editor and translator of Modest Tchai-
> kovsky's biography of Tchaikovsky. She visited Russia many times,
> starting from 1897, where she had established contacts with contem-
> porary Russian musicians and scholars.

Several sensational accounts of the composer's end were widely circulated and received credence, but in view of the medical opinions, clearly
expressed, and the numerous trustworthy witnesses of his last days, the
foregoing account [Tchaikovsky's death from cholera] may be accepted
as authentic.

Grove's Dictionary of Music and Musicians, 5th edn., ed.
Eric Blom (London, 1954), viii. 338

1940s

YURY DAVYDOV

The following passage is taken from an unpublished version of his memoirs.

During the festivities to commemorate the centenary of Pyotr Ilyich's birth I had an opportunity to talk personally with a prominent physician, a disciple of Lev [Bertenson], who argued that the cause of Pyotr Ilyich's death had been poison and that Bertenson himself told him about this, saying that with cholera he covered up the true cause of death. But all this is nonsense. I testify with full conviction that the disease that drove Pyotr Ilyich into his grave was very real cholera with subsequent complications affecting the kidneys that caused uraemia, which the weakened organism failed to overcome.

Whether this signified a fact of malpractice is not for me to judge. One may suppose that the delay in taking the necessary measures against the complications in the kidneys was a fact, and the apologists of Dr Prof. Bertenson, by inventing the story of poison, intended thereby to excuse their master; this I may allow, but I do not doubt for a moment that a fact of poisoning never took place.

GDMC, DM^2, no. 26^1; *PBC* 166

The following is from the published version of Yury Davydov's memoirs.

On the pages of certain newspapers, but mainly in common conversation, doubts appeared as to the cause of death. People began to speak of poisoning, suicide, and other foolishness. Within the camp of Lev Bertenson's student's, there spread the version that the illness which had carried off Pyotr Ilyich was not cholera or its consequences, but poisoning, and that Lev Bertenson himself, they said, had told them about this. This is all nonsense. I testify with complete certainty that the illness which placed Pyotr Ilyich in the grave was most genuine cholera with subsequent complications of the kidneys, causing uraemia, with which the weakened organism proved unable to cope. Uraemia is actually the *poisoning* of the blood by the urine—might this have given rise to the false rumours?

VC (1980), 335–6

ALEXANDRA BOTKINA

Wife of St Petersburg physician Sergey Botkin.

I remember the bitter feeling that enveloped all of us during Pyotr Ilyich's stormy illness. The diagnosis of the doctors who attended him was cholera. But I remember deep doubts expressed by a group of physicians, the colleagues of my husband. It rather resembled an inflammation of the kidneys. The mystery was never revealed. His family physician Bertenson [Vasily] consulted only with his elder brother, but nobody besides them was admitted to the patient.[1] I remember Nevsky Prospect flooded with the sea of those who accompanied Pyotr Ilyich [i.e. the coffin with his body] to the Alexander Nevsky Monastery. Afterwards I often visited his grave when seventeen years later my husband was buried at the same cemetery.

A. P. Botkina, *Pavel Mikhailovich Tretyakov v zhizni i iskusstve* (Moscow, 1993), 218

1950s

OLGA TCHAIKOVSKAYA

Contemporary Russian journalist and distant relative of Tchaikovsky, who has heard suicide stories from the artistic circles in Moscow.

In 1949 *Literaturnaia Gazeta* [the *Literary Gazette*] received a letter from a woman who informed the paper that 'Tchaikovsky was murdered' and that she 'could tell this story of yet another disgraceful crime committed by the Tsarist government in every detail . . .'. Tchaikovsky's family physician and friend Vasily Bertenson administered poison to the composer at regular intervals on the orders of the Tsar. This nightmarish story reached the letter's author in the form of a family tradition according to which Bertenson, suffering from the pangs of conscience, confessed his crime when he was in his cups.

Ol'ga Chaikovskaia, 'Pikovye damy', *Novyi mir*, 10 (1986), 244

---

[1] This is an obvious error: we know that two more physicians and a medical attendant took part in the composer's treatment.

20. Tchaikovsky's grave at the Alexander Nevsky Monastery in St
Petersburg

NIKOLAY AVYERINO

Russian musician, a graduate of the Moscow Conservatoire, who
after 1917 lived in New York.

Lately even Pyotr Ilyich's death from natural causes has been subjected
to doubt. A persistent story started to circulate in which Tchaikovsky
committed suicide. It seemed that the poor Pyotr Ilyich was not allowed
even to die peacefully from natural causes; meanwhile, Tchaikovsky's
illness and its fatal outcome took place before the eyes of all and were
confirmed by the official testimony of such an authority as the late court
physician Lev Bertenson. On the other hand, and such formulation will
appear ridiculous to the sceptics who are convinced that medical evidence exists only for the purpose of being forgotten and that attention
paid to an artist and a creator may be caused only by some intimate
drama, by suicide. . . .

After Pyotr Ilyich's death the Sixth Symphony had been performed
again, this time under the conductorship of Eduard Nápravník. The symphony made a profound impression owing to its sombre, tragic character.
There were many reminiscences of the author's moods and presentiments
at the time of his composition. A prophetic character was ascribed to the
Sixth Symphony, but nobody doubted that the actual death of Pyotr
Ilyich was a natural, tragic accident. Nobody within the circle of friends
admitted any mention, or even a hint, of suicide. This version appeared
abroad and took on the character of a seductive sensation.

N. Av'erino, 'Moi vospominaniia o Chaikovskom',
Vozrozhdenie, 16 (1951), 104–5

JULIEN GREEN

French writer; the following is from his published diary of 28
September 1959.

Count Zubov [a Russian *émigré*] told me the other day that Tchaikovsky
did not die from cholera as it was said, but that he was poisoned because
of a scandal 'of which I can tell you no more' that was on the point of
exploding and reaching the ear of the Emperor.

Julien Green, *Journal: années 1946–1966* (Paris, 1967),
1380

1960s

NICOLAS SLONIMSKY

Distinguished Russian-born American musicographer, who never gave any credence to the rumours of Tchaikovsky's suicide.

A strange mass of unfounded rumours began circulating both in Russia and abroad shortly after Tchaikovsky's death that he committed 'suicide by cholera,' that he deliberately drank unboiled water during a raging cholera epidemic in St Petersburg, and this despite his fear of cholera, which had been the cause of his mother's death. The stories that I heard during my visit to Russia in 1962 were right out of Gothic horror tales. It seems that Tchaikovsky became involved in a homosexual affair with a young member of the Russian Imperial family, and that when Czar Alexander III got wind of it, he served the Tchaikovsky family an ultimatum: either have Tchaikovsky take poison, or have him tried for sodomy and sent to Siberia. Tchaikovsky accepted the verdict, and with connivance of his personal physician, Dr Bertenson, was given a poison that produced symptoms similar to those of cholera. As additional evidence that Tchaikovsky did not die of cholera, the proponents of this theory argue, is the fact that his body was allowed to lie in state and that several of his intimates kissed him on the mouth, as the Russian death ritual allows, whereas cholera victims were buried in zinc-lined sealed coffins to prevent contagion.

Baker's Biographical Dictionary of Musicians, ed. N. Slonimsky, 7th edn. (New York, 1984), p. xxviii

ALEXANDER VOITOV

A numismatist, self-styled historian of St Petersburg's Imperial School of Jurisprudence, from which he graduated in 1914. The following was written down by the musicographer Alexandra Orlova from Voitov's oral account shortly before his death in 1966.

Among the pupils who completed their studies at the School of Jurisprudence at the same time as Tchaikovsky there occurs the name Jacobi. When I was at school I spent all my holidays in Tsarskoe Selo with the family of Nikolay . . . Jacobi, who had been senior procurator to the Senate in the 1890s and who died in 1902. Jacobi's widow, Elizaveta . . . was connected with my parents by ties of affinity and friendship. She was very fond of me and welcomed me warmly. In 1913, when I was in the last but one class at the school, the twentieth anniversary of Tchaikovsky's death was widely commemorated. It was then, apparently under the influence of surging recollections, that Mrs. Jacobi, in great secrecy, told me the story which, she confessed, had long tormented her. She said that she had decided to reveal it to me because she was now old and felt that she had not the right to take to the grave such an important and terrible secret. 'You,' she said, 'are interested in the history of the school and in the fate of its pupils, and therefore you ought to know the whole truth, the more so since it is such a sad page in the school's history.' And this is what she told me.

The incident took place in the autumn of 1893. Tchaikovsky was threatened with terrible misfortune. Duke Stenbock-Fermor, disturbed by the attention which the composer was paying his young nephew, wrote a letter of accusation to the Tsar and handed the letter to Jacobi to pass on to Alexander III. Through exposure Tchaikovsky was threatened with the loss of his rights, with exile to Siberia, with inevitable disgrace. Exposure would also bring disgrace upon the School of Jurisprudence and upon all old boys of the school, Tchaikovsky's fellow students. Yet the honour of the school uniform was sacred. To avoid publicity Jacobi decided upon the following: he invited all Tchaikovsky's former schoolfriends [whom he could trace in St Petersburg] and set up a court of honour which included himself. Altogether there were eight people present. Elizaveta . . . sat with her needlework in her usual place alongside her husband's study. From time to time from within she could hear voices, sometimes loud and agitated, sometimes dropping apparently to a whisper. This went on for a very long time, almost five hours. Then Tchaikovsky came headlong out of the study. He was very white and agitated. All the others stayed for a long time in the study talking quietly. When they had gone, Jacobi told his wife, having made her swear absolute silence, what they had decided about the Stenbock-Fermor letter to the Tsar. Jacobi could not withhold it. And so the old boys [of the school] had come to a decision by which Tchaikovsky promised to abide. They required him to kill himself. . . . A day or two later, the news of the composer's mortal illness was circulating in St Petersburg.

Orlova, 'Tchaikovsky: The Last Chapter', 133–4

1970s

GALINA VON MECK

Daughter of Nikolay von Meck and Tchaikovsky's niece Anna Davydova. Since she was born in 1891, she had no memories of her great-uncle and heard various stories about Tchaikovsky from their mutual friends and relatives.

[On 21 October] the composer came back home seemingly very upset by something—we shall never really know what—and not feeling very well. He asked his brother for a glass of water. When told that he would have to wait for the water to be boiled (Petersburg water not being fit to drink unboiled as the town stood on boggy ground) he ignored his brother's protests, went into the kitchen, filled a glass of water from the tap and drank it, saying something like: 'Who cares anyway!'

That same evening he felt quite ill; the doctor who was sent for the next morning diagnosed cholera, which was then ever-present in Petersburg. Three days later the composer died in great agony.

I am not going here into full details about these last days of Tchaikovsky's life. There were, besides his brother Modest and the doctor, several other people present and the interpretation of some of the things said by the dying man in his agony, according to what I know from the composer's nephew, young Count Alexander Litke (Sania Litke) who was present, was completely different from the way his brother Modest related them. Anyway, the curse which Modest said was meant for my grandmother, Nadezhda von Meck, could not possibly have been directed towards her as Modest wanted it to be thought.

> P. I. Tchaikovsky, *Letters to his Family: An*
> *Autobiography*, trans. Galina von Meck (London, 1981),
> 555

1980s

ALEXANDRA ORLOVA

Soviet musicographer who emigrated to the West in 1979, bringing with her the above-mentioned 'court-of-honour' story.

By the 1920s Vasily Bertenson no longer concealed the truth about the cause of Tchaikovsky's death. And so he told the musicologist, Georgy Orlov, a friend of the now aged doctors's son, the pianist Nikolay Bertenson, that Tchaikovsky commited suicide. At about the same time the doctor Alexander Zander told the same story to his son Yury (Yury Zander was also a friend of Georgy Orlov and told him what his father had to said to him). All this became known to me too, since in the 1930s Georgy Orlov married me and we talked a lot about Tchaikovsky's death. Professor Alexander Ossovsky, the Director of the Research Institute for Music and Drama, where I worked after the war, also talked of Tchaikovsky's suicide. In other words the fact of the composer's suicide had long ceased to be a secret.

> Orlova, *Tchaikovsky: A Self-Portrait*, 411

NATALIYA KUZNETSOVA-VLADIMOVA

Granddaughter of Vera Kuznetsova (née Denisyeva), a younger
sister of the wife of Tchaikovsky's eldest brother Nikolay.

From my childhood I know for certain of Pyotr Ilyich Tchaikovsky's
suicide through my paternal grandmother, Vera Kuznetsova. . . . Her elder
sister, Olga, was married to Tchaikovsky's brother, Nikolay. Vera told
the very same version. . . . She lived in Leningrad . . . dying at the beginning of 1953 at a great age, but sound in mind and good in memory. [She
had heard it] probably from Olga, but in fact spoke of it most reluctantly,
seeing in this court a kind of besmirching of a gentleman's honour for
Tchaikovsky. But more than once she referred to Jacobi [the convener of
the court of honour] very aggressively. . . . Vera said that Alexander III
knew of the letter *after* Tchaikovsky's death.

I well remember that at our home in 1952 my grandmother talked with
Yury Slonimsky, the author of books on ballet, and when he said that the
cause of Tchaikovsky's suicide was that he had paid improper attention
to the heir [to the throne] she had corrected him. 'No, it was to the nephew
of Count Stenbok and not to the heir.'

Comment & Chronicle, 19th Century Music, 13 (1989), 74

Without any pretence at disclosing any new details, I want to tell what
I know from my family. Starting with my childhood I confidently knew
about Pyotr Ilyich Tchaikovsky's suicide and of its cause—and this is
why. My grandmother on my father's side—he was the theatre critic
Evgeny Kuznetsov . . . was Vera [Kuznetsova], née Denisyeva. Her elder
sister Olga was married to Nikolay Tchaikovsky, the brother of the composer. Olga died long before my birth; only from my family (most of all,
from Vera) I know that she was an intelligent woman, deeply religious
(without affectation), restrained, with firm character, by no means talkative, who often knew how to resolve problems that appeared insoluble.
Thus, she actively participated in the concealment of another 'secret'
linked to the Tchaikovsky brothers—she adopted an illegitimate child of
their niece Tanya Davydova, Georgy. His godfather was Pyotr Ilyich
who valued Olga highly and repeatedly wrote this in his letters to Modest.

I intentionally dwell on the personality of Olga in order to give an idea
of whose testimonies, in the form of my father's diary entries, were preserved in our family. In short, these testimonies are as follows: (1) The
death of P[yotr] I[lyich] Tchaikovsky did not result from cholera, but was
caused by suicide. (2) He himself chose the means of suicide and he himself

took the lethal dose of poison. (3) Tchaikovsky's family (in any event, his brother Nikolay who was present at P[yotr] I[lyich]'s death and Olga) knew about this. In Tchaikovsky's family and those of their in-laws this was kept secret: in it they saw enormous damage to the honour of their noble family, and to the great name of the composer himself. (4) As regards Tsar Alexander III, his connection to Tchaikovsky's death was rejected resolutely. I remember that when writers or actors visiting my father would imprudently touch on the version of the story that Pyotr Ilyich Tchaikovsky was compelled to depart from this life because of his exaggerated attention to the young heir apparent, my grandmother Vera used violently and aggressively to interfere. She liked to repeat the words of the Tsar (cited in Alexandra Orlova's article): 'We have many counts and barons, but only one Tchaikovsky.' She also used to say that there had proven to have been only two true noblemen in the whole tragedy— Tchaikovsky and Tsar Alexander III.

Kontinent, 58 (1989), 372–3

1990s

ANTHONY HOLDEN

An award-winning journalist and a popular biographer.

There were many different versions of Tchaikovsky's suicide doing the rounds. One maintained that he had been conducting a homosexual affair with a member of the imperial family—the Tsar's nephew, in some versions, even his son. Ordered by Alexander III to choose between standing trial for sodomy and committing suicide, the composer had ruefully compared himself with Socrates (the charge against whom was, after all, 'corrupting the youth') and opted for a slightly different version of the same dignified death. The Tsar had given him a revolver for the purpose, or a ring filled with arsenic, or both. Lacking the nerve to use the former, the composer had emptied the poison into a last glass of wine. . . . In the St Petersburg of 1993, the present author was even told that Modest had poisoned his brother, for stealing away his lover Lucien Guitry.

Holden, *Tchaikovsky*, 374–5

In nineteenth-century Russia the notion of homosexuality was often fraught with both medical and criminal connotations. Such associations posed a particular problem in the public mind when linked to a person whom well-deserved and world-wide fame had raised much above the ordinary. The public had to resolve this paradox according a psychological need not to denigrate, but rather to elevate the composer in the eyes of his audience, to enhance his share of national sympathy and universal affection. This could easily be achieved by postulating that he had suffered a constant, agonizing, and tragic crisis on account of his unorthodox—and thereby compromising—sexual tendencies. The man of genius, proven an unwilling pawn of forbidden passions, is found worthy then of compassion, not condemnation. He acquires a romantic halo, and through this, with its implied tragic catharsis, the conflict is resolved. And what could be more tragic and more cathartic in such circumstances than suicide?

Thus, regardless of actual events, mass psychology was already predisposed in Tchaikovsky's case to follow archetypal mythological patterns, which were needed to relieve the emotional tensions surrounding his personality and behaviour, and myth operated, in accordance with the formula of Lévi-Strauss, in its natural role of mediator. As regards the figure of Tchaikovsky, who was never an exclusively élite artist but, like no one else, a widely known great national composer, this mechanism of popular myth-making proved particularly apposite.

One accidental circumstance further contributed to such talk. Tchaikovsky's Sixth Symphony was performed on 16 October 1893, just eight days before his death. The reaction of the audience was mixed and somewhat perplexed. But the circumstances of the composer's illness and its aftermath altered drastically the subsequent public response to its music. At the memorial concert of 6 November under the direction of Eduard Nápravník, this same symphony created a tremendous sensation. The public read into this music not only a requiem that the composer had sung for himself, or a mere prophecy of his own imminent end, but even a tragic decision, born of inconsolable despair, to take his own life.

As result, a collection of bizarre and self-contradictory rumours circulated, in the course of several decades, within the same narrow stratum of the two capitals' artistic and semi-bohemian intelligentsia. In this chapter we decided to bring together chronologically the records of the suicide rumour. In contrast to the earlier parts of this book that are based almost solely on documents written by eyewitnesses, the material assembled here belongs to oral tradition that is at best second-hand.

One hopes that the evidence I have so far presented and discussed did demonstrate beyond any reasonable doubt that Tchaikovsky died from the complication of cholera. Consequently, the 'court of honour' tale would not even stand in need of rebuttal if it had not received such broad recognition in the West. But before one proceeds to analyse it further, the

reliability of its sources, as well as some other versions of the suicide legend must be assessed.

In the first place, all those rumours can be easily traced to the same
breeding ground, the bohemian and artistic, or sub-artistic, milieu of both
St Petersburg and Moscow, that is to say, a milieu fraught with a peculiar
mixture of philistinism and libertinage and singularly prone to the perpetuation of all manner of gossip and real or imagined psychodramas.
Although none of them are documented and they are known to us only
through oral transmission, such rumours are often wilfully attributed to
a source with a link, however tenuous, to Tchaikovsky's environment
(but never immediate), be it a member of the composer's extended family
(cf. Nataliya Kuznetsova-Vladimova), his professional colleagues (Aloys
Mooser), medical circles (Georgy Orlov), or his former schoolmates from
the School of Jurisprudence (Alexander Ossovsky and, indeed, the allegedly chief informant Alexander Voitov). It is true that as far as the plausible is concerned, the criteria are loose, and what seems utter nonsense
to one person will make perfect sense to another. Thus, to a promoter of
the 'court of honour' theory the idea that the composer was forced to kill
himself by his brother would seem totally wild whereas an adherent of
that latter theory could with equal legitimacy claim that the convoluted
tale of 'conspiracy-cum-suicide' sounds even wilder. From a scholarly point
of view, however, in the absence of documentary evidence, none of this
merits greater consideration than any fantasy one might care to invent—
for instance, that Tchaikovsky was murdered by a Rimsky-Korsakov,
gnawed by artistic envy, just as Mozart was allegedly poisoned by Salieri.

One must also point out the virtual incompatibility of the rumours.
Mooser heard that Tchaikovsky's removal was ordered personally by
the Tsar on account of the complaint made by the custodian about the
composer's relationship with his son. In another version it was Vasily
Bertenson who acted on the Tsar's orders. Others take pains entirely to
deny the Tsar's involvement: thus, according to Kuznetsova-Vladimova,
her informant Vera Denisyeva went so far as to claim that there were
only two 'true noblemen' in the whole affair—Tchaikovsky and Alexander III. The custodian's son was elevated meanwhile to a member of
the aristocratic Stenbock-Fermors and even the Imperial family, as Ni-
colas Slonimsky was told. Conversely, it appears that neither Alexander
Ossovsky nor Georgy Orlov knew or had anything to say about the 'old
boys' conspiracy' or the 'court of honour'.

What must be resolutely ruled out is the idea that the suicide rumours
could have originated from, or been supported by some 'confession of
truth' or 'confidences' by one of the Bertenson brothers, allegedly shared
with various individuals. The earlier cited documents, namely, Modest

Tchaikovsky's telegram to Vasily Bertenson on Sunday, 24 October on the course of his brother's treatment, and Vasily Bertenson's private letter to Modest of 20 June 1905 on the subject of cholera prove that this doctor must have believed it was the very disease from which his famous patient died.[2] If the story of Vasily Bertenson's 'confession' in his old age is not entirely invented, he must have made it in a state of senility, when people are prone to play out their fantasies and appropriate experiences not their own. Whatever Dr Zander's son may have said to Georgy Orlov must rest with his own conscience. Common sense suggests, however, that if the four physicians were guilty of such gross professional misconduct as covering up a crime, be it a suicide or a murder, to acknowledge this to even their immediate family or close friends would have courted disaster. On the other hand, as Yury Davydov not unreasonably implies, the rumours may well have been encouraged by Lev Bertenson's disciples and admirers in order to exculpate the doctor from the charge of malpractice.

Aside from Alexander Voitov's story, which will be given due consideration later, only two other extant accounts of the composer's supposed suicide offer a variety of detail—one by Aloys Mooser, citing the ballet conductor Riccardo Drigo as his source, and another by Nataliya Kuznetsova-Vladimova, with the reference to her grandmother, Vera Denisyeva, who was in turn a sister of Olga (née Denisyeva), married to Tchaikovsky's elder brother Nikolay. The story told by Mooser about Tchaikovsky's alleged affair with the son of a custodian and the subsequent punishment inflicted by the Tsar makes little sense although it better conforms to the actual pattern of the composer's sexual behaviour than Voitov's claim of his involvement with a young aristocrat: over the years he made it his habit to seek erotic encounters primarily with members of the lower classes and to avoid those of his own or of higher social standing. It is not inconceivable that during his visits to the capital in the course of the last year Tchaikovsky did develop a liaison with some such young man: this would have concurred with the not entirely reliable piece of evidence that can be traced, via Galina von Meck, to Alexander Litke, according to which shortly before, or even on the day when he became ill, the composer was harassed on the street by an apparently common woman who accused him 'of having something to do' with her son.[3] But, as it was earlier demonstrated, any prosecution of a prominent member of the society on such grounds would have been impossible, while the chance that a complaint registered by a simple caretaker might ever reach the

---

[2] GDMC, B[10], no. 468

[3] BBC Archives, LP 35621, front, band 2; this episode is also mentioned in John Warrack, *Tchaikovsky* (London, 1973), 269. I am particularly grateful to Leonard Forman, who provided me with the transcript of Galina von Mech's BBC interviews.

attention of the Emperor was virtually non-existent. Even less likely is
the reaction attributed to Alexander III, who is known to have covered
up several homosexual scandals involving various of his relatives and
associates. In fact, both the state and private papers of the Imperial family (Alexander III's note on the petition about Tchaikovsky's funeral; the
entries from the diaries of the Grand Duke Konstantin Konstantinovich
and the future Nicholas II) prove that their grief was entirely genuine. As
for the reported confirmation of Drigo's story by Alexander Glazunov,
Mooser's report is fraught with another set of logical and psychological
inconsistencies. Given the fact, repeatedly emphasized by Mooser and
others, of Glazunov's high moral probity, he could not have confirmed
the suicide story unless he had heard it from an unimpeachable source.
Such a source could only have been someone from Tchaikovsky's most
intimate circle, someone who had been present at the composer's death-
bed and who, presumably, had participated in the alleged cover-up. It is
obvious that anyone from this group who dared to reveal the 'truth' to
Glazunov would have done so only after swearing him to the strictest
secrecy—which makes it inconceivable that Glazunov would then turn
round and share this information with Mooser, whom he barely knew. If,
then, Mooser's account of his conversation with Glazunov is to be cred-
ited at all, one must assume that the latter confirmed simply the fact of
Tchaikovsky's homosexuality (which was an open secret anyway) and
the existence of the suicide rumours.[4] It is also possible, of course, that,
being unfamiliar with the exact and more recent findings about the spread
of cholera, he might have been, like Rimsky-Korsakov, somewhat troubled to see the open casket at the early requiems. Yet it would be preposterous to maintain that he could have possessed any first-hand knowledge
about such matters as a custodian's complaint or the Emperor's alleged
response to it. In any event, Glazunov's own memoirs, which appeared in
Russia in 1924 during a period when censorship was negligible, speak
only of Tchaikovsky's 'fatal illness' and contain no hint of a supposed
suicide. Nor did he mention it in private communications with Nina
Berberova when, working on her biography of the composer, she met
Glazunov in Paris in the early 1930s.[5]

Mooser's memoirs offer one other curious postscript, introducing a
person described as the composer's great-nephew by the name of Yaroslav

[4] The same applies to the information on Tchaikovsky's alleged suicide which, according to
André Lischke, Glazunov shared with his father; see Brown, *Tchaikovsky Remembered*, 223;
Lischke, *Tchaikovski*, 326, 1103.

[5] Nina Berberova, 'Looking Back at *Tchaikovsky*', 62; Nina Berberova, Malcolm H. Brown,
Simon Karlinsky, 'Tchaikovsky's Suicide Reconsidered: A Rebuttal', *High Fidelity*, 31 (1981),
49.

Tchaikovsky who died in Geneva in 1966 and left a lengthy autobio-
graphical manuscript.[6] It has thus far proved impossible to place this
Yaroslav within the Tchaikovsky family tree, so one cannot rule out that
he may have been an impostor. Be that as it may, his manuscript was
made available to Mooser, who reports that in it Yaroslav, while acknow-
ledging the composer's homosexuality, claimed, however, that Tchaikovsky never yielded to his erotic desires (which we know to have been
patently untrue) but rather, driven to suicide because of the torment he
felt over these 'abnormal impulses', ended his life by purposely drinking
a glass of unboiled water during the cholera epidemics, that is to say, by
playing 'Russian roulette'. In itself, this was a kind of idea bound to
capture the imagination of certain authors and thus join what constitutes
now the lore of 'Tchaikovskiana'.

   Unlike Mooser, Nataliya Kuznetsova-Vladimova, hailed by the supporters of the suicide theory as provider of new evidence confirming
Voitov's story, is not Tchaikovsky's but our contemporary, which means
that the family tradition to which she refers was passed across two gen-
erations. Her letters on this matter were published in both English and
Russian, and anyone looking to uncover inconsistencies there is certain to
find them. (Thus, for instance, her Russian statement does not mention
at all the Jacobis, the Stenbocks, or even the 'court of honour'). She
herself was born long after the death of her great-aunt Olga Denisyeva,
the wife of Nikolay Tchaikovsky, who is said to have been the ultimate
source of the tradition regarding the composer's death. Consequently,
Mrs Kuznetsova-Vladimova's immediate informant was her grandmother
and Olga's sister Vera, through whom, we are told, she knew of Tchaikovsky's suicide 'from childhood'—along with the 'conspiracy-cum-suicide'—and even that he himself had chosen the manner of his death. The
English text tells us that Vera 'probably' heard the story from Olga, while
in the Russian version we read that Olga's testimony was preserved in
the diary of Mrs Kuznetsova-Vladimova's father and Vera's son, the art
and theatre critic Evgeny Kuznetsov, who belonged to the same circles of
the intelligentsia as all the other promoters of the suicide rumours. However, any belief that Tchaikovsky's eldest brother (who was present at
the composer's bedside) or, by extension, his wife may have known about
the alleged 'conspiracy-cum-suicide' is disproved by the recently published notes made by Nikolay Tchaikovsky for strictly private use in May
1894 in which, apparently with a view to magical numerology, he tried to
calculate the significance of numbers 3 and 13 in the late composer's life

---

[6] Mooser's memoirs were graciously made available to me by their translator, Professor Mary
Woodside, of the University of Guelph, Canada.

and twice mentions the 'illness' that carried him away.[7] To conclude, the 'evidence' supplied by Mrs Kuznetsova-Vladimova offers nothing 'new' and, at best, only allows one to infer that the rumour linking Tchaikovsky's death with the School of Jurisprudence and the Counts Stenbock-Fermor may have existed independently from Voitov. No rumour can be given credence unless it is authenticated by documents, regardless of whether it circulates within or without a closely knit group of people, such as a family or a circle of friends. In this connection, it is worth observing that most of Tchaikovsky's relatives—among them Alexander Litke, Galina von Meck, and Praskoviya Tchaikovsky—seem to have been appalled by the perpetuation of the rumours of suicide.[8] In print and in private conversation, in both official statements and informal remarks, they have all denounced each new and unwarranted version of the suicide theory as utterly groundless. As in the case of Tchaikovsky's physicians, to propose that this same group of people, who were allegedly guarding an explosive family secret, would then turn round and let it be leaked to a variety of individuals with a risk of it becoming public knowledge, would defy both psychology and common sense.

One more comment is required to elucidate a piece of information which in appearance pertains to the incident that may or may not have occurred fifteen years before Tchaikovsky's death, namely, Nikolay Kashkin's testimony, written in 1918, regarding the conversation he had with the composer during one of his visits to Klin.[9] According to Kashkin, Tchaikovsky confided in him the story of his failed attempt to commit suicide sometime in the midst of his marital crisis in the autumn of 1877, before he made up his mind to leave his wife for good and flee abroad. In his singular confession the composer is said to have described how one night, in a moment of dark despair, he purposely waded into the freezing waters of the Moskva River in the hope of contracting a fatal case of pneumonia. In this way, he reportedly told Kashkin, his death might appear to be the result of natural causes, thereby sparing his family any

---

[7] *PBC* 190–1.

[8] Tchaikovsky's nephew, Yury Davydov represents a special case; he obviously suffered from an excess of imagination, inventing stories about his uncle, such as the famous episode of the glass of water in Leiner's restaurant, although he was not even present on that occasion, and collaborating with Yury Yuryev in regard to the latter's equally fraudulent memoirs about the same episode. This tendency for myth-making explains why Yury Davydov, while firmly denying, both in public lectures and published reminiscences, any truth in the suicide rumours, was none the less capable, in the course of private conversation, and for the sake of dramatic effect, suddenly to declare that Tchaikovsky had indeed taken poison.

[9] N. D. Kashkin, 'Iz vospominanii o P. I. Chaikovskom', *Proshloe russkoi muzyki: materialy i issledovaniia*, i. *P. I. Chaikovskii* (Petrograd, 1920), 99–132; English translation: David Brown, *Tchaikovsky Remembered* (London, 1993), 50–63.

unnecessary additional pain. Fortunately, the adventure passed with no consequences.

Not surprisingly, the supporters of the suicide theory exploited the episode to the utmost. If Tchaikovsky had the heart to wade into the icy river in that moment of trial, runs their thesis, he would have surely have had no compunction in poisoning himself in an hour of even greater stress or if ordered to do so. Their argument disregards even for a moment a possibility that, told in retrospect, the story could have been imagined, embellished, or drawn out of proportion, by Kashkin or even Tchaikovsky himself. Most important, however, is to recognize that even if everything did take place exactly as reported, this still does not warrant the conclusion reached by the champions of the composer's suicide. If one compares the two stories—that of Tchaikovsky wading into the river in the hope of contracting pneumonia and that of the same man taking poison with the purpose of appearing to have died of cholera—one discerns perhaps subtle but essential differences in the supposed pattern of behaviour. In the former case, Tchaikovsky could not have known whether his plan world succeed, that is, whether he would actually fall ill and die. In the latter case, there would be no room for uncertainty: arsenic poison is a decidedly lethal agent. Moreover, when taking poison the composer could in no way have ensured or indeed foreseen that his physicians would have agreed to falsify the medical records by declaring him dead from cholera so that no disgrace would be brought to his family—which was, after all, a chief point in the pneumonia plan.[10] Psychologists tell us that behavioural patterns in response to the challenge of crisis belong to fixed individual faculties and do not change. As his conduct at the time of his marriage shows, Tchaikovsky's prevailing pattern of response was to flee from danger, not to kill himself. As for the story of his botched attempt to give himself pneumonia, it suggests, if taken at face value, not so much a suicidal determination as the idea of *amor fati*, a reliance on fate, and is indeed more consonant with the view that the composer may have played some game of 'Russian roulette' by deliberately drinking a glass of unboiled water in the midst of a cholera epidemic—with the outcome of which he could not be certain. But then this particular theory clearly does not square with the belief in poison or a 'court of honour'. Furthermore, since there exists not a single scrap of evidence to the effect that in the autumn of 1893 Tchaikovsky actually faced a crisis which might have impelled him to court death, it must be firmly put to rest.

---

[10] Holden goes so far as to propose that it was in fact the doctors 'who advised Tchaikovsky that counterfeiting cholera by taking arsenic was the way to avoid disgrace and exposure'. This is a preposterous notion, charging four respected physicians with accessory to suicide *before* the event! (Holden, *Tchaikovsky*, 399).

It is now time to address the most picturesque and detailed version of the suicide legend, ascribed by its popularizer Alexandra Orlova to one Alexander Voitov, a self-styled historian of the School of Jurisprudence from which he graduated in 1914. It means that he was born three years after Tchaikovsky's death and had reached 17 when he is supposed to have heard the 'court of honour' story. Consequently, Voitov did not belong among the composer's contemporaries, as did Aloys Mooser, but was one generation closer to him than Nataliya Kuznetsova-Vladimova. On the other hand, Voitov's immediate informant, Ekaterina Jacobi, must have been of advanced age by the time of their encounter, at least, over 70, when she was speaking about the events which had allegedly occurred twenty years earlier.

What strikes us in the various arguments put forth so far by the champions of the 'conspiracy-cum-suicide' theory is their failure to abide by the elementary rules of scholarly procedure and to test their sensational 'findings' against the known and established facts. Elsewhere I took pains to refute in minute detail their so-called 'evidence' related to medical matters such as the epidemiology of cholera, precautionary measures, and the operation of poisons.[11] Similarly, they never bothered to verify even the biographical data regarding the very dramatis personae of the tale, the Jacobis and the Stenbock-Fermors, confusing such particulars as the first name of Nikolay Jacobi's widow or his own rank and office. None of them actually made an enquiry into the circumstances of the Stenbock-Fermor family who, according to the story, set the entire tragedy in motion, although this could elucidate important aspects of the controversy and conceivably even sober up some of the gullible.[12] No one by the name

---

[11] Poznansky, 'Tchaikovsky's Suicide', 206–12.

[12] Anthony Holden merely reproduces my own findings on Stenbock-Fermor's family with the addition of a few irrelevant details. But his attempt to identify the addressee of Tchaikovsky's short undated note, which he claims to have discovered in St Petersburg public library, as the young Alexander Stenbock-Fermor is entirely without foundation. The note runs: 'Much respected Alexander Vladimirovich, I can come to you tomorrow only at 11 o'clock. It is impossible for me to come before that. If it is not convenient for you, please let me know. I am all yours P. I. Tchaikovsky' (Holden, *Tchaikovsky*, 382). Known by Tchaikovsky's scholars for quite some time and published in the composer's collected letters in 1981, this note is nothing but an ordinary business letter and, despite Holden's (who has no knowledge of Russian) assertion to the contrary, makes not the slightest hint at intimacy. The letter is entirely official in tone and Holden is mistaken in the belief that Russian 'ves' vash' [all yours] (incorrectly translated 'I am all yours') is any more affectionate an expression than 'yours always' in English. In reality it is merely a calque from the French 'tout à vous' and the same formula was used by Tchaikovsky in many other official letters. Moreover, this note comes not from the Stenbock-Fermors but from the archive deposition of the Adlerberg family and must have been addressed to Count Alexander Vladimirovich Adlerberg, who was an official in the Directorate of Imperial Russian Theatres and in 1886 negotiated with Tchaikovsky on the matter of the singer Alexandra Panaeva-Kartseva, who was the composer's relative, and her further theatrical career.

Stenbock-Fermor is mentioned in any known source relevant to Tchaikovsky, although at least six families so called (that is, the two branches, the Stenbocks and the Stenbock-Fermors) resided in St Petersburg and its environs in the 1890s. Genealogical research shows that the only young man who might conceivably fit within the framework of the 'old boys, conspiracy' theory would have been Alexander Stenbock-Fermor, the son of Count (not 'Duke'—there were no dukes in Russia!) Vladimir Stenbock-Fermor. In that case, the enraged uncle who allegedly proceeded to bring a complaint before the Tsar could only have been Alexey Stenbock-Fermor, Equerry at the court of Alexander III. This man was clearly an influential figure and could easily have handed his complaint to the Tsar personally, without resorting to an intermediary in the person of Nikolay Jacobi. But his very status indicates that he was an experienced courtier who must have been well aware of the homosexual practices prevalent both within the Imperial family itself and among the highest echelons of the bureaucratic establishment. Another member of the clan, Herman Stenbock, was actually Superintendent of the Household of the homosexual Grand Duke Sergey Aleksandrovich and a cousin of the distinguished court official, Count Vladimir Lamsdorf, a future foreign minister and another homosexual. Through Herman and Alexey alone, all the Stenbocks and Stenbock-Fermors alike would certainly have been aware of how unpropitious the situation at court would be for any attempt at the homosexual exposure of someone enjoying social, political, or cultural prominence. In fact, the conduct ascribed to them in Voitov's story would have been self-destructive. By creating an atmosphere of scandal around so delicate an issue they would have endangered the interests and prestige of their entire family.[13]

Enough has been said here and elsewhere on the attitudes to homosexuality in nineteenth-century Russia to warrant the conclusion that Tchaikovsky had nothing to fear even in the case of an impending scandal. It must be further emphasized, however, that the School of Jurisprudence was by no means a bastion of moral probity as the believers in the 'old boys' conspiracy' wish to portray it. Adolescent debauchery of every description flourished at the School. We have an obscene paean to the joys of homosexuality written by its students, which was published in a limited edition of Russian pornographic poetry in 1879 with the note that the hymn was very much in vogue within the School's walls. It is true that in 1860 there occurred a travesty of a 'court' convoked at the instigation of one Vladimir Taneyev (the elder brother of the composer Sergey Taneyev, one of Tchaikovsky's close friends) in order to deliberate on a

---

[13] Ibid. 203–4.

case of homosexual rape committed by a fellow student Vladimir Zubov.[14] An accurate study of this mock trial reveals, however, in the first place, the extreme indifference of the participants to the moral aspects of the affair and, in the second, that the final verdict was objectively made in favour of the accused.[15] Furthermore, it can be established that this so-called trial was the only one in the annals of the School of Jurisprudence.

In addition to his own homosexual brother Modest, at least four of Tchaikovsky's friends who were also homosexual graduated from the School of Jurisprudence: Vladimir Adamov, who became an official in the Ministry of Justice, the landowner Nikolay Kondratyev, as well as two very prominent men, the repeatedly mentioned poet Alexey Apukhtin and the statesman Prince Vladimir Meshchersky, the former known for his provocative behaviour and mordant wit, the latter grown to become the *éminence grise* behind the throne during the reigns of both Alexander III and Nicholas II.

Against all this background it seems most unlikely that anyone associated with the School of Jurisprudence, least of all the group of learned lawyers, would have been inclined to risk ruining their careers by undertaking a moral crusade that included the twofold crime of blackmail and murder in order to 'save' the prestige of that institution, not to mention the incommensurability of the alleged fault (a mere courtship) and punishment with death.

A further absurdity of the alleged conspiracy becomes clear with the recognition that Modest did request several of his late brother's classmates, such as Vladimir Gerard and Ivan Turchaninov, whom the supporters of the suicide theory number among his 'judges' and actual executioners, to produce their reminiscences of his years in the School.

Earlier I listed the options Tchaikovsky could have pursued if he had wished to avoid an impending scandal—from the appeal to the high-placed patrons to temporary withdrawal abroad. The nonsense inherent in the 'court of honour story' becomes all the more palpable when one contrasts the alleged conduct of his persecutors with at least one infinitely more plausible alternative which would almost certainly have been the advice to them of a professional lawyer such as Nikolay Jacobi. The fact of the matter is that were the Stenbock-Fermors truly determined to safeguard the chastity of their young relative from the composer's advances, no appeal to the Emperor was necessary. They needed only to negotiate with Tchaikovsky himself either directly or through an intermediary, which would fully conform to accepted norms of behaviour. Knowing

---

[14] V. I. Taneev, *Detstvo. Iunost'. Mysli o budushchem* (Moscow, 1959), 399–401.
[15] Poznansky, *Tchaikovsky*, 36–7.

Tchaikovsky's character, there can be no doubt that he would have pledged to leave the young Stenbock alone, whoever he may have been.

That the 'court of honour' simply could not have happened in the period where it is placed by its defenders clearly follows from an accurate reading of the chronology. The material presented in this book leaves no room at all for five or more hours of Tchaikovsky's unaccounted movements during his entire stay in St Petersburg. One remembers that, according to Voitov, the gathering took place in Nikolay Jacobi's house in Tsarskoe Selo: the round trip to this suburb of the capital would have taken four hours at the very least, and the same Voitov insisted that the proceedings 'went on for a very long time, almost five hours'. One cannot even allow that the informant made an error and that the meeting occurred in St Petersburg: it can be easily ascertained that Nikolay Jacobi had no other address besides Tsarskoe Selo, that is to say, he possessed no residence in the capital.[16] A further possibility that the group might have been convened elsewhere, for instance, in the city apartment of another conspirator, must be similarly ruled out as it would have excluded the presence of Mrs Jacobi with her needlework, who is claimed by Voitov as the principal eyewitness.

At the earlier stage of the controversy Tuesday, 19 October was proposed as the only possible date of the alleged trial on the grounds, we were told, that it was the only day for which we do not possess the full account of the composer's whereabouts except that in the evening he attended the performance of Rubinstein's *Die Makkabäer*.[17] This proved, however, wrong since it is documented that in the afternoon the composer was visited in his apartment by the managers of the Kononov company who negotiated with him over the revision and production of his opera *The Oprichnik*, to which he agreed. Later a truly improbable dating was claimed that resembles more a gesture of desperation, namely, that the entire affair occurred on Thursday, 21 October, the very day when Tchaikovsky was taken ill.[18] This simply would not do: several of his activities during that day were observed by witnesses other than Modest who, according to the logic of the suicide theory, cannot be trusted at all: the composer's abortive visit at eleven o'clock to Eduard Nápravník is confirmed by the independent testimony of the latter's son Vladimir; he had lunch with the piano manufacturer Fyodor Mülbach, and around five in the afternoon he was found at home by the visitor Alexander Glazunov already quite ill. This leaves only the night and early morning for a visit

---

[16] See under the name Jacobi in the city directory *Ves' Peterburg*.
[17] Orlova, 'Tchaikovsky: The Last Chapter', 134.
[18] Orlova, *Tchaikovsky*, 413.

to Tsarskoe Selo which means that he had to depart from the city almost immediately after the meal at Leiner's restaurant, and one is required to imagine that several very busy men spent the start of their workday debating the blackmail and murder of Russia's most famous composer, while the wife of one of the men all the time 'sat with her needlework in her usual place alongside her husband's study'! Incidentally, both Tuesday and Thursday were regular business days, and it follows that the alleged instigator of the proceedings, Nikolay Jacobi, would have had to go to considerable trouble to persuade seven other prominent civil servants to neglect their duty and join him in Tsarskoe Selo. A far more logical course of action would have been for him to schedule the event, for instance, for the weekend since no one could anticipate that in a few days Tchaikovsky, a sudden victim of cholera, would be suffering the throes of agony and fighting death.

Since it was demonstrated that no 'trial' could have conceivably taken place in the period under discussion, any speculation about when the composer might have received and consumed the poison, thus submitting to an imaginary verdict of a self-appointed 'court', is a priori idle. The suggestion that the actual carrier of the deadly stuff was the lawyer August Gerke, an old acquaintance whom Tchaikovsky visited on the day before he fell ill to consult him on a matter of business, is totally incompatible with the archival material that includes Gerke's private papers showing desperate concern about his friend's condition and unquestioned belief in cholera. As a footnote, one has to mention in this context a quote from Galina von Meck, which the suicide theorists tried to exploit in support of their views arguing that if on 21 October Tchaikovsky was prepared to drink the glass of unboiled water, despite his brother's protests, with the cry 'Who cares anyway!', he must have already swallowed by then the fatal poison, or prepared to do so shortly. But in fact, the episode reported by the composer's great-niece (who was born only two years before his death), reiterating the familiar motif of unboiled water, means nothing of the sort. Even if one considers it authentic, it merely confirms Modest's claim of his brother's growing indisposition on that day after his abortive visit to the Nápravníks. Obviously, Tchaikovsky was upset by stomach spasms and diarrhoea as well as by thirst (another symptom of cholera) which may easily explain both his utterance and impatience. One observes that Galina von Meck named no source in regard to this particular episode, although she specifies that it was Alexander Litke who told her about 'some of the things said by the dying man in his agony' and was present at the composer's bedside. It must be added that both she and Litke repeatedly spoke against suicide rumours with an unequivocal insistence that Tchaikovsky died from cholera.

As was the case with the 'court of honour', it is demonstrable that the alleged subsequent cover-up could not conceivably have happened. All four physicians who treated Tchaikovsky enjoyed flawless reputations. After Mussorgsky's death, whom he tried to help battle with his chronic alcoholism, Lev Bertenson was always extremely sensitive to anything that might affect his medical prestige. For someone of his professional and social stature to preside over the cover-up of a criminal venture that involved blackmail, sexual scandal, and virtual murder would have meant not only the desecration of his Hippocratic oath, but the risk of utterly ruining his career and forever staining his name in the eyes of posterity— a risk which would have far outweighed any sympathy he might have felt for the composer or for Modest. The same applies also to the three other doctors. Furthermore, it is clear that any cover-up on the scale needed by the circumstances would have required the complicity not only of Tchaikovsky's physicians, relatives, and friends, but that of many more individuals including public and government officials, clergy, and journalists. The very belief that members of the medical or ecclesiastical profession can easily be forced, against their conscience, into full submission by the order of the state bears an indelible stamp of Soviet mentality. This was indeed almost universally true under the Bolshevik rule. It is also true that in pre-revolutionary Russia the Orthodox Church functioned to a large extent as a branch of the state and was supervised by Imperial appointment—but only so far as it concerned political and ideological issues, and not matters of individual Christian conscience where the clergy were adamant and would have hardly consented to bury a suicide on sacred ground and in accordance with the canonical rites. It is also worth emphasizing that not a single newspaper publication that covered Tchaikovsky's death or its aftermath contains even the remotest hint of any activities behind the scenes, and this is true not only of official or respectable periodicals, but also of what would today be called tabloids, which would not have hesitated to create a sensation. The conclusive evidence against any attempts at cover-up are, however, found in the private papers of Tchaikovsky's family and friends which were never intended for publication, such as Modest's telegram to Vasily Bertenson and their later exchange on the subject of cholera; entries in the Grand Duke Konstantin's diary; the private notes of August Gerke and Nikolay Tchaikovsky; and the correspondence of Modest and Bob Davydov dated July 1898, in which they discussed in some detail problems of the composer's health, such as the recurrent stomach disorder, which prepared, in Bob Davydov's own words, 'the ultimate ground for terminal illness'.

In the end, one must address, albeit very tentatively, the question of who might have been responsible for the birth and spread of the rumours alleging Tchaikovsky's suicide. There is no doubt that the suicide myth concurred with psychological exigencies of popular imagination troubled by the fact that the famous man whose private life was shrouded in some kind of secrecy suddenly died from a disease usually associated with the poor and the needy. As it happens, the myth served as the mediator between public romanticism in response to the composer's exalted social and cultural status, and the mundane character of the way he died.

There seem to have been at least three stages in the development of the suicide rumours and several axes along which they evolved. Judging by the hints in such sources as the testimonies of Ivan Klimenko and Ekaterina Kakhanova, the original gossip, that must have arisen soon after the composer's death from the powerful impact made on the audience by the first posthumous performance of the *Pathétique*, concerned a sort of 'fatal attraction', that is, the claim that Tchaikovsky took his life because of unrequited love, presumably for his nephew Bob Davydov, to whom the 'morbid' Symphony is dedicated. It was said that Rimsky-Korsakov's relatives and descendants (although he himself seems never to have given credence to such talk) used to disseminate the suicide version in Russia, and later in Paris, which is probably how it later made its way into various circles of the Russian *émigré* community.

By the middle and late 1890s, when Mooser made his stay in St Petersburg, the original idea of a 'fatal attraction' had been given a somewhat different slant with the introduction of a new figure, the custodian's son, and the reference to Tchaikovsky's supposed fear of reprisal from the authorities. On the one hand, it is characteristic of rumour as a phenomenon, in each stage of its operation, to be embroidered by concrete, supposedly authentic, detail which seems to enhance its credibility, but cannot, as in this case, withstand close scrutiny: the object of Tchaikovsky's infatuation could hardly have been, as it was alleged, the son of the custodian attached to Modest's apartment building since Modest moved there only a month earlier, and Tchaikovsky had never visited the place before. On the other hand, the new version made him less the simple prey of his own passion and more the victim of a repressive government, which well accords with the growing political radicalism in Russian society. Subsequent events, such as the publication of Modest's biography in 1902–3, and Bob Davydov's suicide in 1906, caused by drug abuse, must have served to revive the same rumours.

The emergence of the 'court of honour' legend must have been, at least in part, the Russian public's opportunistic response to the trial of Oscar Wilde of 1895. The parallels are too obvious for mere accident: the famous writer is replaced by a no less famous composer, Lord Alfred Douglas by the young aristocrat Stenbock-Fermor, and the Marquess of

Queensberry by an enraged uncle. As Laura Engelstein points out in her recent study, in late nineteenth-century Russia 'on the public stage, homosexuality never served as a vehicle for symbolic politics, as it did in England and Germany during the same period'.[19] Accordingly, since no official trial could have happened, it needed to be made unofficial, staged by Tchaikovsky's own former schoolmates on whom, as the instigators of his suicide, and not on his own sexual tastes, the principal blame could be now placed. It seems logical to surmise that this final blend of hearsay and fantasy originated—either strand by strand or altogether—within quarters hostile to the School of Jurisprudence, whose graduates occupied some of the highest posts in the Imperial government (according to some memoirists, Nikolay Jacobi, incidentally, seems to have been a rather odious character), or hostile to the Stenbock-Fermors, or both.

Although the gist of the enforced suicide rumour must have been in existence for about a century, the elaborate version we now possess, theoretically speaking, could have been invented or embellished by any or all of our known informants such as, for instance, Ekaterina (not Elizaveta!) Jacobi, or Alexander Voitov. It will be idle to speculate on Mrs Jacobi's possible motives, such as perhaps resentment against her late husband, his colleagues, or the Stenbock-Fermors, who in fact lived in the same neighbourhood. Voitov's involvement with the legend and his revelations invite such questions as why a man so dedicated to the memory of his Alma Mater would have chosen to disclose this quite damning information about it to someone with whom he was apparently not intimate; or why an elderly woman would have shared this singularly shameful story with a boy of 17 in the first place. Finally, it does seem, at the very least, unusual that, though a professional archivist and biographer and presumably concerned with the value of documentation, Mrs Orlova apparently made no effort to obtain written testimony from Voitov as to the veracity of the transcript she claims to have made of his narrative.[20]

Suicide, to say nothing of unauthorized execution (which is what the 'court of honour' story amounts to), is a juridical matter by definition. This implies that the presumption of innocence must be honoured and

---

[19] Engelstein, *The Keys to Happiness*, 58.

[20] Holden claims that Voitov's wife Inna, whom he interviewed for BBC TV's *Omnibus* film 'Who killed Tchaikovsky?' shown on 4 December 1993, confirmed that 'he [her husband] told her too the details of the "court of honour"—exactly as relayed by Orlova' (Holden, *Tchaikovsky*, 392). This contradicts his own and the film director's statements elsewhere, that she denied such knowledge, which also clearly transpires in her own words, heavily edited for film. (See Holden, 'The Death of Tchaikovsky: Cholera or Suicide?', *Čajkovskij-Studien*, i (Mainz, 1995), 150; Richard Fawkes, 'Anatomy of Death', *Classical Music*, 4 Dec. (1993), 33.) In a recent telephone conversation with the present author, Inna Voitova reiterated that she never heard the 'court of honour story' from her husband at all.

that the burden of proof must rest with the prosecution—in this instance, with those charging Tchaikovsky's former classmates (themselves lawyers) with a list of crimes including conspiracy, blackmail, fraud, and inducement to commit suicide. Any jury today, forced to deliberate on this peculiar case of 'non-sense in uniform' and presented with the pack of rumour and hearsay assembled by some biographers, would almost certainly render a verdict of 'not guilty' for lack of proof. Indeed, it is doubtful that one could find a legal expert anywhere who would dare to initiate proceedings on the basis of such flimsy evidence. As for any inquest into the composer's death, provided it were impartially conducted and all the pros and cons carefully weighed, the coroner's report is equally predictable: death by natural or accidental causes.

When all is said and done, we are left with the hope that further exploration in Russian archives may unearth new evidence which will shed light on the ultimately mythopoeic process behind the formation of this grotesque scenario about the departure from the world of one of its great composers. But, however it arose, the resulting 'Gothic tale' corresponded, as it happened, all too perfectly with the popular sensibilities that developed within Soviet Russia, in consequence of which it easily persisted through several decades. On the one hand, it had little or nothing in common with the official accounts and pronouncements which the public, and in particular the intelligentsia, learned to distrust; on the other, it pretended to 'expose' the alleged atrocities of the old Tsarist regime, in which the majority still tended to believe.

Epilogue

─────

One has to agree that contracting infection and dying in the time of a cholera epidemic is tragic, but by no means unnatural. It was the stature of the dead man that explains why the otherwise unspectacular death in St Petersburg, even irrespective of the rumours that surrounded it, made a lasting impression on the makers of our culture. It was of the great Russian composer and his fate, among others (Wagner, Nietzsche, Mahler), that Thomas Mann must have thought when he worked on *Death in Venice*. And one must admit that by drawing the modernist icon in the figure of Gustav Aschenbach, with the latter's absorption in art, and the stoic endurance of adversity, and the quest for the sublime, he came closer to understanding Tchaikovsky's character than most of the biographers. This image considerably deteriorated in all subsequent fictional treatments of the composer: in the novel written by Thomas Mann's son Klaus, *Symphonie Pathétique*, Tchaikovsky is made to play Russian roulette with the glass of unboiled water (a view favoured, incidentally, by George Balanchine); Ken Russell's cinematographic fantasy *The Music Lovers* makes of him a neurotic *bon vivant*, terrorized by women, and hideously expiring when plunged in the hot bath. By now we already have plays and even operas based on the 'court of honour' absurdity, and there is talk that Hollywood is considering screening a film with the same plot.

All this, however, belongs to the realm of imagination and cannot be helped: in our age, one does not fulminate against the lack of authenticity in literature or art. Biographical scholarship, on the other hand, is quite a different matter. To resolve a quandary of the sort that was generated by the circumstances of Tchaikovsky's death, the biographer should follow the principle by eliminating the impossible and introducing valid evidence, which constitutes the chief purpose of this book.

The pathetic figure of the 'mad gay Russian', perpetually on the verge of nervous breakdown, that was until very recently an almost unanimous view of Tchaikovsky, both among critics and the general public, owes its existence in the first place to his treatment by biographers plagued by ethnic and sexual stereotypes. As Richard Taruskin astutely pointed out, in this case 'the essentializing discourses of nationality and sexuality reappeared in tandem'.[1] No less does this reflect on the misconception and misrepresentation of his music, and the blame must be placed, to a very considerable degree, on many Western musicologists and music critics who not only essentialized the composer as 'just a Russian', but failed properly to enquire into the artistic and emotional connotations of that very Russianness which they liked to talk about.

That quality of Tchaikovsky's music which is usually described as 'morbid' or 'despondent' has little to do with his presumed personal preoccupation with anguish and death. Rather, it bears on the psychological phenomenon recurrent in the Russian tradition and best described by the word *toska* which is something quite different from the French *ennui* or the British *spleen*. The word that probably comes closest is what the German Romantics called *Weltschmerz*. In the Russian context, this means a passionate nostalgia for higher spirituality, which arises from disaffection with earthly pursuits, a craving for the experience outside the human grasp, and this is what endows Tchaikovsky's best work with the 'celestial' resonance that reaches far beyond familiar dichotomies, such as pessimism versus optimism, and the like.

Tchaikovsky was never an artist of the élite, whose fate might be of little or no interest to the masses of the population. Rather, he enjoyed, like no one else, enthusiastic acclaim in every stratum of Russian society both during his lifetime and long afterwards. Within the peculiar conditions of the 'classical' Soviet Union, where access to data on many topics, including the lives of prominent people, however long dead, was often deliberately restricted by the authorities, oral tradition tended to be viewed as the chief, or even only, source of information. Anything, even truth, was suspect if confirmed by government sources, and the popular mind was ever willing to reject such officially sanctioned information in favour of some extravagant rumour. With the advent of *glasnost*, an entire flood of such lore about famed figures of the past burst from the underground and inundated newspaper pages and radio broadcasts. Both Peter the Great and Catherine the Great had been murdered in outlandish fashion by their favourites; Nicholas I had committed suicide, while Nicholas II, by contrast, had been rescued from Bolshevik captivity by the Americans and died in Florida only recently; Lenin's elder brother

---

[1] Richard Taruskin, 'Pathetic Symphonist', *New Republic*, 216 (6 Feb. 1995), 29.

was an illegitimate son of Alexander III; Stalin had met secretly with Hitler off the coast of the Black Sea in the middle of the war (this last having been heard by someone from someone else who had been told it by the self-proclaimed captain of the cutter which allegedly hosted the momentous summit). The three great Russian poets of this century who committed suicide, Sergey Esenin, Vladimir Mayakovsky, and Marina Tsvetaeva, were now said to have been killed by the KGB or by Jewish Freemasons (depending on the political bias of the credulous), or perhaps by both. These and similar examples illustrate how popular sensationalism tends, with respect to the interpretation of past events, to function in outright defiance of the logical principle known as Ockham's Razor, that is, how it replaces simple and self-sufficient propositions with the needlessly complex: thus, a death from natural causes is transformed into a suicide, a suicide into a murder, and a murder into a full-blown conspiracy.

This tendency towards the sensational is not, of course, an exclusively Russian trait. The ongoing debate about John F. Kennedy's assassination comes immediately to mind, but we might also mention the recent furore raised over the corpse of America's twelfth President, Zachary Taylor. On the insistence of one resolute researcher who had become convinced that Mr Taylor had been poisoned by his political enemies, his remains were exhumed in June 1991 and subjected to forensic analysis. The results, to everyone's embarrassment, were negative. Zachary Taylor, the press was told by Kentucky's chief medical examiner, died just as it had been said that he did, from natural causes, not arsenic poisoning.

Perhaps there are those who might argue for resorting to a similar course of action as a way of settling the current controversy over the death of Pyotr Ilyich Tchaikovsky. We can only hope that good taste and common sense will prevail, that the truth, however lacking in melodrama, may be recognized on the grounds of the irrefutable evidence, and that the composer's shade remains undisturbed.

Select Bibliography

———

ARENSON, A., *P. I. Chaikovsky: biograficheskii ocherk* [*Biographical Sketch*], (Riga, 1898).

AUER, LEOPOLD, *My Long Life in Music* (London, 1924).

AV'ERINO, N., 'Moi vospominaniia o Chaikovskom' ['My Recollections of Tchaikovsky'], *Vozrozhdenie* [*Renaissance*], 16 (1951).

BERBEROVA, NINA, 'Looking Back at Tchaikovsky', *Yale Review*, 80 (1992).

—— Malcolm H. Brown, and Simon Karlinsky, 'Tchaikovsky's Suicide Reconsidered: A Rebuttal', *High Fidelity*, 31 (1981).

BERTENSON, SERGEI, *Vokrug isskusstva* [*Around Art*] (Hollywood, 1957).

BERTENSON, V. B., *O kholere* [*On Cholera*] (St Petersburg, 1905).

BLINOV, N. O., *Posledniaia bolezn'i smert' P. I. Chaikovskogo* [*Tchaikovsky's Last Illness and Death*] (Moscow, 1994).

BOGDANOVICH, A. V., *Tri poslednikh samoderzhtsa* [*The Three Last Autocrats*] (Moscow/Leningrad, 1924).

BOTKINA, A. P., *Pavel Mikhailovich Tret'yakov v zhizni i iskusstve* [*Pavel Mikhailovich Tretyakov in Life and Art*] (Moscow, 1993).

BROWN, DAVID, 'Tchaikovsky', *The New Grove: Russian Masters*, i (London, 1986).

—— *Tchaikovsky: A Biographical and Critcal Study*, iv: *The Final Years (1885–93)* (London, 1991).

—— *Tchaikovsky Remembered* (London, 1993).

BROWN, MALCOLM H., 'Tchaikovsky: The Early Years, 1840–1874 by David Brown', *Journal of the American Musicological Society*, 33 (1980).

BUCKLE, RICHARD, *Diaghilev* (New York, 1979).

CHAIKOVSKAIA, OL'GA, 'Pikovye damy' ['Queens of Spades'], *Novyi mir* [*New World*], 10 (1986).

CHEKHOV, A. P., *Polnoe sobranie sochinenii* [*Complete Works*], 12 vols. (Moscow, 1974).

ENGELSTEIN, LAURA, *The Keys to Happiness: Sex and the Search for Modernity in fin-de-siècle Russia* (Ithaca, NY, 1992).

EVANS, RICHARD J., *Death in Hamburg: Society and Politics in the Cholera Years 1839–1910* (Oxford, 1987).

FAWKES, RICHARD, 'Anatomy of a Death', *Classical Music* (4 Dec. 1993), 33.

GAY, PETER, *The Bourgeois Experience: Victoria to Freud*, ii (Oxford, 1986).

GRECHANINOV, A., *Moia muzykal'naia zhizn'* [*My Musical Life*] (Paris, 1934).

GREEN, JULIEN, *Journal: années 1946–1966* (Paris, 1967).

HASKELL, ARNOLD, L., in collaboration with Walter Nouvel, *Diaghileff* (New York, 1935).

HOLDEN, ANTHONY, 'The Death of Tchaikovsky: Cholera or Suicide', *Čajkovskij-Studien*, i (Mainz, 1995), 141–53.

—— *Tchaikovsky* (London, 1995).

IASTREBTSEV, V. V., *N. A. Rimskii-Korsakov: Vospominaniia* [*Recollections*], 2 vols. [Leningrad, 1959–60).

IUR'EV, I. M., *Zapiski* [*Notes*] , 2 vols. (Moscow/Leningrad, 1939–45).

KASHKIN, N. D., 'Iz vospominanii o P. I. Chaikovskom' ['From Memories of P. I. Tchaikovsky'], *Proshloe russkoi muzyki: materialy i issledovaniia*, i: *P. I. Chaikovskii* [*The Past in Russian Music: Documents and Research*, i: *P. I. Tchaikovsky*] (Petrograd, 1920); English trans. David Brown, *Tchaikovsky Remembered* (London, 1993).

—— *Vospominaniia o P. I. Chaikovskom* [*Memories of P. I. Tchaikovsky*] (Moscow, 1954).

KENDALL, ALAN, *Tchaikovsky* (London, 1988).

KLEIN, HERMAN, *Thirty Years of Musical Life in London* (New York, 1903).

KLIMENKO, I. A., *Moi vospominaniia o P. I. Chaikovskom* [*My Memories of P. I. Tchaikovsky*] (Riazan, 1908).

—— *Piotr Il'ich Chaikovskii. Kratkii biograficheskii ocherk* [*Tchaikovsky: A Short Biographical Sketch*] (Moscow, 1909).

KOLOMIITSOV, V., *Stat'i i pis'ma* (Leningrad, 1971).

LAMOND, FREDERIC, *The Memoirs of Frederic Lamond* (Glasgow, 1949).

LEVIN, EVA, *Sex and Society in the World of the Orthodox Slavs, 900–1700* (Ithaca, NY, 1989).

LISCHKE, ANDRÉ, *Piotr Ilyitch Tchaikovsky* (Paris, 1993).

NABOKOV, V. D., 'Plotskie prestupleniia po proektu ugolovnogo ulozheniia' ['Carnal Offences in the Draft of the Criminal Code'], *Sbornik statei po ugolovnomu pravu* [*A Collection of Articles on Criminal Law*] (St Petersburg, 1904), 102–25.

[OBNINSKII, V. P.], *Poslednii samoderzhets* [The Last Autocrat] (Berlin, 1912).

ORLOVA, ALEXANDRA, 'Tchaikovsky: The Last Chapter', *Music & Letters*, 62 (1981), 125–45.

—— *Tchaikovsky: A Self-Portrait* (Oxford, 1990).

POZNANSKY, ALEXANDER, 'Tchaikovsky's Suicide: Myth and Reality', *19th Century Music*, 11 (1988), 199–220.

—— *Tchaikovsky: The Quest for the Inner Man* (London, 1993).

—— *Samoubiistvo Chaikovskogo: mif i realnost'* [*Tchaikovsky's Suicide: Myth and Reality*] (Moscow, 1993).

—— 'Tchaikovsky as Communist Icon', *For SK: In Celebration of the Life and Career of Simon Karlinsky* (Berkeley, 1994).

—— 'Tchaikovsky: The Man behind the Myth', *Musical Times*, 4 (1995), 175–82.

PROTOPOPOV, V. V. (ed.), *Vospominaniia o P. I. Chaikovskom* [*Recollections of Tchaikovsky*] (Moscow, 1962, 4th edn., 1980).

RIMSKY-KORSAKOV, N. A., 'Letopis′ moei muzykal′noi zhizni' ['Chronicle of my Musical Life'], *Polnoe sobranie sochinenii* [*Complete Works*], i (Moscow, 1955).

RUBINSHTEIN, A. G., *Literaturnoie nasledie* [*A Literary Heritage*], 3 vols. (Moscow, 1986).

SABANEEV, LEONID, *S. I. Taneev: Mysli o tvorchestve i vospominaniia o zhizni* [*S. I. Taneev: Thoughts on his Creative Work and Memories of his Life*] (Paris, 1930).

SOKOLOV, V. S., *Antonina Chaikovskaia: istoriia zabytoi zhizni* [*Antonina Tchaikovskaia: The Story of a Forgotten Life*] (Moscow, 1994).

SPECHT, RICHARD, *Johannes Brahms* (London, 1930).

STRAVINSKY, IGOR, and CRAFT, ROBERT, *Expositions and Developments* (London, 1962).

SUVORIN, A. S., *Dnevnik* [*Diary*] (Moscow/Petrograd, 1923).

TANEEV, V. I., *Detstvo. Iunost′. Mysli o budushchem* [*Childhood, Youth, Thoughts on the Future*] (Moscow, 1959).

TARUSKIN, RICHARD, 'Pathetic Symphonist', *New Republic*, 6 Feb. (1995).

TCHAIKOVSKY, M. I., *Zhizn′ P. I. Chaikovskogo* [*Life of Tchaikovsky*], 3 vols. (Moscow, 1900–3).

TCHAIKOVSKY, P. I., *Letters to his Family: An Autobiography*, trans. Galina von Meck (London, 1981).

—— 'To my best friend': Correspondence between Tchaikovsky and Nadezhka von Meck, 1876–1878, trans. Galina von Meck, ed. Edward Garden and Nigel Gotteri (Oxford, 1993).

TOLSTOY, L. N., *Polnoe sobranie sochinenii* [*Complete Works*], 90 vols. (Moscow, 1929–64).

VINOGRADOFF, IGOR, 'Some Russian Imperial Letters to Prince V. P. Meshchersky (1839–1914)', *Oxford Slavonic Papers*, 10 (1962).

WARRACK, JOHN, *Tchaikovsky* (London, 1973).

WITTE, S. I., *Vospominaniia* [*Memories*], 3 vols. (Berlin, 1922).

ZAJACZKOWSKI, HENRY, 'Tchaikovsky: The Quest for the Inner Man by Alexander Poznansky', *Musical Times*, 11 (1992).

Index